Lecture Notes in Computer Science

Lecture Notes in Artificial Intelligence 14991

Founding Editor

Jörg Siekmann

Series Editors

The series Lecture Notes in Artificial Intelligence (LNAI) was established in 1988 as a topical subseries of LNCS devoted to artificial intelligence.

The series publishes state-of-the-art research results at a high level. As with the LNCS mother series, the mission of the series is to serve the international R & D community by providing an invaluable service, mainly focused on the publication of conference and workshop proceedings and postproceedings.

Stephen M. Watt · Tetsuo Ida
Editors

Symbolic Computation in Software Science

10th International Symposium, SCSS 2024
Tokyo, Japan, August 28–30, 2024
Proceedings

Springer

Editors
Stephen M. Watt
University of Waterloo
Waterloo, ON, Canada

Tetsuo Ida
Computer Science
University of Tsukuba
Tsukuba, Japan

ISSN 0302-9743 ISSN 1611-3349 (electronic)
Lecture Notes in Artificial Intelligence
ISBN 978-3-031-69041-9 ISBN 978-3-031-69042-6 (eBook)
https://doi.org/10.1007/978-3-031-69042-6

LNCS Sublibrary: SL7 – Artificial Intelligence

This Springer imprint is published by the registered company Springer Nature Switzerland AG
The registered company address is: Gewerbestrasse 11, 6330 Cham, Switzerland

Preface

These are the proceedings of SCSS 2024, the *10th International Symposium on Symbolic Computation in Software Science*. The symposium aimed to promote research on the theoretical and practical aspects of symbolic computation in software science in the context of modern computational and artificial intelligence techniques.

Symbolic computation is the science of computing with symbolic objects (terms, formulae, programs, representations of algebraic objects, and so on). Powerful algorithms have been developed during recent decades for the significant subareas of symbolic computation: computer algebra and computational logic. These include resolution proving, model checking, provers for various inductive domains, rewriting techniques, cylindrical algebraic decomposition, Gröbner bases, characteristic sets, and telescoping for recurrence relations. These algorithms and methods have been successfully applied in various fields. Software science has the goal of applying scientific principles in the development of software and covers a broad range of topics in software construction and analysis. One of the main objectives is to enhance software quality. The SCSS meetings bring these fields together, allowing the ideas from each to enhance the other.

The inaugural SCSS workshop in 2008 was an international collaboration, a joint effort among three partners: Bruno Buchberger (Johannes Kepler University), Tetsuo Ida (University of Tsukuba), and Masahiko Sato (Kyoto University). This initiative was made possible by the bilateral research program between JSPS (Japan) and FWF (Austria). The workshop grew out of internal workshops that brought together researchers from the associated groups:

- Theorema Group at RISC, Johannes Kepler University Linz, Austria
- Symbolic Computation Research Group at University of Tsukuba, Japan
- Software Science Foundation Group at Kyoto University, Japan
- Sup'Com (Higher School of Communication of Tunis) at University of November 7th at Carthage, Tunisia.

This composition clearly shows that the meetings intended an intersection of theory and application. Since the first instance, the meetings have been held in Austria, Japan, and Tunisia, except one online at the time of COVID-19:

2008 First International Workshop on Symbolic Computation in Software Science (SCSS 2008), Hagenberg, Austria
2009 Second International Workshop (also known as the Tunisia-Japan Workshop) on SCSS, Gammarth, Tunisia
2010 Third International Workshop on SCSS, Hagenberg, Austria
2012 Fourth International Symposium on SCSS, Gammarth, Tunisia
2013 Fifth International Symposium on SCSS, Hagenberg, Austria
2014 Sixth International Symposium on SCSS, Gammarth, Tunisia
2016 Seventh International Symposium on SCSS, Tokyo, Japan
2017 Eighth International Symposium on SCSS, Gammarth, Tunisia
2021 Ninth International Symposium on SCSS, online.

Over the years, the scope of SCSS has evolved, incorporating new research themes that drive progress in symbolic computation in software science. Some of the recurring topics in the SCSS meetings have been:

- Theorem proving methods and techniques
- Algorithm synthesis and verification
- Formal methods, including for the analysis of network security
- Complexity analysis and termination analysis of algorithms
- Extraction of specifications from algorithms
- Generation of inductive assertions for algorithms
- Algorithm transformations
- Component-based programming
- Symbolic methods for semantic web and cloud computing.

The present instance of SCSS builds on these themes. In response to the SCSS 2024 call for papers, a total of 11 full papers were received. All full papers received three single-blind reviews by program committee members or other reviewers. Four of the papers were accepted, and another three were accepted on condition that specific revisions be made. These seven are included in this volume. In addition, the symposium featured 17 papers accepted to a "work in progress" track.

The papers presented here emphasize formal analysis and proof of theorems in various applications, foundational work on rewrite systems, and sound handling of branches of inverse functions. After fifteen years, the foundational framework stands firm, continually incorporating innovative developments in SCSS domains.

July 2024

Stephen M. Watt
Tetsuo Ida

Organization

SCSS Steering Committee *as of August 2023*

Adel Bouhoula	Arabian Gulf University, Bahrain
Bruno Buchberger	RISC Johannes Kepler University, Austria
Hoon Hong	North Carolina State University, USA
Tetsuo Ida	University of Tsukuba, Japan
Laura Kovács	TU Wien, Austria
Temur Kutsia	RISC Johannes Kepler University, Austria
Mohamed Mosbah	LABRI, France
Michael Rusinowitch	Inria, France
Masahiko Sato	Kyoto University, Japan
Carsten Schneider	RISC Johannes Kepler University, Austria
Dongming Wang	Beihang University, China, and CNRS, France

SCSS 2024 Organizing Committee

General Chair

Tetsuo Ida	U. Tsukuba

Program Committee Chair

Stephen Watt	U. Waterloo

Local Arrangements Chair

Katsusuke Nabeshima	Tokyo U. of Science

Program Committee

David Cerna	Czech Academy of Sciences, Czechia
Changbo Chen	Chinese Academy of Sciences, China
Rachid Echahed	CNRS and University of Grenoble, France
David Jeffrey	University of Western Ontario, Canada

Cezary Kaliszyk	University of Innsbruck, Austria
Yukiyoshi Kameyama	University of Tsukuba, Japan
Laura Kovács	TU Wien, Austria
Temur Kutsia	RISC Johannes Kepler University, Austria
Christopher Lynch	Clarkson University, USA
Yasuhiko Minamide	Tokyo Institute of Technology, Japan
Julien Narboux	CNRS and Université de Strasbourg, France
Wolfgang Schreiner	RISC Johannes Kepler University, Austria
Sofiène Tahar	Concordia University, Canada
Stephen Watt (Chair)	University of Waterloo, Canada
Lihong Zhi	AMSS Chinese Academy of Sciences, China

Ph.D. Student Session Committee

Xavier Dahan	Tohoku University, Japan

Local Arrangements Committee

Yuki Ishihara	Nihon University, Japan
Katsusuke Nabeshima (Chair)	Tokyo University of Science, Japan
Yosuke Sato	Tokyo University of Science, Japan
Hiroshi Sekigawa	Tokyo University of Science, Japan
Akira Terui	University of Tsukuba, Japan

Additional Reviewers

Robin Coutelier
Petra Hozzová
Zijia Li
Adnan Rashid
Johannes Schoisswohl
Jonas Schöpf
Nicolas Smoot
Liao Zhang

Sponsors

SCSS 2024 gratefully acknowledges the support of our sponsors, the Kayamori foundation of informational science advancement and Maplesoft.

Keynote Speaker

Algorithmic Intelligence

Bruno Buchberger

RISC Johannes Kepler University, Austria

Consciousness, Reflexion, Intelligence, Mathematics, Models, Knowledge, Algorithms, Machines, Computation, Software, Symbolics, Numerics, Programming, Automated Reasoning, Automated Programming, Machine Learning, Artificial Intelligence, Algorithmic Intelligence, ... In this talk, I try to clarify these notions and how they relate to each other. I will draw some conclusions about the power of mathematics for the future, which is expressed (and hidden) in changing wording. In particular, I will speak about the critical importance of mathematical education for the future of the world.

Invited Speakers

From Computer Algebra to Signal Processing

Wenshin Lee

University of Stirling, UK

In 1795, the French mathematician de Prony published a method to fit a real-valued exponential model to some uniformly collected samples [1]. This classical method in approximation theory is based on a linear recurrence relation among the data. After two centuries, in the field of computer algebra, Ben-Or and Tiwari presented an algorithm for interpolating sparse multivariate polynomials [2]. Interestingly, these two methods are closely related [3]. The cross-fertilization between these two has led to a series of exciting developments in exponential analysis and its applications in signal processing, including a multivariate exponential analysis method that does not suffer from the well-known curse of dimensionality [4], a validated exponential analysis approach based on subsampling [5], and the breaking of the Nyquist constraint [6] that has underpinned almost all digital signal applications so far.

The Nyquist constraint was formulated at the beginning of the 20th century [7]. It is the digital signal processing equivalent of the statement that the argument of a complex exponential $\exp(\phi\Delta)$ with $\phi \in \mathbb{C}$ and $\Delta \in \mathbb{R}^+$ can only be retrieved uniquely when $|\Im(\phi)\Delta| < \pi$. In the past decade, this constraint was first broken by using randomly collected signal samples [8, 9] and later with the use of regularly spaced samples [6]. The techniques used in the latter are closely related to sparse interpolation in symbolic computation. Being able to circumvent the Nyquist constraint from a set of regularly spaced samples offers new possibilities in many practical signal processing applications, among them antenna design for estimating directions of arrival (DOA) of signals.

Estimating the directions of simultaneously arriving signals is crucial in applications such as radar, remote sensing, radio frequency interference mitigation, wireless networks, and machine perception of unmanned aerial vehicles or self-driving cars. In designing a regularly spaced antenna system for estimating the DOA, a main constraint is the spatial Nyquist criterion that requires the space between two sensors to be less than half of the signal wavelength. A disadvantage of densely spaced antenna elements is the effect of mutual coupling, which is normally reduced through costly extensive calibration of the system. In addition, sparse arrays are desirable for an increased resolution compared to a dense array with the same number of antenna elements.

Using a regularly spaced antenna system for DOA estimation can be formulated as an exponential analysis problem, which can be tackled by the classical Prony method. Recent advances in exponential analysis, stemming from its connection to sparse interpolation in symbolic computation, enable us to completely eliminate the dense Nyquist spacing requirement for DOA [10]. Building upon recent results in one-dimensional DOA estimation [10] and multivariate exponential analysis [4], we are developing new sparse solutions for estimating planar DOA in antenna design. Our aim is to offer significant improvements in performance and cost efficiency.

References

1. de Prony, R.: Essai expérimental et analytique sur les lois de la dilatabilité des fluides élastiques, et sur celles de la force expansive de la vapeur de l'eau et de la vapeur de l'alkool à différentes températures. J. de l' École Polytechnique **1**(22), 24–76 (1795)
2. Ben-Or, M., Tiwari, P.: A deterministic algorithm for sparse multivariate polynomial interpolation. In: STOC'88: Proceedings of the Twentieth Annual ACM Symposium on Theory of Computing, pp. 301–309 (1988)
3. Giesbrecht, M., Labahn, G., Lee, W.-S.: Symbolic-numeric sparse interpolation of multivariate polynomials. J. Symbol. Comput. **44**(8), 943–959 (2009)
4. Cuyt, A., Lee, W.-S.: Multivariate exponential analysis from the minimal number of samples. Adv. Comput. Math. **44**(4):987–1002 (2018)
5. Briani, M., Cuyt, A., Lee, W.-S.: VEXPA: Validated EXPonential Analysis through regular sub-sampling. Signal Process. **177**, 107722 (2020)
6. Cuyt, A., Lee, W.-S.: How to get high resolution results from sparse and coarsely sampled data. Appl. Comput. Harmon. Anal. **48**(3), 1066–1087 (2020)
7. Nyquist, H.: Certain topics in telegraph transmission theory. Trans. Am. Inst. Electr. Eng. **47**(2), 617–644 (1928)
8. Candés, E.J., Romberg, J., Tao, T.: Robust uncertainty principles: exact signal reconstruction from highly incomplete frequency information. IEEE Trans. Inf. Theory, **52**(2), 489–509 (2006)
9. Donoho, D.L.: Compressed sensing. IEEE Trans. Inf. Theory, **52**(4), 1289–1306 (2006)
10. Knaepkens, F., Cuyt, A., Lee, W.-S., de Villiers, D.I.L.: Regular sparse array direction of arrival estimation in one dimension. IEEE Trans. Antennas Propag. **68**(5), 3997–4006 (2020)

Proof Assistants and Foundations of Mathematics

Masahiko Sato

Kyoto University, Japan

Reflecting on the history of the developments of mathematics and proof assistants, I will propose a design principle of a new proof assistant which provides an environment where mathematics and meta-mathematics can be developed simultaneously in a seamless manner.

Relating Symbolic Computation to the Foundations of Science

Stephen Wolfram

Wolfram Research, USA

It started with a breakthrough in fundamental physics in 2020. And now it's becoming clear that the foundations of science are deeply connected to ideas in symbolic computation. The result is emerging unification that relates term rewriting to black holes, metamathematical space to SETI, biological evolution undecidability, and much more. This talk will discuss both new theoretical perspectives and results, and some of their practical implications, notably in emerging features of the Wolfram Language.

Operations on Parametric Ideals

Kazuhiro Yokoyama

Rikkyo University, Japan

We deal with ideals generated by polynomials with parametric coefficients, and introduce the notion of stabilities on ideal structures based on stability of forms of Gröbner bases. For these computations, we can apply comprehensive Gröbner systems effectively. Then, we consider stabilities on basic operations on ideals, such as intersection, quotient, saturation, and radical, and show that those are computablewith help of comprehensive Gröbner systems. Moreover, as an advanced operation, we consider primary decomposition and discuss its computational tractability.

Contents

Formal Analysis of Vehicular Crash Severity Using KeYmaera X

Oumaima Barhoumi[1(✉)], Mohamed H Zaki[2], and Sofiène Tahar[1]

[1] Concordia University, Montreal, QC, Canada
{o_barh,tahar}@ece.concordia.ca
[2] Western University, London, ON, Canada
mzaki9@uwo.ca

Abstract. In this paper, we integrate formal methods with traffic conflict techniques such as Time-To-Collision and Deceleration Rate, and evasive action indicators, like Jerk Profile and Yaw Rate in order to introduce a practical traffic safety rule. We propose the use of formal methods to prove the correctness of this traffic safety rule and verify road users' compliance with it. To this end, we utilize differential dynamic logic and the KeYmaera X theorem prover for the formalization and verification of this rule. Furthermore, we conduct a formal analysis of crash severity applied to different traffic collision scenarios to determine the optimal evasive actions to be taken during a traffic conflict, along with their appropriate intensity. Using KeYmaera X, we are able to automatically verify the proposed traffic safety rule in three traffic collision scenarios, namely rear-end and head-on and left-side collisions.

Keywords: Formal Verification · Traffic Conflict Techniques · Transportation Safety · Crash Severity · KeYmaera X

1 Introduction

Urban mobility is witnessing a growing reliance on advanced driver-assistance systems for traffic safety mitigation. Yet, these systems and the anticipated deployment of driverless vehicles expose the traffic network to an unprecedented level of technologies that might not be fully mature to deal with the complex nature of the traffic culture. While Artificial Intelligence (AI) systems are known for their complexity and advanced capabilities, a lesser-known fact is that both actual self-driving cars and vehicles equipped with advanced driving-assistance systems (ADAS) operate on principles similar to those underlying ChatGPT and other large language models (LLMs) [13]. Both types of AI leverage statistical reasoning to predict the next word, phrase, or steering input, which places significant emphasis on recently used words or actions in their calculations. This kind of AI lacks a true understanding of the situation, context, or unobserved factors that a human would naturally consider in similar circumstances. However, the critical distinction is that while a language model might produce nonsensical or

S. M. Watt and T. Ida (Eds.): SCSS 2024, LNAI 14991, pp. 1–19, 2024.
https://doi.org/10.1007/978-3-031-69042-6_1

irrelevant output, a self-driving car has the potential to be fatal [13]. One relevant example is the 2018 Uber driverless vehicle fatal incident, where the vehicle could not perform the evasive actions necessary to avoid a pedestrian [19]. Conventional methods for system verification, often relying on testing and simulation, differ significantly from formal verification tools like KeYmaera X and lack the mathematical rigor and formal guarantees provided by tools based on formal methods. Typically, they involve manual testing and debugging, which may not comprehensively address the intricate interactions within hybrid systems that combine discrete events and continuous dynamics. Formal methods refer to mathematically based techniques for the specification, design, verification, and validation of software and hardware systems. These methods use mathematical languages and tools to model and analyze systems, helping to ensure their correctness and reliability. Verification and validation of algorithms for perception, decision-making, and control using formal methods can help ensure that these systems operate safely and reliably. This is particularly important for avoiding accidents and minimizing risks associated with autonomous vehicles navigating in complex traffic scenarios. Therefore, the use of formal methods is essential in addressing safety-related challenges anticipated in road transportation while simultaneously establishing a well defined specification for traffic rules [5].

In the literature, established traffic safety rules define what constitutes safe conditions. However, the deployment of connected autonomous vehicles (CAVs) is presenting unprecedented challenges in adhering to these rules. This challenge is evident in the rising number of rear-end collisions involving automated vehicles compared to conventional human-driven vehicles in 2023 [13]. In this study, we have decided to focus not on defining safe conditions as a safety specification, but rather on identifying unsafe conditions that lead to collisions. Our objective with this approach is to establish a foundational framework that will enable further research to enhance CAVs by identifying clear and well-defined safe regions for operation, informed by understanding the unsafe conditions. To do so, we chose to dive deeper into the causes of these collisions by concentrating on a crucial phase that precedes a collision: traffic conflicts and the actions taken during them. Therefore, we conduct our analysis assuming that the vehicle is already in a traffic conflict. Hence, preventing these conflicts from leading to crashes is one of the main axes to focus on. In this context, Traffic Conflict Techniques (TCTs), also referred to as traffic safety indicators, are employed as a set of methods for identifying, assessing, and analyzing traffic conflicts. By adopting a broader perspective, TCTs enable a reliable traffic analysis that can offer insights into the underlying causes and risk factors associated with traffic conflicts. In this paper, we introduce a practical traffic safety rule based on the combination of TCTs such as Time-To-Collision and Deceleration Rate, and evasive-actions-based indicators, like Jerk Profile and Yaw Rate. Additionally, we propose to formally verify the developed rule using an automated prover in order to conduct a formal analysis of vehicular crashes and their anticipated severity.

In this work, we consider a temporal-proximity and two speed-related traffic safety indicators, namely Time-to-Collision (TTC), Delta-V and Extended

Delta-V, respectively. TTC is a temporal proximity indicator [22] that is defined as the time remaining for a collision to take place between two involved vehicles if no action is taken. Whereas, Delta-V (ΔV) represents the velocity variation of the vehicles prior and post-crash [9]. Extended Delta-V is a more precise indicator for predicting the likelihood and severity of a crash [9], as it calculates a hypothetical value of Delta-V instead of using the true value. In addition to these indicators, evasive action-based indicators such as jerk profile and yaw rate are also utilized to conduct a more accurate analysis of traffic conflicts and assess the success of a maneuver based on the intensity of these indicators. The jerk profile [6] provides a detailed insight into a vehicle's temporal acceleration dynamics. This metric is calculated as the derivative of the vehicle's acceleration, allowing us to capture rapid changes in acceleration over time. The yaw rate [6] quantifies the extent of swerving or rotational motion exhibited by a vehicle during maneuvers. Understanding the yaw rate is essential for evaluating the intensity of a vehicle's response when evading obstacles, navigating curves, or making sharp turns. Our research aims to investigate the effectiveness of these evasive action-based indicators in resolving traffic conflicts by conducting a formal analysis of their intensity using formal methods. The main contribution of the paper lies in the integration and application of formal methods to solve specific safety challenges in transportation by (1) proposing a novel traffic rule established using temporal and spatial indicators along with evasive actions; and (2) using formal methods tool, KeYmaera X, to formally verify the proposed traffic rule in three different traffic scenarios.

Vehicles are complex systems that involve both continuous and discrete dynamics, where the former represents the vehicle's movement and the latter includes events such as gear changes and braking. The behavior of a vehicle in traffic is determined by the interaction between these dynamics. In this paper, we focus on formally verifying the proposed traffic safety rule combining the specified TCTs and evasive actions indicators, i.e., TTC, Extended Delta-V, jerk profile and yaw rate, respectively. To achieve this goal, we require a sufficiently expressive logic capable of reasoning about dynamic behaviors. This is essential for formalizing both the traffic safety indicators and the traffic safety rule, alongside a formal verification tool that ideally supports such logic in an automated fashion. Therefore, first- and higher-order logic theorem proving would be the most convenient formal verification method to achieve this goal. While studying existing automated and interactive theorem provers, we realized that the automated hybrid verification tool KeYmaera X [16] is the most appropriate for our work. In fact, KeYmaera X supports Differential Dynamic Logic (dL) [16] as the specification language, which will enable us to efficiently study the traffic safety rule in different car crash scenarios. Moreover, KeYmaera X provides a rigorous and systematic proof engines suitable for checking whether the vehicle complies with the safety specifications. The TCTs employed in this process will be scrutinized, and based on their evaluation, a decision will be made regarding the safe management of the involved vehicles by determining the appropriate intensity of the evasive actions indicators. In this paper, we aim to improve road safety by developing a better understanding of the causes of traffic conflicts and developing effective strategies to prevent them. This is achieved by adopting a proactive approach that consists of formally analyzing the severity of traffic conflicts and determining the convenient evasive measures to be taken as well as their intensities to prevent potential vehicular crashes. The proof files for the traffic safety rule formalized in KeYmaera X are available online [3].

The rest of the paper is organized as follows. In Sect. 2, we review the works done earlier relating TCTs and formal verification. In Sect. 3, we provide some preliminaries of the employed TCTs and their mathematical representation. Section 4 describes the traffic safety rule formal structure. Whereas Sect. 5 covers the formalization process of the introduced traffic safety rule. Finally, we conclude this work in Sect. 6.

2 Related Work

The use of formal methods in the field of transportation is recognized by researchers based on its own merits in verifying safety critical systems such as vehicles. Thanks to their rigorous nature, formal verification aims to deliver sound systems that meet their specifications by applying various techniques, such as runtime monitoring, model checking and interactive or automated theorem proving. For instance, Mao et al. [12], modeled a cooperative adaptive cruise control system using the CHARON modeling language and applied runtime monitoring to check the model against safety properties defined using the temporal logic MEDL through simulation. Although the authors utilize a formal modeling language (MEDL) for specifying the properties, their approach involves a simulation-based case study for monitoring the safety properties. In the work of Althoff et al. [1], algorithmic verification which is an extension of model checking was applied online to make sure that a self-driving vehicle will avoid static objects as well as dynamic obstacles on the road. In this work, the assumption of the other car strictly adhering to road traffic regulations oversimplifies real-world traffic complexity and uncertainty. Unpredictable behavior and distracting factors are also not considered, limiting the proposed approach's ability to capture dynamic traffic scenarios.

The authors of [17] provided a formally verified checker of the safe distance rule in order to verify if an autonomous vehicle complies with traffic rules using the interactive theorem prover Isabelle/HOL. The study neglects to consider the interactions between the subject vehicle and other vehicles, as well as the surrounding environment. These interactions could be indicated by traffic safety indicators like Time-To-Collision. When it comes to the verification of the entirety of the traffic system, Loos et al. [11] developed a formal proof of a distributed car control system to verify that the control model guarantees collision freedom for arbitrarily many cars using the KeYmaera automated theorem prover. While the study successfully provides formal verification results for collision freedom, accounting for uncertainties in the environment, such as the presence of unpredictable objects or obstacles, is crucial for its real-world deployment. Incorporating these factors into the formal verification process can provide a more accurate assessment of the system's reliability under diverse circumstances. In [14], the work of Mitsch et al. was one of the early attempts to utilize formal verification tools in the modeling of freeway dynamics. The authors used dL for the formulation and verification of the system specifications using KeYmaera. However, it is important to acknowledge that the current approach does not fully address uncertainties in the environment or incorporate real-world constraints and scenarios into the verification process.

The studies mentioned above cover the verification of different safety aspects of the vehicle and its interaction with the outer environment. However, none of them explores the verification of TCTs, which serve as traffic safety indicators. In our work, we are taking interest in the verification of a new traffic safety rule linking TCTs indicators, i.e., TTC, Delta-V, and Extended Delta-V, along with evasive actions indicators, i.e., jerk profile and yaw rate. The formalization of this rule and its verification will introduce accurate safety bounds for driver behaviors during traffic conflicts to avoid collisions by studying different case scenarios and identifying the severity level of crashes if they were to happen. In light of this, and inspired by the work of [11,14] using KeYmaera, we will employ the KeYmaera X hybrid theorem prover which is an extension of KeYmaera to conduct the verification process.

3 Preliminaries

To ease the readability of the paper, in this section we provide a preliminary introduction to relevant notions of TCTs and evasive actions indicators along with their mathematical formulations. We also provide an overview of the KeYmaera X theorem prover and a summary of the used differential dynamic logic syntax.

3.1 Traffic Conflict Techniques

In this paper, we apply different TCTs and evasive action indicators, furthermore, we provide their mathematical formulation for different collision scenarios. In this case, the vehicles involved in the collision are assumed to have identical properties, such as length, i.e., $L_1 = L_2 = L$, and mass, i.e., $m_1 = m_2 = m$. Assuming vehicles have equal masses and lengths is essential for simplifying the analysis of crash severity. Without this assumption, we would need to account for various vehicle shapes, sizes (like SUVs, vans, compacts), and weights, leading to a multitude of sub-cases and a wide range of crash severity levels to analyze. Moreover, we only consider the execution of evasive actions, i.e., braking and swerving, in a sequential manner rather than simultaneously.

Time To Collision: TTC is defined as the time required for two vehicles to collide if they continue at their present speed and on the same path [7]. In the work of [8] a TTC of 4 s signifies the presence of a conflict situation for a

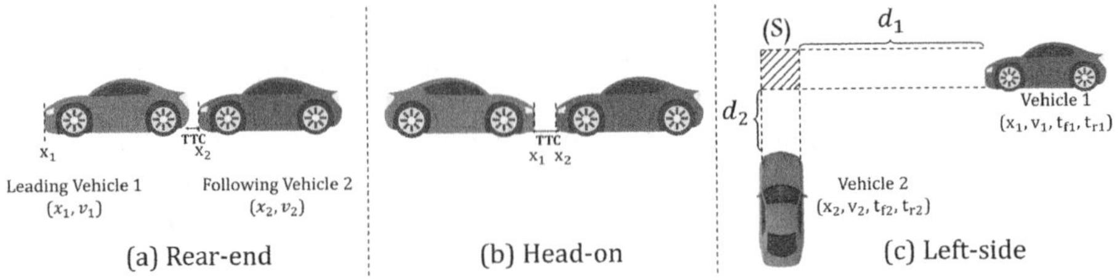

Fig. 1. Collision Scenarios

vehicle. However, the same study revealed that TTC values in the range of 4 to 5 s sometimes led to false positives, indicating potential collisions when, in fact, a typical braking maneuver would have safely resolved the traffic conflict. As a result, it is acknowledged in the literature [8] that setting a TTC threshold at 3 s is appropriate for safety evaluation. TTC can be computed for various traffic interactions. In our case, we define TTC in rear-end, head-on, and left-side collision situations, where we use the indexes *1* and *2* to refer to the leading and following vehicles in traffic as shown by Fig. 1:

1. **Rear-end Collision:** TTC is measured between two consecutive vehicles from the rear bumper of the leading vehicle to the front bumper of the following vehicle as shown by Figure 1.a. The formula to compute TTC for two consecutive vehicles in a rear-end collision scenario is defined as [22]:

$$TTC_1 = \frac{x_1 - x_2 - L_1}{v_2 - v_1}, \qquad v_2 > v_1 \tag{1}$$

   The bumper positions and velocities of vehicles 1 and 2 are represented by the variables x_1, x_2, v_1, and v_2, respectively. Additionally, L_1 represents the length of the leading vehicle, which is vehicle 1, while the following vehicle is represented by vehicle 2.

2. **Head-on Collision:** In this collision scenario, TTC is measured between the front bumpers of the two involved vehicles as reflected by Figure 1.b. Therefore, the formula of TTC is modified as [10]:

$$TTC_2 = \frac{x_1 - x_2}{v_1 + v_2} \tag{2}$$

   where x_1, x_2, v_1 and v_2 are the positions and velocities of vehicles 1 and 2, respectively.

3. **Left-side Collision:** In this case, the definition of TTC, as illustrated by Figure 1.c, is revised by considering the time instances corresponding to the arrival of the front and rear-ends of both vehicles 1 and 2 at the conflict-to-collision region (S), denoted as t_{f1}, t_{r1}, t_{f2} and t_{r2}, respectively. The TTC in this case is determined as follows [10]:

$$t_{f1} < t_{f2} < t_{r1}; \quad TTC_3 = \frac{d_2}{v_2} \tag{3}$$

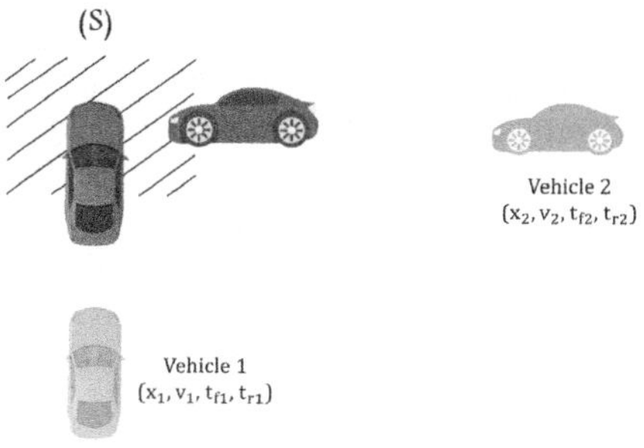

Fig. 2. Left-Side Traffic Conflict

$$t_{f2} < t_{f1} < t_{r2}; \quad TTC_3 = \frac{d_1}{v_1} \tag{4}$$

where v_1 and v_2 represent the vehicles' velocities and d_1 and d_2 are defined as the x-distance and y-distance separating vehicles 1 and 2 from the region (S) respectively.

In this scenario, we are examining a left-side collision, where either vehicle 1 reaches the conflict-to-collision region (S) after vehicle 2, or vice-versa. If TTC is less than 3 s, both vehicles are considered to be involved in a traffic conflict. The time intervals specified in Eqs. 3 and 4 are conditions that define a mathematical formulation of TTC, enabling a continuous TTC calculation during traffic conflicts. In this study, we will proceed with the Time-To-Collision given by Eq. 3, i.e., TTC_3, where vehicle 1 arrives at the conflict-to-collision region (S) while vehicle 2 has not yet left this region which leads to a traffic conflict, as shown by Figure 1.c. This is described by the arrival of the front of vehicle 2, i.e., t_{f2}, before the arrival of the rear of vehicle 1, i.e., t_{r1}, and after the arrival of the front of vehicle 1, i.e., t_{f1}, reflecting a traffic conflict during which TTC can be computed as given by Eq. 3. This relationship is depicted schematically in Figure 2.

Extended Delta-V: Extended Delta-V (Ext-ΔV) is a speed-related indicator describing the speed reduction rate of vehicles due to an unexpected event, e.g., conflict, collision [9]. It is used as an informative measure of the possibility of a crash occurrence and whether or not a preventive action was taken. The value of this indicator foresees the severity of the collision should it happen. For this, Extended Delta-V represents the theoretical value of Delta-V if the taken evasive action was successful. In the case where the collision takes place, the value of Extended Delta-V converges to the true value of Delta-V. Whereas, Extended Delta-V abides by the same general rule to determine the value of Delta-V, given by Eq. 5 to determine its value. The specificity of this indicator compared to the classical Delta-V lies in the vehicle's speed definition prior to a conflict.

This indicator as defined in Eq. 6, incorporates braking as an evasive measure linked to a temporal indicator. In a traffic conflict, the chosen temporal indicator within a collision course is TTC. It gauges the proximity to collision, multiplied by a deceleration rate, in order to determine the required evasive action for crash avoidance. Severity assessment is based on the aggressiveness and remaining time to the collision.

$$Ext\text{-}\Delta V = V_{post} - V \tag{5}$$

$$V = v_0 - a * TTC \tag{6}$$

Under the assumption that it is an *inelastic collision* [18] and in the case of two vehicles colliding, those vehicles will stick together after the crash, i.e., $V_{1post} = V_{2post} = V_{post}$. Mathematically, an inelastic collision is translated by [18]:

$$m_1 * v_1 + m_2 * v_2 = (m_1 + m_2) * V_{post} \tag{7}$$

Given our assumption that the masses of vehicle 1 and vehicle 2 are equal, i.e., $m_1 = m_2 = m$, V_{post} is deduced as:

$$V_{post} = \frac{v_1 + v_2}{2} \tag{8}$$

Jerk Profile: The studies in [2,21] reveal that acceleration patterns in normal driving situations can resemble those in conflict situations. Relying solely on the deceleration profile may not accurately evaluate the severity of vehicle interactions. Instead, the jerk profile, which measures the rate of change of acceleration, can detect transitions from light braking to sudden and intense braking. The jerk profile is defined as a function of the vehicle's acceleration, i.e., a:

$$J = \frac{da}{dt} \tag{9}$$

Analyzing the jerk profile allows differentiation between traffic conflict situations and normal or near-miss situations. For instance, a traffic conflict is characterized by a strong negative value of the jerk, where the highest value computed by the jerk is found to be -15 m/s^3 seeing that any greater value will be considered mechanically unfeasible [21]. As for a situation where normal braking is executed, the highest value of jerk computed is at -8 m/s^3. Based on the findings of multiple researchers, such as [15] and [2], a threshold value of the jerk profile is defined in Eq. 10, to be equal to -9.82 m/s^3, as an indicator of safety-critical driving behavior. Mathematically, the jerk profile is defined as follows:

$$-9.82 m/s^3 \leq J < -15\, m/s^3 \tag{10}$$

Yaw Rate: Braking, as an evasive action, is not always sufficient to avoid a crash. Swerving is a variation of the heading angle in a chosen direction once the vehicle is found in a conflict situation. The yaw rate is used as the indicator to quantify this, it is used to describe the change of the heading angle in a

Table 1. Statements of Hybrid Programs [16]

Statement	Effect
$x := e$	discrete assignment of the current value of term e to variable x
$x:=*$	nondeterministic assignment of an arbitrary real number to x
$?P$	continue if first-order formula P holds in the current state, abort otherwise
$x'=f(x)$ & Q	follow differential equation $x' = f(x)$ within evolution domain Q for any duration
$\alpha; \beta$	sequential composition, first performs α and then β afterwards
$\alpha \cup \beta$	nondeterministic choice, following either α or β
α^*	nondeterministic repetition, repeating α $n \geq 0$ times

short period. Mathematically, the yaw rate and the vehicle's heading angle θ are defined as follows [20]:

$$r(t) = \frac{d\theta}{dt} \tag{11}$$

$$\theta = \frac{x}{rd} \tag{12}$$

with x as the vehicles position and rd representing the radius of the curve. The range of the yaw rate is defined based on the safety of the action after its execution. With regards to resolving a traffic conflict by swerving, we propose a range of [0, 45] degrees, i.e., [0, 0.785] radians [4], for effective maneuvering in response to a traffic conflict while maintaining control of the vehicle:

$$0 < r \leq 0.785 \tag{13}$$

3.2 KeYmaera X Theorem Prover

KeYmaera X is an interactive theorem prover for hybrid systems supporting differential dynamic logic (dL) that is based on first-order logic, along with a program notation for hybrid systems [16]. dL is a single language that integrates operational system models and formulas. In dL, a hybrid program (HP) is a compositional program notation for hybrid systems, which include both discrete and continuous behaviors. A HP consist of various program statements, including differential equations that describe continuous behaviors. A summary of the used syntax and informal semantics of hybrid programs is given in Table 1, where HPs are composed of different elements such as α and β, which are also HPs, x represents variables that can be used within an HP, e denotes a term that may contain x, and P and Q are formulas of first-order logic of real arithmetic [16]. Thanks to its interfacing with several provers and tools that are invoked transparently in the background, e.g., Mathematica or Z3 SMT Solver, KeYmaera X stands out by implementing automatic proof strategies to enable the compositional verification of large systems. To verify the proposed safety traffic rule in

KeYmaera X, the proving process is based on a series of applied automatic proof strategies. For instance, the rule of the hybrid program including a differential equation requires solving the dynamics of hybrid systems, i.e., vehicles. Afterwards, the obtained solutions are used to prove each sub-goal of the rule until reaching the main goal. Eventually, KeYmaera's verification process results in either a proven rule or an error that disables the prover from continuing the process. In our case, the correctness of the rule is proved for the three different scenarios of rear-end, head-on, and left-side collision.

4 Crash Severity Analysis

In this section, we discuss in detail the proposed methodology for crash severity analysis using the KeYmaera X theorem prover, followed by a detailed description of the traffic safety rule specification.

4.1 Proposed Methodology

The proposed methodology for the formal analysis of crash severity is depicted in Figure 3. As illustrated in the figure, the first step of our approach involves the formulation of traffic conflict indicators, including Time-To-Collision, Extended Delta-V, and deceleration rate. Additionally, we define evasive action indicators such as jerk profile and yaw rate. These indicators are then formalized using dL, which serves as the specification logic in our approach. Subsequently, we establish a traffic safety rule that specifies safe conditions, defined by predefined thresholds for each indicator, and the consequences of their violation, i.e., an Imminent collision. In this context, we examine three distinct collision scenarios: rear-end, head-on, and right-side. The collision scenarios presented in this study are illustrative of basic cases, yet they serve as an illustration of potential real-world interactions involving two different vehicles. This traffic safety rule states that"If these thresholds are violated and appropriate evasive actions are not taken with the correct level of intensity, a collision will occur". The first step in defining this rule is to introduce its pre-conditions based on the inputs for the system, such as the vehicle's environment parameters. The next step is to model the hybrid system, given the vehicle's dynamics, using an ordinary differential equation (ODE) due to the continuous evolution of the system. Lastly, the post-conditions are introduced to describe every speed interval and its association with a deceleration variable. These steps are carried out in the KeYmaera X theorem prover where the verification process will take place.

The evaluation of the consequences of violating traffic safety rules is based on predefined thresholds of safety traffic indicators (cf. Section 3.1). The impact of such violations is studied in three distinct traffic scenarios. In each scenario, a formal analysis is conducted to assess the severity of potential crashes based on the specific situation. To deduce the severity level of a crash, we rely on the values of TTC and Delta-V as well as the speeds of the vehicles involved in a traffic conflict. These severity levels include categories such as *property damage only*,

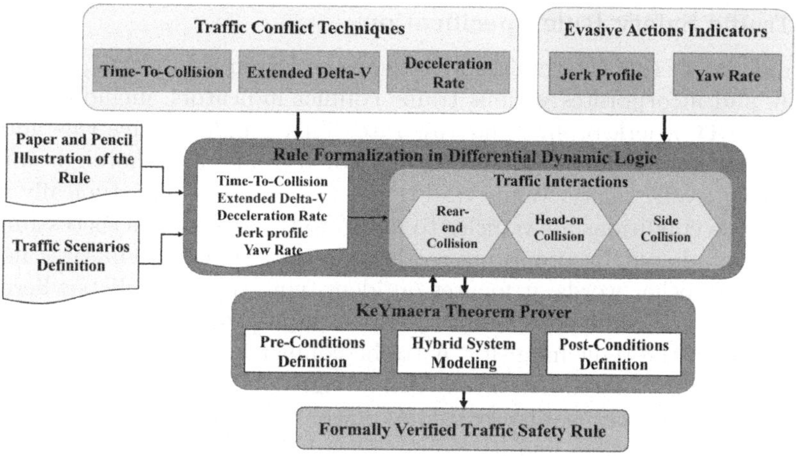

Fig. 3. Methodology for Formal Crash Severity Analysis

potential injury, *non-severe injury*, and *severe injury* depending on the speeds of the vehicles involved in the traffic conflict. We achieve this by monitoring the variation of the value of Extended Delta-V and the speeds of the two involved vehicles entering the traffic conflict. Once the involved vehicles are found in a traffic conflict, the interpretation of the values of the safety indicators determines the severity level of the crash should it happen.

In this study, we evaluate crash severity by categorizing involved vehicles into speed intervals. The speed ranges are as follows, increasing in 20 km/h increments: [0, 20), [20, 40), [40, 60), [60, 80). The final interval, [80, 150), encompasses speeds starting from 80 km/h, and extends up to 150 km/h. This range is chosen to represent speeds for standard vehicles, with 150 km/h being the maximum speed considered for this category. While formalizing speed and defining deceleration as a function of speed can result in a more concise and self-contained formalization, in our approach, we opted for explicitly representing speed values to emphasize the significance of the severity analysis and its importance. In the course of our study, we consider different speed intervals to account for different deceleration rates as given by Equation 14, which is applied in the event of a traffic conflict, where the variable a refers to the assigned deceleration and $b_0 < b_1 < b_2 < b_3 < b_4$. However, it is important to note that these rates are approximations, as the precise intensity of braking cannot be determined without additional information about the surrounding conditions and environment of the conflict.

$$a = \begin{cases} b_0, & 0 < v \leq 20 \\ b_1, & 20 < v \leq 40 \\ b_2, & 40 < v \leq 60 \\ b_3, & 60 < v \leq 80 \\ b_4, & 80 < v \end{cases} \tag{14}$$

4.2 Traffic Safety Rule Specification

The traffic safety rule is formulated based on the Extended Delta-V, as described in Eq. 6, and incorporates various traffic conflict indicators, including Time-to-Collision (TTC), jerk profile, and yaw rate. This comprehensive rule addresses multiple collision scenarios in order to provide a robust and thorough approach for ensuring traffic safety. While traditional traffic safety rules typically aim to establish safe conditions for vehicles to navigate traffic conflicts successfully, our approach stands out by proposing a traffic safety rule that delineates non-safe conditions. In other words, it focuses on identifying traffic conflicts wherein the involved vehicles could potentially collide if appropriate evasive measures are not taken with the right intensity. A traffic conflict happens if one or all of the involved vehicles violate a traffic rule, show signs of bad driving, or simply join a zone where a conflict is already taking place. In this context, our reasoning is based on the TTC value and its defined threshold to start studying the safety of the involved vehicles. Once the computed value of TTC is less than 3 sec, the first tested evasive action is braking. The rate of deceleration is chosen based on the speed of the vehicle. Furthermore, the intensity of this rate is evaluated using the jerk profile to determine the sufficiency of the action. Should the deceleration rate prove inadequate to prevent a collision, an additional evasive action must be undertaken to ensure that the collision does not occur. The complementing action, i.e., swerving, is inspected using the defined yaw rate indicator, and its effectiveness is also evaluated. In the analysis, the speed of the involved vehicles plays a crucial role in determining the type and intensity of the required evasive action. In instances where these actions fall short, a potential collision becomes likely. The severity level of each collision is established by considering the speeds of the vehicles involved at the time of the traffic conflict. The sketch of the defined traffic safety rule is represented as follows: `(Initial State` $\wedge$ `TCTs thresholds violated)` $\longrightarrow$ $\big[$`{(control);(Vehicles' Dynamics)}*`$\big]$`(TCTs thresholds violated)` $\longrightarrow$ `Collision)`, starting from an initial state, i.e., `Initial State`, where the thresholds defined for the TCTs indicators are violated, i.e., `TCTs thresholds violated`, a collision, i.e., `Collision`, is bound to take place. This occurs if the execution of the control part, `control`, reflected by the braking and/or governed by its dynamics (`Vehicles' Dynamics`), proves insufficient in safely mitigating the traffic conflict [3].

5 Verification of the Traffic Safety Rule

In this section, a formal description of the traffic safety rule structure is detailed along with its formalization in differential Dynamic Logic (dL). Furthermore, the verification process of the formalized rule in KeYmaera X is described in different traffic scenarios.

5.1 Formal Specification of the Traffic Safety Rule

In this section, we provide a description of the conditions that can lead to a collision, where we cover the corner cases that a driver can face during a traffic conflict. Furthermore, we present a comprehensive formal definition that provides a formalized understanding of these conditions. For a TTC less than 3 sec, we consider the following corner cases.

1. **Ext-Δ V_p < Ext-ΔV:** In this context, Ext-ΔV_p represents the speed change calculated after deceleration. This condition specifies that when a conflict is detected, an imminent collision is likely if the speed variation, denoted as Ext-ΔV_p, is less than the initial Extended-Delta V value, denoted as Ext-ΔV, which is typically computed under normal traffic conditions. This situation prompts further investigation into the following scenarios:
2. **(Jerk profile $\geq$ 0) $\wedge$ ((Yaw rate $\leq$ 0) $\vee$ (Yaw rate > 0.785)):** These values represent the failure to execute evasive actions; no braking and no swerving which leads immediately to an accident, should the situation remain unchanged during the conflict situation.
3. **(-9.9 < Jerk profile < 0) $\wedge$ ((Yaw rate $\leq$ 0) $\vee$ (Yaw rate > 0.785)):** In this case, the braking action reflects a deceleration rate demonstrating a normal braking situation which is not substantial enough to mitigate the conflict at hand safely. Furthermore, the yaw rate indicates that the trajectory was unchanged meaning no swerving was done. Once combined, these conditions eventually will lead to a collision that may or may not be severe depending on the involved vehicles' speed.
4. **(-15 < Jerk profile $\leq$ -9.9) $\wedge$ ((Yaw rate $\leq$ 0) $\vee$ (Yaw rate > 0.785)):** A jerk profile falling in the defined interval does not necessarily translate into a successful deceleration rate. In fact, the braking might not be enough to stop the vehicle before engaging in the collision. For this to be avoided, the deceleration can be accompanied with a minimum of swerving to make sure that the accident is avoided. The absence of the swerving in this case might be critical and can even lead to a collision that will have a certain impact depending on the vehicles' speeds.

The four aforementioned corner cases are formally represented in dL as follows, where J indicates the jerk profile, while r represents the yaw rate.

Definition 1: $\texttt{TCT}_{violated} \equiv (\texttt{TTC} \leq 3) \wedge (\texttt{Ext-}\Delta\texttt{V}_p < \texttt{Ext-}\Delta\texttt{V}) \wedge \Big(((\texttt{J} \geq 0) \vee ((\texttt{r} \leq 0) \vee (\texttt{r} > 0.785))\Big) \vee \Big((-9.9 < \texttt{J} < 0) \wedge ((\texttt{r} \leq 0) \vee (\texttt{r} > 0.785))\Big) \vee \Big((-15 < \texttt{J} \leq -9.9) \wedge ((\texttt{r} \leq 0) \vee (\texttt{r} > 0.785))\Big)\Big)$

5.2 Formalization of Traffic Collision Scenarios

For every traffic interaction, i.e., rear-end, head-on and left-side collision, the mathematical modeling of the pre-conditions and vehicle dynamics differ. Therefore, the formalization of *Pre-conditions (init)* and *Vehicle Dynamics (dyn)* is given below for every traffic interaction.

1. **Rear-end Collision:** For a rear-end collision, the speed of the following vehicle and its evasive actions in a traffic conflict play a crucial role in assessing

the potential crash severity. Denoting the assumed speeds of vehicles 1 and 2 as v_1 and v_2, respectively (where $v_2 > v_1$), the process begins with the calculation of the Extended Delta-V before a conflict. The monitoring of Time-To-Collision, i.e., TTC_1, comes into play, and when it equals or falls under 3 sec [8], an evasive action will be taken based on the value of v_2. Subsequently, the Extended Delta-V is recalculated and compared to the initial value to determine its strength in averting a potential collision. The formalization of the pre-conditions in dL, i.e., *init*, given below, establishes different bounds for the defined parameters.

Definition 2: $\texttt{init} \equiv (\texttt{v}_0 > 0) \wedge (\texttt{v}_{post} \geq 0) \wedge (\texttt{v}_1 \geq 0) \wedge (\texttt{v}_2 \geq 0) \wedge (\texttt{b}_0 > 0) \wedge (\texttt{b}_1 > \texttt{b}_0) \wedge (\texttt{b}_2 > \texttt{b}_1) \wedge (\texttt{b}_3 > \texttt{b}_2) \wedge (\texttt{b}_4 > \texttt{b}_3) \wedge (\texttt{m}_1 > 0) \wedge (\texttt{m}_2 > 0)\ (\texttt{rd} > 0) \wedge (\texttt{x}_2 < \texttt{x}_1) \wedge (\theta_2 = \frac{x_2}{rd}) \wedge (\texttt{TTC}_1 = \frac{x_1 - x_2 - L_1}{v_2 - v_1})$

The dynamics of the vehicle, given below, are modeled using its position x_2, velocity v_2 and acceleration a_2. The formalization of the ordinary differential equation (ODE) linking these parameters in KeYmaera X is given along with the derivation of the jerk profile J_2 and yaw rate r_2.

Definition 3: $\texttt{dyn} \equiv \texttt{x}_2' = \texttt{v}_2,\ \texttt{v}_2' = \texttt{a}_2,\ \texttt{a}_2' = \texttt{J}_2,\ \theta_2' = \texttt{r}_2$

The proof structure of the traffic safety rule in this collision scenario is depicted in Figure 4, where achieving a *No Collision* outcome (represented by the green leaf) is contingent on adhering to the TCTs thresholds and executing the required evasive actions. Failure to comply may lead to a collision, the severity of which can be determined by assessing the value of TTC_1, the speed of the vehicles and the Extended Delta-V value, as well as considering whether an evasive maneuver was attempted.

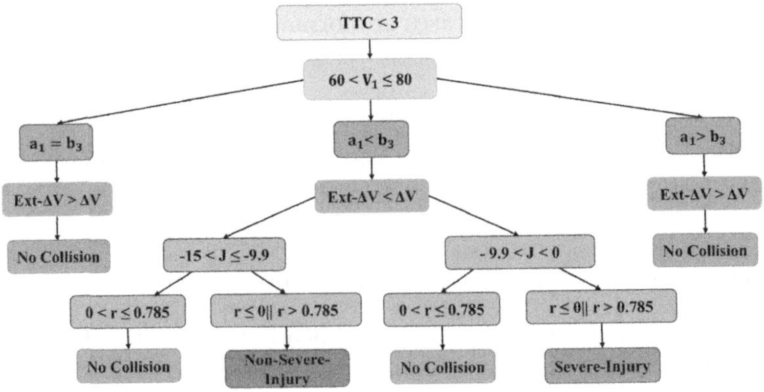

Fig. 4. Proof Structure and Formal Analysis of Crash Severity in a Rear-end Collision Scenario

2. **Head-on Collision:** For a head-on collision, once a traffic conflict situation is identified by Time-To-Collision $\text{TTC}_2 < 3$, the magnitude of the evasive action is carried out based on the speed interval. This magnitude is analyzed to conclude if the crash will happen or not and determine its severity in both cases. Based on the computed value of Extended Delta-V, a series of actions, i.e., braking and swerving, are executed to avoid the conflict safely. However, the execution of evasive actions in some cases proves either insufficient to avoid a collision or too strong for the situation at hand leading to further complications. For this, we build our study on analyzing the intensity of the taken actions by analyzing the obtained values for the rates indicators, jerk profile, and yaw rate, as measures for braking and swerving intensities, respectively. The formalization of the pre-conditions definition for this traffic scenario is described below:

Definition 4: $\texttt{init} \equiv (\texttt{v}_0 > 0) \wedge (\texttt{v}_{post} \geq 0) \wedge (\texttt{v}_1 \geq 0) \wedge (\texttt{v}_2 \geq 0) \wedge (\texttt{b}_0 > 0) \wedge (\texttt{b}_1 > \texttt{b}_0) \wedge (\texttt{b}_2 > \texttt{b}_1) \wedge (\texttt{b}_3 > \texttt{b}_2) \wedge (\texttt{b}_4 > \texttt{b}_3) \wedge (\texttt{m}_1 > 0) \wedge (\texttt{m}_2 > 0) \wedge (\texttt{rd} > 0) \wedge (\texttt{x}_2 \neq \texttt{x}_1) \wedge (\theta_1 = \frac{x_1}{rd}) \wedge (\theta_2 = \frac{x_2}{rd}) \wedge (\text{TTC}_2 = \frac{x_1 - x_2}{v_1 + v_2})$

As for modeling the system dynamics, the corresponding ODE is given for the involved vehicles, i.e., vehicle 1 and vehicle 2, using their positions x_1 and x_2, velocities v_1 and v_2, and accelerations a_1 and a_2, respectively. Furthermore, the jerk profile and yaw rate are computed for both vehicles and denoted as J_2, J_2, r_1 and r_2, respectively. The formalization of the dynamics of the system in dL is given below:

Definition 5: $\texttt{dyn} \equiv \texttt{x}_1' = \texttt{v}_1,\ \texttt{v}_1' = \texttt{a}_1,\ \texttt{a}_1' = \texttt{J}_1,\ \theta_1' = \texttt{r}_1,\ \texttt{x}_2' = \texttt{v}_2,\ \texttt{v}_2' = \texttt{a}_2,\ \texttt{a}_2' = \texttt{J}_2,\ \theta_2' = \texttt{r}_2$

3. **Left-side Collision:** A conflict situation taking place from the driver's left/right side on the main street is prone to happen under many favorable conditions. In this scenario, the defined Delta-V formula explicitly defines the angle using its *cosine* value. Using the formula defined in [9], the Extended Delta-V is calculated as:

$$Ext - \Delta V_i = \frac{m_i}{m_1 + m_2} \cdot \sqrt{v_1^2 + v_2^2 - 2v_1 v_2 \cos\alpha} \tag{15}$$

where m_i and v_i denote the mass and speed of vehicle i, with $i \in \{1, 2\}$ representing either vehicle 1 or 2, and α is the approaching angle. In this traffic scenario, Time-To-Collision, i.e., TTC_3, is defined based on vehicles positioning, as described by Eqs. 3 and 4. For this case, $\alpha = 90°$ is used to simplify things with a conflict-to-collision region, where the two involved vehicles will intercept each other if the crash is not avoided as shown by Figure 1.c. The formalization of the defined parameters as pre-conditions, *init*, is given below.

Definition 6: $\texttt{init} \equiv (\texttt{v}_0 > 0) \wedge (\texttt{v}_{post} \geq 0) \wedge (\texttt{v}_1 \geq 0) \wedge (\texttt{v}_2 \geq 0) \wedge (\texttt{b}_0 > 0) \wedge (\texttt{b}_1 > \texttt{b}_0) \wedge (\texttt{b}_2 > \texttt{b}_1) \wedge (\texttt{b}_3 > \texttt{b}_2) \wedge (\texttt{b}_4 > \texttt{b}_3) \wedge (\texttt{m}_1 > 0) \wedge$

$(\mathtt{m}_2 > 0) \wedge (\mathtt{c} \geq -1) \wedge (\mathtt{t}_{f1} > 0) \wedge (\mathtt{t}_{f2} > 0) \wedge (\mathtt{t}_{r1} > 0) \wedge (\mathtt{t}_{r2} > 0) \wedge (\mathtt{t}_{r1} > \mathtt{t}_{f1}) \wedge (\mathtt{t}_{r2} > \mathtt{t}_{f2}) \wedge (\mathtt{x}_2 \neq \mathtt{x}_1) \wedge (\mathtt{c} \leq 1) \wedge (\mathtt{rd} > 0) \wedge (\theta_1 = \frac{x_1}{rd}) \wedge (\theta_2 = \frac{x_2}{rd}) \wedge (\mathtt{TTC}_3 = \frac{d_2}{v_2})$

The formalization of the ODE modeling the system dynamics is given below for the involved vehicles, i.e., vehicle 1 and vehicle 2, using their positions x_1 and x_2, velocities v_1 and v_2, and accelerations a_1 and a_2, respectively. Moreover, the jerk profile and yaw rate are computed for both vehicles and denoted as J_1, J_2, r_1 and r_2, respectively.

Definition 7: $\mathtt{dyn} \equiv \mathtt{x}_1' = \mathtt{v}_1,\ \mathtt{v}_1' = \mathtt{a}_1,\ \mathtt{a}_1' = \mathtt{J}_1,\ \theta_1' = \mathtt{r}_1,$
$\mathtt{x}_2' = \mathtt{v}_2,\ \mathtt{v}_2' = \mathtt{a}_2,\ \mathtt{a}_2' = \mathtt{J}_2,\ \theta_2' = \mathtt{r}_2$

5.3 Formal Verification of the Traffic Safety Rule

When the conditions outlined in Definition 1 are met, it indicates an inevitable collision between the vehicles involved in the traffic conflict. In the context of a head-on collision, this is formally defined when the position of front bumper of vehicle 1, denoted as x_1, is equal to the position of the front bumper vehicle 2, denoted as x_2, as defined in Definition 8.

Definition 8: $\mathtt{Collision} \equiv \mathtt{x}_1 = \mathtt{x}_2$

The same definition is valid for a left-side collision as given below:

Definition 9: $\mathtt{Collision} \equiv \mathtt{x}_1 = \mathtt{x}_2$

In a rear-end collision, it is, however, important to note that the impact takes place at the rear bumper of the leading vehicle. Therefore, a collision is defined by the position of the rear bumper of vehicle 1 (x_1 - L_1) being equal to the position of the front bumper of vehicle 2 (x_2) as given by Definition 10.

Definition 10: $\mathtt{Collision} \equiv \mathtt{x}_1 - \mathtt{L}_1 = \mathtt{x}_2$

Using Definitions 1-10, we express in KeYmaera X the following main theorem as the target traffic safety rule. The proposed traffic safety rule is composed of three parts: (1) initial state characterization; (2) definition of multiple speed intervals with the severity level associated with each interval; and (3) post-condition as an expression of the expected outcome if the rule holds.

Theorem:
$\vdash \mathtt{init} \wedge \mathtt{TCT}_{violated} \longrightarrow [\{(\mathtt{ctrl});(\mathtt{dyn})\}^*](\mathtt{TCT}_{violated} \longrightarrow \mathtt{Collision})$
The traffic safety rule is given by the above theorem where `init` is determined based on the collision scenario, as described in Definitions 2, 4, and 6. Definition 1 provides the formal definition of $\mathtt{TCT}_{violated}$. The control component, represented as `ctrl`, involves the allocation of specific deceleration rates along with swerving maneuvers, contingent upon the speed of the vehicles. For more detailed information, please refer to the proof files [3]. Definitions 3, 5, and 7

specify the vehicle dynamics `dyn` depending on the collision scenario. Since there are no evolution domain constraints in `dyn` that limit the duration, each continuous evolution has an arbitrary duration $t \in \mathbb{R}_{\geq 0}$. The operator *, as described in Table 1, signifies a nondeterministic repetition of the program. Lastly, the collision definition `Collision` is given by Definitions 8, 9 and 10. The symbol $\longrightarrow$ denotes an implication relation connecting two formulas, the antecedent and the consequent. It asserts that the truth of the antecedent implies the truth of the consequent.

5.4 Discussion

We succeeded in verifying the above theorem in KeYmaera X (version 5.0.1). The considered collision scenarios exhibit varying levels of complexity given the number of vehicles involved. In our formalization, we consider the dynamics of all involved vehicles as well as their potential evasive actions based on their respective speeds which adds more complexity to the verification process. This complexity is reflected by the number of tactics needed to prove the theorem as well as the verification time. For instance, the verification of the head-on collision scenario involves modeling the two vehicles implicated and the possible actions executed by each vehicle. This led to applying more tactics and rules to prove this scenario in KeYmaera X. As for rear-end and left side-collision, the systems modeled are less complicated, and therefore, easier to be verified. The verification process was carried out using KeYmaera X's automated strategies, which allowed for a fully automated process. This means that no manual intervention was required during the verification process, which resulted in a more efficient and accurate verification. The KeYmaera X proof files are available online [3].

6 Conclusion

In this paper, we proposed to integrate formal methods with TCTs in order to obtain guarantees of a rigorous analysis of vehicular crash severity. In particular, we provided the formalization and verification of a traffic safety rule using the hybrid theorem prover KeYmaera X. The proposed rule combines crucial TCTs, namely Time-To-Collision and Extended Delta-V, along with relevant evasive actions indicators, i.e., jerk profile and yaw rate. These indicators are employed to formally analyze crash severity based on their computed values. By performing a comprehensive analysis of traffic conflict techniques, the proposed traffic safety rule helps in identifying the suitable evasive actions with the right intensity. This proactive approach holds the potential to significantly reduce the occurrence of actual traffic crashes. However, knowing that traffic conflicts differ from one situation to another, we proposed to conduct our analysis in three different traffic scenarios, i.e., rear-end, head-on, and left-side collision. The work developed in this paper demonstrates the importance of combining different traffic conflict indicators as a unified safety rule, where each indicator provides a complementary safety aspect of the interactions. The use of formal methods to formally verify the safety rule is of great importance to guarantee the reliability and soundness of the system. This work can be a great asset in the decision-making process for autonomous vehicles during traffic conflicts. As future work, we plan to extend the proposed crash analysis to incorporate connectivity by considering autonomous and connected vehicles, including the inter-communication between them. It will also be interesting to consider other traffic behaviors than those presented in this paper, such as lane changing or weaving.

Future Directions: Considering that AI is increasingly becoming the dominant technology underlying many systems, particularly safety-critical systems, our future work aims to explore the integration of traffic safety rules as formal safety constraints directly into the objective function of Reinforcement Learning algorithms. This approach is intended to ensure that safety becomes an inherent and prioritized aspect of AI algorithms, especially in the context of autonomous systems and intelligent decision-making processes.

Acknowledgement. We would like to extend our thanks to Dr. André Platzer (Karlsruhe Institute of Technology) and Dr. Stefan Mitsch (DePaul University) for their availability to answer our inquiries about KeYmaera.

References

1. Althoff, M., Stursberg, O., Buss, M.: Safety assessment of autonomous cars using verification techniques. In: American Control Conference, pp. 4154–4159 (2007)
2. Bagdadi, O., Várhelyi, A.: Jerky driving-an indicator of accident proneness? Accid. Anal. Prev. **43**(4), 1359–1363 (2011)
3. Barhoumi, O.: KeYmaera X proof files for the traffic safety rule (2024). https://github.com/OumaimaBarhoumi/Traffic-Safety-Rule/
4. Cao, X., Young, W., Sarvi, M.: Exploring duration of lane change execution. In: Australasian Transport Research Forum, pp. 1–17 (2013)
5. Garcia, J., Feng, Y.: A comprehensive study of autonomous vehicle bugs. In: International Conference on Software Engineering, pp. 385–396. ACM (2020)
6. Guo, Y., Sayed, T., Zaki, M.H.: Exploring evasive action–based indicators for PTW conflicts in shared traffic facility environments. J. Transp. Eng. Part A: Syst. **144**(11), 04018065 (2018)
7. Hayward, J.: Near-miss determination through use of a scale of danger. In: Highway Research Record, pp. 24–34 (1972)
8. Hirst, S., Graham, R.: The format and presentation of collision warnings. In: Ergonomics and Safety of Intelligent Driver Interfaces, pp. 203–219. CRC Press (1997)
9. Laureshyn, A., De Ceunynck, T., Karlsson, C., Svensson, Å., Daniels, S.: In search of the severity dimension of traffic events: Extended Delta-V as a traffic conflict indicator. Accid. Anal. Prev. **98**, 46–56 (2017)
10. Laureshyn, A., Svensson, Å., Hydén, C.: Evaluation of traffic safety, based on micro-level behavioural data. Accid. Anal. Prev. **42**(6), 1637–1646 (2010)
11. Loos, S.M., Platzer, A., Nistor, L.: Adaptive cruise control: hybrid, distributed, and now formally verified. In: Butler, M., Schulte, W. (eds.) : Formal Methods, pp. 42–56. Springer, Berlin, Heidelberg (2011). https://doi.org/10.1007/978-3-642-21437-0_6

12. Mao, J., Chen, L.: Runtime monitoring for cyber-physical systems: a case study of cooperative adaptive cruise control. In: International Conference on Intelligent System Design and Engineering Application, pp. 509–515 (2012)
13. Mary, L.: 5 conclusions from an automation expert with firsthand knowledge of highway regulation what self-driving cars tell us about AI risks: "missy" cummings. IEEE Spectrum **60**(10), 30–35 (2023)
14. Mitsch, S., Loos, S.M., Platzer, A.: Towards formal verification of freeway traffic control. In: International Conference on Cyber-Physical Systems, pp. 171–180 (2012)
15. Nygård, M.: A method for analysing traffic safety with help of speed profiles. Ph.D. thesis, Tampere University of Technology, Finland (1999)
16. Platzer, A.: Differential dynamic logic for verifying parametric hybrid systems. In: Olivetti, N. (ed.) Automated Reasoning with Analytic Tableaux and Related Methods, pp. 216–232. Springer, Berlin, Heidelberg (2007). https://doi.org/10.1007/978-3-540-73099-6_17
17. Rizaldi, A., Immler, F., Althoff, M.: A formally verified checker of the safe distance traffic rules for autonomous vehicles. In: Rayadurgam, S., Tkachuk, O. (eds.) NASA Formal Methods, pp. 175–190. Springer International Publishing, Cham (2016). https://doi.org/10.1007/978-3-319-40648-0_14
18. Shelby, S.: Delta-V as a measure of traffic conflict severity. In: International Conference on Road Safety and Simulation, pp. 14–16 (2011)
19. Stanton, N.A., Salmon, P.M., Walker, G.H., Stanton, M.: Models and methods for collision analysis: a comparison study based on the Uber collision with a pedestrian. In: Safety Science **120**, 117–128 (2019)
20. Tageldin, A., Sayed, T., Wang, X.: Can time proximity measures be used as safety indicators in all driving cultures? Transp. Res. Record **2520**(1), 165–174 (2015)
21. Zaki, M.H., Sayed, T., Shaaban, K.: Use of drivers' jerk profiles in computer vision-based traffic safety evaluations. Transp. Res. Record **2434**(1), 103–112 (2014)
22. Zheng, L., Ismail, K., Meng, X.: Traffic conflict techniques for road safety analysis: open questions and some insights. Can. J. Civil Eng. **41**(7), 633–641 (2014)

Formal Verification of ABCD Parameters Based Models for Transmission Lines

Elif Deniz[1(✉)], Adnan Rashid[1], Osman Hasan[2], and Sofiène Tahar[1]

[1] Department of Electrical and Computer Engineering, Concordia University, Montreal, Quebec, Canada
{e_deniz,rashid,tahar}@ece.concordia.ca

[2] School of Electrical Engineering and Computer Science, National University of Sciences and Technology, Islamabad, Pakistan
osman.hasan@seecs.nust.edu.pk

Abstract. Transmission lines are widely used in many safety-critical applications, such as embedded systems (printed circuit boards) and power grids. They are generally represented as two-port networks and ABCD parameters are used to develop mathematical models (system of equations) capturing the relationship between the sending and receiving quantities, i.e., voltages and currents. In this paper, we propose to use higher-order-logic theorem proving for formally verifying the ABCD parameters based models of transmission lines. In particular, we use the HOL Light theorem prover to formalize transmission lines as systems consisting of these two-port network models, such as short, medium and cascaded, and various constraints on components of networks. Next, we formalize the Kirchhoff's voltage and current laws capturing dynamics of voltages and currents in these two-port networks. Moreover, we use these laws for formally verifying the ABCD parameters based models of transmission lines. To demonstrate the practical effectiveness of our proposed approach, we formally verify the ABCD parameter based medium transmission line model of a Wireless Power Transfer (WPT) system, which is widely used in electric vehicles and embedded devices.

Keywords: Transmission Lines · ABCD Parameters · Higher-Order Logic · Theorem Proving · HOL Light · Wireless Power Transfer

1 Introduction

Transmission lines [12] are used to transmit electrical energy from source to destination in the form of electromagnetic waves and are considered as essential components of power transmission/distribution networks. Based on their length, they are categorized as short, medium or long transmission lines. Moreover, to represent some scenarios, like impedance matching and operational flexibility, a single classification may not be adequate, necessitating the use of cascaded transmission lines, where these lines are connected in series, such as short-short or short-medium and vice versa [12]. This categorization of transmission lines

S. M. Watt and T. Ida (Eds.): SCSS 2024, LNAI 14991, pp. 20–37, 2024.
https://doi.org/10.1007/978-3-031-69042-6_2

enables us to model them using their equivalent lumped circuit representations and thus greatly facilitates a precise modeling of currents and voltages. Furthermore, the applications of these transmission lines extend across various domains including power distribution, medical imaging, telecommunications and aerospace. For instance, transmission lines can be used in the design of power distribution systems in aircrafts to ensure the reliable supply of electrical energy to various avionic subsytems, contributing to the overall functionality, safety and performance of the aircraft [15].

Transmission lines are generally represented as two-port networks that are electrical circuits comprising of lumped elements, such as resistors, capacitors and inductors, with pairs of terminals on sending and receiving ends, enabling a connection to the external networks [4]. These networks are characterized by their ABCD parameters, also known as chain or transmission line parameters ensuring a systematic modelling of the transmission lines [12]. In particular, the ABCD parameters enable developing the mathematical models (system of equations) of these networks capturing a relationship between the sending and receiving quantities, i.e., voltages and currents, by incorporating their characteristics like impedance and admittance. Moreover, these mathematical models can also be derived from the application of the physical laws, such as the Kirchhoff's Current Law (KCL) and the Kirchhoff's Voltage Law (KVL) on the two-port networks corresponding to the transmission lines [14].

In this paper, we propose to use the HOL Light theorem prover for the formalization of the ABCD parameters based models of transmission lines and their analysis. One of the main motivations for choosing HOL Light is the availability of the required theories of linear algebra, vector and matrices. Moreover, its underlying logic kernel has been verified in the CakeML project [11], which raises the level of soundness of our work.

The main contributions of the paper are as follows:

- Deep embedded formalization of transmission lines and their two-port network models along with related ABCD matrices and associated circuit models.
- Formal verification of the KCL and KVL capturing the dynamics the circuit models of the transmission lines using the formalized libraries of multivariate calculus [6] in the HOL Light theorem prover.
- Formal verification of the ABCD parameters based models of transmission lines (short, medium and cascaded) based on the KCL and KVL implementations verified in the last step.
- Formal verification of the T-shaped circuit model [3] for Wireless Power Transfer (WPT) [10] that is widely used in electric vehicles and embedded devices.

To the best of our knowledge, no formalization of the ABCD parameters based modeling of transmission lines exists in the literature and thus, for safety-critical applications this type of analysis in HOL theorem proving is utmost important. The source code of our formalization is available for download at [1] and can be used by other researchers and engineers for analysis and further enhancements.

The rest of the paper is organized as follows: In Sect. 2, we provide preliminaries introducing the notion of ABCD parameters of transmission lines, as well as briefly describing the HOL Light theorem prover. In Sect. 3, we present the formalization of the ABCD parameters based models of transmission lines. Section 4 provides the formal verification of the short, medium and cascaded transmission lines captured by the ABCD matrix. We provide the formal analysis of a WPT system in Sect. 5. Finally, Sect. 6 concludes the paper.

2 Preliminaries

In this section, we present the fundamental concepts of modeling transmission lines through ABCD parameters and matrices. We also briefly describe the HOL Light theorem prover and associated functions and symbols that are necessary for understanding the rest of the paper.

2.1 ABCD Parameters of a Transmission Line

A two-port network refers to a system with two input and two output terminals. Figure 1 illustrates a generic two-port network, which is to be characterized using ABCD parameters.

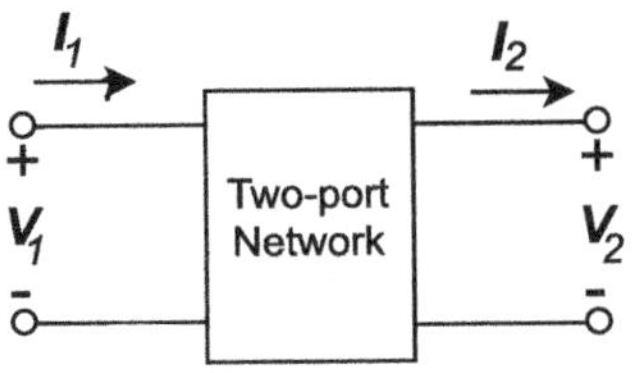

Fig. 1. Two-Port Network

In the context of the two-port transmission line model, port 1 is characterized by an input current, denoted as I_1, and a corresponding input voltage, V_1. The resulting output voltage and current at port 2 are labeled as V_2 and I_2, respectively. It is essential to note that the chosen current directions designate I_1 as entering and I_2 as leaving the two-port network. Here, V_1 and I_1 are dependent variables whereas V_2 and I_2 are considered independent. Let A, B, C and D be constants that characterize the above network. These *ABCD parameters* relate the input variables V_1 and I_1 as functions of the output variables V_2 and I_2 as follows:

$$V_1 = AV_2 + BI_2$$

$$I_1 = CV_2 + DI_2$$

The above equations can be written in matrix form:

$$\begin{bmatrix} V_1 \\ I_1 \end{bmatrix} = \begin{bmatrix} A & B \\ C & D \end{bmatrix} \begin{bmatrix} V_2 \\ I_2 \end{bmatrix}$$

These parameters play an important role in the analysis and comprehension of the transmission of electrical signals through intricate networks. It is also utilized to evaluate the performance of input, output voltage, and current within the transmission network.

2.2 HOL Light Theorem Prover

HOL Light [5] is an interactive theorem proving environment for the development of mathematical proofs using higher-order logic. It is implemented in Objective CAML (OCaml) [13], which is a variant of the ML (Meta-Language) functional programming language. The significance of theorem proving systems lies in their ability to verify general properties of software and hardware systems. For example, they can help in verifying and establishing the accuracy of diverse properties of a digital circuit, ensuring that the circuit operates as intended and complies with the specified design criteria. Furthermore, HOL Light provides a variety of automated proof procedures and proof assistants to assist users in guiding and completing their proofs. In addition, users have the flexibility to craft and implement their own personalized automation methods. Table 1 summarizes some HOL Light functions/symbols and their meanings that are frequently used in our proposed formalization.

Table 1. HOL Light Functions and Symbols

HOL Light Functions/ Symbols	Standard Functions/ Symbols	Description
`&a`	$\mathbb{N} \rightarrow \mathbb{R}$	Type casting from Natural numbers to Reals
`&num`	{0,1,2..}	Positive Integers data type
`Cx a`	$\mathbb{R} \rightarrow \mathbb{C}$	Type casting from Reals to Complex
`real`	$\mathbb{R}$	Real data type
`complex`	$\mathbb{C}$	Complex data type
`A ** B`	**AB**	Matrix-matrix multiplication
`A ** x`	**Ax**	Matrix-vector multiplication

In the rest of the paper, we will use standard mathematical notations rather than pure HOL Light syntax notations to facilitate the understanding of the paper for a non-HOL Light user. Readers interested in viewing the original HOL Light formalization can see the source code for our formalization at [1].

3 Formalization of the ABCD Parameters Based Models

A transmission line is used to carry electrical energy from a generating source to various distribution units by transmitting voltage and current waves from one end to the other. Transmission lines can be represented by two-port networks (circuit models having lumped elements). They can be single transmission lines, such as, short and medium lines based on their lengths or cascaded depending on the number of lines connected in series. Single transmission line models can further be categorised based on the arrangement of various lumped components of the circuits. For example, a short circuit representation, where a resistor R is connected in series to a capacitor Ca is commonly known as a *series impedance model* for the short transmission line. Similarly, medium transmission lines can be represented by their Π or T models based on the connection of various circuit components [4]. Therefore, it is sufficient to model single transmission lines that can further be used in the cascaded transmission lines, connected in series.

In our formalization, we present these transmission lines models, based on their type, as an enumerated type definition in HOL Light as:

```
define_type "tl_models = ShortTL_SerImp | ShortTL_ShuAdm |
                         MediumTL_TCir | MediumTL_PiCir"
```

Next, in order to capture an interaction between various components and their impact on the equivalent circuit models, we need to model the voltage and current functions and their associated representations in the mathematical model. In this regard, we first model the types of the voltage and current functions, and the complex vectors and matrices using the type abbreviation based on the available types in HOL Light as follows:

```
new_type_abbrev ("vol_fun",`:(ℂ → ℂ)`)
new_type_abbrev ("cur_fun",`:(ℂ → ℂ)`)
new_type_abbrev ("comp_vec",`:ℂ^2`)
new_type_abbrev ("comp_mat",`:ℂ^2^2`)
```

The type vol_fun is used to model a voltage function Vx that accepts a variable x of complex type $\mathbb{C}$ and returns a complex-valued function V. Similarly, the type comp_mat captures a 2×2 matrix having every entry as a complex number.

Similarly, we model the ABCD parameters and transmission line constants as 4-tuples in HOL Light. Moreover, we model the types of the sending and receiving end quantities as follows:

```
new_type_abbrev ("abcd_param",`:(A × B × C × D)`)
new_type_abbrev ("trans_lines_const",`:(R × L × Ca × G)`)
new_type_abbrev ("send_end_quan",`:(Vs × Is)`)
new_type_abbrev ("recei_end_quan",`:(VR × IR)`)
```

where the types of A, B, C, D, R, L, Ca, G, Vs, Is, VR and IR are given in Table 2. A transmission line is valid if it is represented by a valid ABCD parameters based model and satisfies various constraints on transmission line constants.
We formalize the validity of a transmission line in HOL Light as follows:

Definition 1. Valid Transmission Line

```
⊢def ∀tlc tlm.      valid_transmission_line (tlm,tlc) ⇔
                 valid_transm_line_model tlm ∧ valid_tl_const tlc
```

Table 2. Parameters, and their Standard and HOL Light Symbols

Parameter Description	Standard Symbol	HOL Light Symbol:Type	Parameter Description	Standard Symbol	HOL Light Symbol:Type
Parameter A	A	A:ℝ	Parameter B	B	B:ℝ
Parameter C	C	C:ℝ	Parameter D	D	D:ℝ
Resistance	R	R:ℝ	Inductance	L	L:ℝ
Capacitance	Ca	Ca:ℝ	Conductance	G	G:ℝ
Sending End Voltage	V_s	Vs:vol_fun	Sending End Current	I_s	Is:cur_fun
Receiving End Voltage	V_R	VR:vol_fun	Receiving End Current	I_R	IR:cur_fun

where the function valid_transm_line_model accepts a transmission line model, i.e., short or medium and provides its validity. This is formalized as:

Definition 2. Valid Transmission Line Models

⊢$_{def}$ (valid_transm_line_model (ShortTL_SerImp) ⇔ T) ∧
  (valid_transm_line_model (ShortTL_ShuAdm) ⇔ T) ∧
  (valid_transm_line_model (MediumTL_TCir) ⇔ T) ∧
  (valid_transm_line_model (MediumTL_PiCir) ⇔ T)

Similarly, the function valid_tl_const in Definition 1 models the validity of the transmission line constants as follows:

Definition 3. Valid Transmission Line Constants
⊢$_{def}$ ∀R L Ca G.
  valid_tl_const ((R,L,Ca,G):trans_lines_const) ⇔
    &0 < R ∧ &0 < L ∧ &0 < Ca ∧ &0 < G

The verification of a relationship between the sending and receiving end quantities (voltages and currents) ensures the correct working of the ABCD parameters based models of transmission lines. To verify this relationship, we first model the generalized ABCD matrix as follows:

Definition 4. Generalized ABCD Matrix
⊢$_{def}$ ∀A B C D.

$$\text{abcd\_mat\_gen ((A,B,C,D):abcd\_param)} = \begin{bmatrix} \mathtt{A} & \mathtt{B} \\ \mathtt{C} & \mathtt{D} \end{bmatrix}$$

Next, we model the sending and receiving quantities as two-dimensional vectors in HOL Light:

Definition 5. Sending End Vector
⊢$_{def}$ ∀Vs Is z.

$$\text{send\_end\_vec ((Vs,Is):send\_end\_quan) z} = \begin{bmatrix} \mathtt{Vs(z)} \\ \mathtt{Is(z)} \end{bmatrix}$$

Definition 6. Receiving End Vector
$\vdash_{def}$ ∀VR IR z.

$$\text{recei\_end\_vec ((Vs,Is):recei\_end\_quan) z} = \begin{bmatrix} \texttt{VR(z)} \\ \texttt{IR(z)} \end{bmatrix}$$

Now, we use Definitions 4, 5 and 6 to formalize a generalized relationship between the sending and receiving quantities of transmission lines as:

Definition 7. Relationship Between Sending/Receiving Quantities
$\vdash_{def}$ ∀Vs Is VR IR A B C D.
relat_send_receiv_quan_gen (Vs,Is) (VR,IR) (A,B,C,D) z ⇔
(send_end_vec (Vs,Is) z = ((abcd_mat_gen (A,B,C,D)):comp_mat) **
recei_end_vec (VR,IR) z)

Finally, we formalize KCL and KVL, capturing the dynamics of voltage and current in the circuit models, as follows:

Definition 8. KCL and KVL
$\vdash_{def}$ ∀cur_list z. kcl (cur_list:cur_fun list) (z:complex) =
((vsum (0..(LENGTH (cur_list) - 1)) (λn. EL n cur_list z)) = Cx (&0))
$\vdash_{def}$ ∀vol_list z. kvl (vol_list:vol_fun list) (z:complex) =
((vsum (0..(LENGTH (vol_list) - 1)) (λn. EL n vol_list z)) = Cx (&0))

where the functions kcl and kvl accept lists of currents and voltages across the components of circuits, cur_list and vol_list, a complex variable z, and return the implementations of KCL and KVL, respectively. For example, kcl ensures that the sum of all currents leaving a particular node is zero. Here, the function vsum accepts a vector-valued function f and provides the summation $\sum_{i=0}^{n} fi$. Similarly, the function EL n l extracts the nth element from a list l.

4 Formalization of the Transmission Lines Models

This section presents the formal verification of the ABCD parameters based models of transmission lines, such as short, medium and cascaded transmission lines. To this end, we first formalize the ABCD matrices for the lumped circuits models in HOL Light as follows:

Definition 9. ABCD Matrices of Transmission Lines Models
$\vdash_{def}$ ∀R L Ca G w.
abcd_mat ShortTL_SerImp ((R,L,Ca,G):trans_lines_const) w =

$$\begin{bmatrix} 1 & \mathsf{R} + \mathsf{ii} * \mathsf{w} * \mathsf{L} \\ 0 & 1 \end{bmatrix} \quad \wedge$$

abcd_mat ShortTL_ShuAdm ((R,L,Ca,G):trans_lines_const) w =

$$\begin{bmatrix} 1 & 0 \\ \frac{1}{\mathsf{R}} + \mathsf{ii} * \mathsf{w} * \mathsf{Ca} & 1 \end{bmatrix} \quad \wedge$$

abcd_mat MediumTL_PiCir ((R,L,Ca,G):trans_lines_const) w =

$$\begin{bmatrix} 1 + \dfrac{\mathsf{w} * \mathsf{CaR} + \mathsf{ii} * \mathsf{w} * \mathsf{L}}{2} & 0 \\ \dfrac{1}{\mathsf{R}} + \mathsf{ii} * \mathsf{w} * \mathsf{Ca} & 1 \end{bmatrix} \quad \wedge$$

$$\mathsf{abcd\_mat\ MediumTL\_TCir\ ((R,L,Ca,G):trans\_lines\_const)\ w} =$$

$$\begin{bmatrix} \mathsf{T}\left(1 + \dfrac{\mathsf{w} * \mathsf{CaT}}{4}\right) & \mathsf{w} * \mathsf{Ca} \\ \left(\dfrac{1}{\mathsf{R}}\right) + \mathsf{ii} * \mathsf{w} * \mathsf{Ca} & \left(1 + \dfrac{\mathsf{w} * \mathsf{CaT}}{2}\right) \end{bmatrix}$$

where $\mathsf{T} = \mathsf{R} + \mathsf{ii} * \mathsf{w} * \mathsf{L}$. The function abcd_mat accepts the model, transmission line constants and a variable w, and returns the ABCD matrix corresponding to the given model. Here, the symbol "ii" is used to represent the imaginary number.

4.1 Formalization of Short Transmission Lines

Short transmission lines are implemented by their two circuit representations, namely, series impedance and shunt admittance circuit models. The series impedance model is represented by the circuit given in Fig. 2.

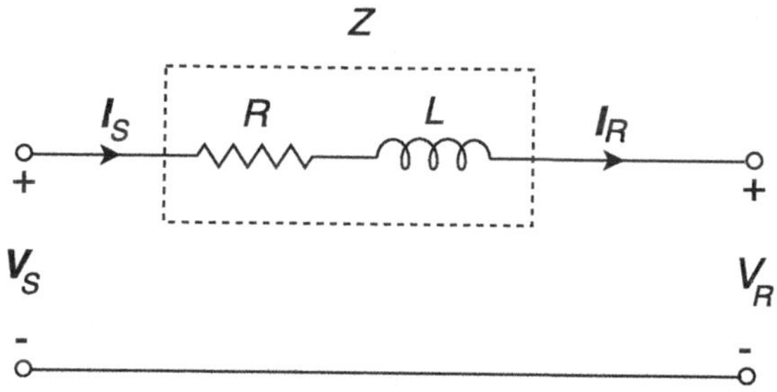

Fig. 2. Short Circuit Series Impedance Transmission Line

Here, the impedance effect is obtained from a series connection of the circuit's components resistor and inductor, respectively. We apply KVL on the series impendence circuit representation to obtain the following equation:

$$V_S = V_R + ZI_R \tag{1}$$

where Z represents the impedance of the circuit. Similarly, KCL for the series impedance circuit (Fig. 2) is mathematically expressed as follows:

$$I_S = I_R \tag{2}$$

Next, the KVL and KCL representations of the series impedance model, i.e., Eq. (1) and (2) can be expressed using the ABCD parameters as follows:

$$V_S = AV_R + BI_R \tag{3}$$

$$I_S = CV_R + DI_R \tag{4}$$

where $A = 1$, $B = Z$, $C = 0$ and $D = 1$.

We start the verification of this model by formalizing the KVL implementation of the circuit in HOL Light as:

Definition 10. KVL for Short Circuit Series Impedance Implementation

```
⊢def ∀Vs Is VR IR w z R L Ca G.
  kvl_implem ShortTL_SerImp ((Vs,Is):send_end_quan)
        ((VR,IR):recei_end_quan) ((R,L,Ca,G):trans_lines_const) (w:real) z =
  (kvl [(λz. Vs z); (λz. −(VR z)); resis_volt R (λz. −(IR z));
                                   induct_volt L w (λz. −(IR z))] z)
```

where the functions resis_volt and induct_volt model the voltages across the resistor and inductor, respectively and their formalization is given as Entries 1 and 2 of Table 3. The function kvl_implem mainly accepts a transmission line model (here, ShortTL_SerImp), input and output quantities and transmission line constants, and return the KVL implementation corresponding to the given model[1].

Table 3. Voltage and Currents Across Various Components

Components' Names	Formal Models
Voltage across Resistance	⊢def ∀R Ir. resis_volt R (Ir:cur_fun) = (λz. Ir z ∗ R)
Voltage across Inductance	⊢def ∀L w Il. induct_volt L w (Il:cur_fun) = (λz. ii ∗ w ∗ L ∗ Il (z))
Series Impedance Voltage	⊢def ∀R L w Isi. series_imped_volt R L w (Isi:cur_fun) = (λz. (resis_volt R Isi) z + (induct_volt L w Isi) z)
Admittance Current	⊢def ∀Ca w Va. admit_curr_med Va Ca w = (λz. w ∗ $\frac{\text{Ca}}{2}$ ∗ (V z))

Our next step is to verify the equivalence of our formalization of the KVL for the short circuit series impedance implementation to its mathematical representation, which is captured as the following HOL Light theorem.

[1] Here, we only present the implementation of the short circuit series impendence model for brevity.

Theorem 1. KVL for Short Circuit Series Implementation Equivalence
$\vdash_{thm}$ ∀Vs Is VR IR w z R L Ca G.
  let se = ((Vs,Is):send_end_quan) and
    re = ((VR,IR):recei_end_quan) and
    tlc = ((R,L,Ca,G):trans_lines_const) in
    [A] valid_transmission_line (ShortTL_SerImp,tlc)
      ⇒ kvl_implem ShortTL_SerImp se re tlc w z ⇔
          (Vs z = ((series_imped_volt R L w IR) z) + VR z)

where the function series_imped_volt (given as Entry 3 of Table 3) models the voltage across the series combination of the resistor and inductor, as depicted in Fig. 2. The only assumption A provides the validity of the transmission line for the short circuit series impedance model. The HOL Light proof for the verification of Theorem 1 is given as follows[2]:

```
let SHORT_TL_SERIES_IMPED_KVL = prove(
`∀Vs Is VR IR Ca G L R w z.
  kvl_implem ShortTL_SerImp ((Vs,Is):send_end_quan)
   ((VR,IR):recei_end_quan)((R,L,Ca,G):trans_lines_const) w z =
      (Vs z = ((series_imped_volt R L w (IR:cur_fun)) z) + VR z)`,

REPEAT GEN_TAC THEN SIMP_TAC [series_imped_volt] THEN
  REWRITE_TAC [kvl_implem; kvl] THEN REWRITE_TAC [LENGTH] THEN
  SIMP_TAC [GSYM ONE; GSYM TWO; GSYM THREE] THEN
  SIMP_TAC [SUC_SUB1] THEN SIMP_TAC [VSUM_4_LIST] THEN
  SUBGOAL_THEN `induct_volt L w (λz. --(IR:cur_fun) z) z =
                --(induct_volt L w (λz. IR z) z)` ASSUME_TAC
  THENL [REWRITE_TAC [induct_volt] THEN CONV_TAC COMPLEX_FIELD;ALL_TAC]
  THEN ASM_SIMP_TAC[] THEN POP_ASSUM (K ALL_TAC) THEN
  SUBGOAL_THEN `resis_volt R (λz. --(IR:cur_fun) z) z =
                --(resis_volt R (λz. IR z) z)` ASSUME_TAC
  THENL [REWRITE_TAC [resis_volt] THEN CONV_TAC COMPLEX_FIELD;ALL_TAC]
  THEN ASM_SIMP_TAC[] THEN POP_ASSUM (K ALL_TAC) THEN
  SIMP_TAC [ETA_AX] THEN CONV_TAC COMPLEX_FIELD)
```

We start the proof by eliminating the universal quantifications using a repeated application of the tactic GEN_TAC. We use the tactical REPEAT to repeatedly apply a tactic (In this case, it is GEN_TAC). Subsequently, we simplfy our goal by employing our definition of series impedance voltage (Entry 3 of Table 3) through the tactic SIMP_TAC. We then utilize REWRITE_TAC to rewrite our goal (proof state) using functions about KVL (Definitions 8 and 10). Moreover, we continue the proof process by leveraging the theorems regarding number arithmetic, summation and lists, which are proven as a part of this formalization.
It is important to note that the ASM variants of tactics REWRITE_TAC and SIMP_TAC

[2] Here, we only provide a detailed proof process of Theorem 1 and the details about verification of the rest of theorems can be found in our proof script [1].

provide rewriting and simplification tactics by incorporating the assumptions of the theorem to be proved. Finally, we use a decision procedure `COMPLEX_FIELD`, which automatically proves the basic field facts over complex numbers. Here, `CONV_TAC` is used to make a tactic from a conversion, which is `COMPLEX_FIELD` in our case. Additionally, we use the `THEN-THENL` structure to combine the whole proof, where the tactic `THEN` is used to combine two or more tactics applied to a goal. In case, if a tactic generates multiple subgoals *g1,..,gn*, one can utilize the `THENL` [*tac1;...;tacn*] to apply same set of tactics to different subgoals. Therefore, this structure provides a more compact representation of the proof as shown above in the HOL Light proof of Theorem 1.

Similarly, we formalize the KCL implementation of the short circuit series impedance implementation in HOL Light as follows:

Definition 11. KCL for Short Circuit Series Implementation

$\vdash_{def}$ ∀Vs Is VR IR w z R L Ca G.
  kcl_implem ShortTL_SerImp (Vs,Is) (VR,IR) (R,L,Ca,G) (w:real) z =
    (kcl [(λz. Is z); (λz. −(IR z))] z)

Next, we verify the equivalence of the above KCL implementation with its mathematical representation as the following HOL Light theorem.

Theorem 2. KCL for Short Circuit Series Implementation Equivalence

$\vdash_{thm}$ ∀Vs Is VR IR w z R L Ca G.
  let se = ((Vs,Is):send_end_quan) and
    re = ((VR,IR):recei_end_quan) and
    tlc = ((R,L,Ca,G):trans_lines_const) in
    [A] valid_transmission_line (ShortTL_SerImp,tlc)
      ⇒ kcl_implem ShortTL_SerImp se re w z tlc ⇔ (Is z = IR z)

The verification of the above theorem is very similar to that of Theorem 1.

Now, we verify a relationship between the sending and receiving quantities (voltages and currents) for the series impedance implementation of the short transmission line based on its KCL and KVL implementations as:

Theorem 3. Verification of the Short Transmission Line Model

$\vdash_{thm}$ ∀Vs Is VR IR w z R L Ca G.
  let se = ((Vs,Is):send_end_quan) and
    re = ((VR,IR):recei_end_quan) and
    tlc = ((R,L,Ca,G):trans_lines_const) in
    [A] valid_transmission_line (ShortTL_SerImp,tlc)
      ⇒ ((kvl_implem ShortTL_SerImp se re w z tlc) ∧
        (kcl_implem ShortTL_SerImp se re w z tlc)) ⇔
        (relat_send_receiv_quan ShortTL_SerImp se re tlc w z)

Assumption A ensures the validity of the short transmission line model. The proof process of Theorem 3 is mainly based on Theorems 1 and 2, and properties of matrices and vectors, alongwith some complex arithmetic reasoning.

We now formally verify the ABCD matrix based model of the series impendence circuit implementation of the short transmission line as:

Theorem 4. Verification of ABCD Matrix for Short Transmission Line
$\vdash_{thm}$ ∀Vs Is VR IR w z R L Ca G.
let se = ((Vs,Is):send_end_quan) and
re = ((VR,IR):recei_end_quan) and
abcd = ((A,B,C,D):abcd_param) and
tlc = ((R,L,Ca,G):trans_lines_const) in
[A1] valid_transmission_line (ShortTL_SerImp,tlc) ∧
[A2] A = 1 ∧ [A3] B = R + ii * w * L ∧ [A4] C = 0 ∧ [A5] D = 1
⇒ ((relat_send_receiv_quan_gen se re abcd z) =
(relat_send_receiv_quan ShortTL_SerImp se re tlc w z))

Assumption A1 ensures that the series impedance model corresponds to a valid transmission line. Assumptions A2-A5 capture the ABCD parameters of the model. Finally, the conclusion of Theorem 4 ensures that the generalized ABCD parameters based transmission line model is equal to the short circuit series impedance implementation. The verification of the above theorem is mainly based on properties of vectors and matrices alongside some complex arithmetic reasoning. We also formally verify the shunt admittance circuit model for the short transmission lines and the details about its verification can be found in the HOL Light code available at [1].

4.2 Formalization of Medium Transmission Lines

The medium transmission lines are implemented by their two circuit representations, namely, the *Nominal* Π and T-circuit models, based on configurations of lumped components of the circuit. The nominal Π-circuit model for the medium transmission line is depicted in Fig. 3.

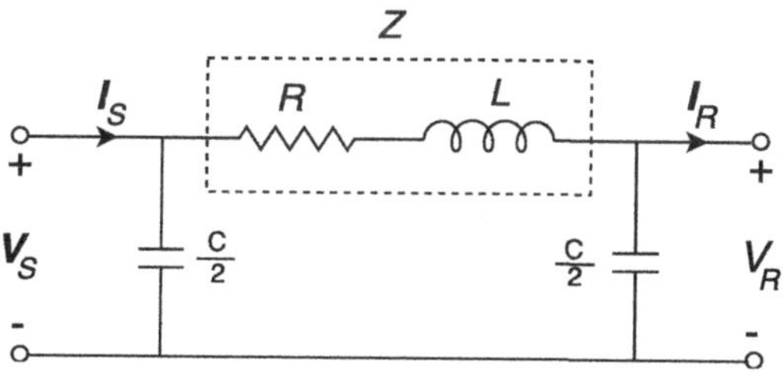

Fig. 3. Π-circuit Medium Transmission Line

Here, the impedance effect is obtained from a series connection of the circuit's elements resistor and inductor, and the admittance effect is inherited from the capacitor. We start the verification of this model by formalizing the KVL implementation of the circuit in HOL Light as:

Definition 12. KVL for Medium Line Nominal Π Circuit Implementation

```
⊢def ∀Vs Is VR IR.
kvl_implem MediumTL_NomPi (Vs,Is) (VR,IR) w z =
        (kvl [(λz. Vs z); (λz. -(VR z)); resis_volt R (λz. -(IR z));
              induct_volt L w (λz. -(IR z));
              resis_volt R (admit_curr_med (λz. -(VR z)) Ca w);
              induct_volt L w (admit_curr_med (λz. -(VR z)) Ca w)] z)
```

where the function admit_curr_med models the admittance current for the medium transmission line and its formalization is given as Entry 4 of Table 3.

Our next step is to verify the equivalence of the formalization of KVL for the nominal Π-circuit implementation to its mathematical representation, which is represented as the following HOL Light theorem.

Theorem 5. KVL for Medium Line Nominal Π Circuit Equivalence

```
⊢thm ∀Vs Is VR IR R L Ca G w z.
   let se = ((Vs,Is):send_end_quan) and
       re = ((VR,IR):recei_end_quan) and
       tlc = ((R,L,Ca,G):trans_lines_const) in
       [A] valid_transmission_line (MediumTL_NomPi,tlc)
         ⇒ kvl_implem MediumTL_NomPi se re tlc w z ⇔
             (Vs z = VR z + (R + ii * w * L) * IR z +
                          (R + ii * w * L) * ((w * Ca) / 2) * VR z)
```

The only assumption A provides the validity of the transmission line for the nominal Π-circuit model. The proof process of Theorem 5 is mainly based on some properties of list and summation of complex-valued functions alongside some complex arithmetic reasoning.

Similarly, we formalize the KCL implementation of the nominal Π-circuit implementation. Here, we only show its implementation on the sending end only.

Definition 13. KCL for Medium Line Nominal Π-circuit Implementation

```
⊢def ∀Vs Is Iz VR IR w z R L Ca G.
   kcl_implem_s_end MediumTL_NomPi (Vs,Is)
  (VR,IR) (Iz:cur_fun) w z (R,L,Ca,G) =
        (kcl [(λz. Is z); (λz. -(Iz z)); admit_curr_med (λz. -(Vs z)) Ca w] z)
```

Next, we verify the equivalence of the above KCL implementation with its mathematical representation as the following HOL Light theorem.

Theorem 6. KCL for Medium Line Nominal Π-circuit Equivalence

```
⊢thm ∀Vs Is VR IR Iz w z R L Ca G.
   let se = ((Vs,Is):send_end_quan) and
       re = ((VR,IR):recei_end_quan) and
       tlc = ((R,L,Ca,G):trans_lines_const) in
  kcl_implem_s_end MediumTL_NomPi se re (Iz:cur_fun) w z tlc ⇔
    (Is z = Iz z + (admit_curr_med Vs Ca w) z)
```

The verification of the above theorem is very similar to that of Theorem 5. We further formalized the KCL on the receiving end of the model and combined both of these to obtain the final KCL implementation.

Next, we formally verify the ABCD parameters based representation of the nominal Π-circuit based model. We also formally verify the nominal T-circuit model for the medium transmission lines and the details about these formalizations are skipped here due to the space limitation and can be found in the HOL Light code available at [1].

4.3 Formalization of Cascaded Transmission Lines

When multiple transmission lines models are connected in series, it results into a cascaded transmission line as depicted in Fig. 4. Here, n transmission lines are connected in series and a relationship between the sending and receiving end quantities is mathematically expressed as follows:

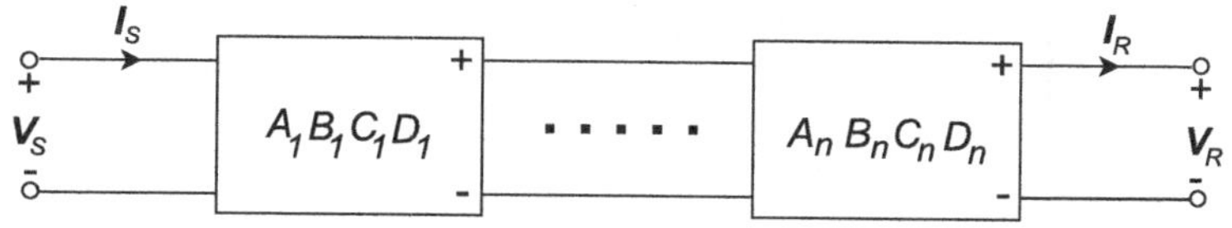

Fig. 4. Cascaded Transmission Line

$$\begin{bmatrix} V_S \\ I_S \end{bmatrix} = \begin{bmatrix} A_1 & B_1 \\ C_1 & D_1 \end{bmatrix} \cdots \begin{bmatrix} A_n & B_n \\ C_n & D_n \end{bmatrix} \begin{bmatrix} V_R \\ I_R \end{bmatrix} \tag{5}$$

where the ABCD matrix for the cascaded transmission line is a multiplication of matrices for each of the individual transmission line models. To formalize this ABCD matrix, we use the type abbreviation to model a collection of parameters for the individual transmission line models as:

```
new_type_abbrev ("w",`:ℝ`)
new_type_abbrev ("tl_models_param",`:(tl_models × trans_lines_const)`)
new_type_abbrev ("tl_models_param_all",`:(tl_models_param list × w)`)
```

where tl_models_param is a pair with its first element presenting a single transmission line model and the second element providing the transmission lines constants for the same transmission line present in the cascaded transmission line. Similarly, tl_models_param_all is a pair with its first element representing a list of parameters for all transmission line models present in the cascaded transmission line. The second element captures a variable w having a real data-type. Now, we use this type abbreviation to formalize the ABCD matrix for the cascaded transmission line in HOL Light as follows:

Definition 14. Cascaded ABCD Matrix
$\vdash_{def}$ ∀tlms tlmpa w R L Ca G.
  cascaded_abcd_matrix ([ ],w) = cidentity_mat ∧
  cascaded_abcd_matrix (CONS (tlms,(R,L,Ca,G)) tlmpa,w) =
    (abcd_mat tlms (R,L,Ca,G) w) ** cascaded_abcd_matrix (tlmpa,w)

where the function cascaded_abcd_matrix uses a variable of type tl_models_param_all and models the ABCD matrix of the cascaded transmission line using a recursive definition in HOL Light. We use the above definition to verify the ABCD matrix of a cascaded transmission line (medium and short transmission lines) as:

Theorem 7. ABCD Matrix of Cascaded Two Port Circuit/ Transmission Line
$\vdash_{thm}$ ∀R1 R2 L1 L2 Ca1 Ca2 G1 G2 w.
  let tlc1 = ((R1,L1,Ca1,G1):trans_lines_const) and
    tlc2 = ((R2,L2,Ca2,G2):trans_lines_const) in
    [A] valid_cascaded_tl ([MediumTL_PiCir,tlc1; ShortTL_SerImp,tlc2], w)
  ⇒ cascaded_abcd_matrix ([MediumTL_PiCir,tlc1; ShortTL_SerImp,tlc2], w) =

$$\begin{bmatrix} \mathsf{T3} & \mathsf{T3} * \mathsf{T2} + \mathsf{T1} \\ \mathsf{w} * \mathsf{Ca1} * \mathsf{T4} & \mathsf{w} * \mathsf{Ca1} * \mathsf{T4} * \mathsf{T2} + \mathsf{T3} \end{bmatrix}$$

where, $\mathsf{T1} = \mathsf{R1} + \mathsf{ii} * \mathsf{w} * \mathsf{L1}$, $\mathsf{T2} = \mathsf{R2} + \mathsf{ii} * \mathsf{w} * \mathsf{L2}$

$$\mathsf{T3} = 1 + \frac{\mathsf{w} * \mathsf{Ca1} * \mathsf{T1}}{2} \qquad \mathsf{T4} = 1 + \frac{\mathsf{w} * \mathsf{Ca1} * \mathsf{T1}}{4}$$

The only assumption A ensures the validity of the cascaded transmission line. The proof process of the above theorem is mainly based on Definition 14, properties of lists and matrices, alongside some complex arithmetic reasoning. More details about its verification can be found in the code available at [1].

5 Application: Wireless Power Transfer System

A Wireless Power Transfer (WPT) system enables the transmission of electrical energy from source to destination without establishing a physical connection [7]. A WPT system uses the phenomenon of electromagnetic fields based on the induction coils to send energy from the transmitter to the receiver. It has been widely used in Electrical Vehicles (EVs) [2] and implantable medical devices [9]. For example, it is used for charging batteries in EVs, where the placement of wires is not possible due to a restricted space. To analyze the process of the energy transmission, the WPT system is represented as a T-shape transmission line lumped model [10]. Next, the ABCD parameters are analyzed to study the relationship between the voltages and current on the sending and receiving ends. The T-shape lumped medium transmission line model for the series-series compensation WPT system [10] is depicted in Fig. 5. Here, R_1, C_1 and L_{k1} model the resistance, capacitance and leakage inductance on the sending end. Similarly, R_2, C_2 and L_{k2} capture the same quantities on the receiving end. M_{12} is the mutual inductance between the sending and receiving coils.

Similarly, V_1, I_1, V_2 and I_2 represent the sending and receiving end voltages and currents, respectively.

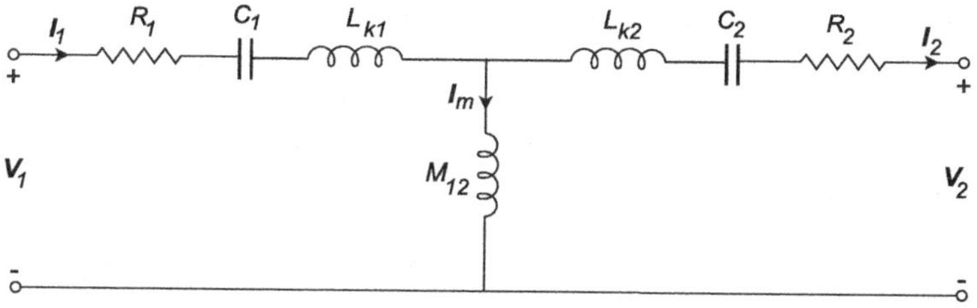

Fig. 5. T-Model for WPT System

Here, for simplicity, we consider the sending and receiving coils are identical. Therefore, the resistance, capacitance and leakage inductance on the sending and receiving ends are equal to each other, i.e., $R_1 = R_2 = R$, $C_1 = C_2 = C$ and $L_{k1} = L_{k2} = L$. Now, we can express a relationship between the sending and receiving quantities for T-shaped lumped model for the WPT system as follows [10]:

$$\begin{bmatrix} V_1 \\ I_1 \end{bmatrix} = \begin{bmatrix} 1 + \frac{K_1}{K_2} & K_1 \left(2 + \frac{K_1}{K_2}\right) \\ \frac{1}{K_2} & 1 + \frac{K_1}{K_2} \end{bmatrix} \begin{bmatrix} V_2 \\ I_2 \end{bmatrix} \tag{6}$$

where,
$K_1 = R + jwL_k + \frac{1}{jwC}$, $K_2 = jwM_{12}$

We formally verify the above ABCD parameters based model of the WPT system (Equation (6)) based on the KCL and KVL implementations as the following theorem in HOL Light:

Theorem 8. ABCD Matrix of WPT System
$\vdash_{thm}$ ∀Vs Is VR IR R Lk Ca G M12 w.
  let se = ((Vs,Is):send_end_quan) and
    re = ((VR,IR):recei_end_quan) and
    tlc = ((R,Lk,Ca,G):trans_lines_const) in
    [A] valid_transmission_line (MediumTL_TCir,tlc)
      ⇒ (kvl_implem_wpt MediumTL_TCir se re tlc w z ∧
        kcl_implem_wpt MediumTL_TCir se re tlc M12 w z) ⇔
          (relat_sr_wpt MediumTL_TCir se re tlc M12 w z)

The proof process of the above theorem is straightforward, thanks to our formalization of ABCD parameters based models presented in Sects. 3 and 4. More details about its verification and the rest of the formalization can be found in the HOL Light code at [1].

5.1 Discussion

We introduced the first formalization of the ABCD parameters based models of transmission lines using an interactive theorem prover to ensure more sound and complete analysis. The main idea is to verify various aspects of transmission line designs, contributing to the development of formal models for power and communication systems. The utilization of HOL Light enabled us to verify generic properties, with universally quantified variables and thus can be reused and applied to different applications, such as printed circuit boards, coplanar waveguides, etc. Another distinguishing feature of our proposed formalization is the development of a systematic approach for analyzing the ABCD parameters based models of the transmission lines, which is easy to follow even for a non-HOL user. One of the challenging parts was the development of the deep embedding based formalization of the transmission lines, where we need to gather all details about the parameters that contribute to the dynamics of the two-port models of transmission lines and packaging them into our formalization. Moreover, it is worth mentioning that the use of higher-order-logic theorem proving in physical systems, particularly, transmission lines poses a significant challenge. This is mainly attributed to the considerable time and effort required for formalizing the underlying theories within higher-order logic. A potential approach to address this challenge involves the ongoing formal development of theories, encompassing libraries of practical and commonly used transmission lines in real-world applications. This approach has the potential to reduce the costs linked to incorporating theorem proving into the crucial stages of designing and verifying transmission line systems. The work presented in this paper can be considered as a foundational step, with the potential to verify numerous applications in related fields.

6 Conclusion

This paper proposed to use higher-order-logic theorem proving for formally analyzing the ABCD parameters based models of transmission lines. In particular, we formalized the lumped circuit models for the short, medium and cascaded transmission lines. Moreover, we formally verify the KVL and KCL implementations of these circuit models. Next, these implementations are used to verify the ABCD parameters based models of transmission lines. Finally, we used our proposed formalization for verifying the T-circuit model representation of a WPT system. In the future, we aim to establish a connection of these models with the telegrapher's equations [8] by formally analyzing the ABCD parameters based model for distributed (long) transmission lines. The formalization of long transmission lines requires the application of advanced mathematical techniques, such as matrix, complex variable analysis and differential equations.

References

1. Rashid, A and Deniz, E.: https://hvg.ece.concordia.ca/code/hol-light/ABCD_Parameters/ABCD_Parameters.php (2024)
2. Bi, Z., Kan, T., Mi, C.C., Zhang, Y., Zhao, Z., Keoleian, G.A.: A review of wireless power transfer for electric vehicles: prospects to enhance sustainable mobility. Appl. Energy **179**, 413–425 (2016)
3. Davidson, C.W.: Transmission Lines for Communications. Springer (1978).https://doi.org/10.1007/978-1-349-19995-2
4. Glover, J.D., Sarma, M.S., Overbye, T.: Power System Analysis and Design. Cengage Learning, SI Version (2012)
5. Harrison, J.: Handbook of Practical Logic and Automated Reasoning. Cambridge University Press (2009)
6. Harrison, J.: The HOL light theory of Euclidean space. J. Autom. Reason. **50**, 173–190 (2013)
7. Imura, T., Imura, T.: Wireless Power Transfer. Springer (2020)
8. Inan, U.S., Inan, A.S., Said, R.K.: Engineering Electromagnetics and Waves. Pearson (2016)
9. Jiang, H., et al.: A low-frequency versatile wireless power transfer technology for biomedical implants. IEEE Trans. Biomed. Circuits Syst. **7**(4), 526–535 (2012)
10. Kim, D.: ABCD Parameters in series-series compensation wireless power transfer system. In: Sustainable Power and Energy Conference, pp. 1–5. IEEE (2022)
11. Kumar, R., Arthan, R., Myreen, M.O., Owens, S.: HOL with definitions: semantics, soundness, and a verified implementation. In: Interactive Theorem Proving, LNCS, vol. 8558, pp. 308–324. Springer (2014). https://doi.org/10.1007/978-3-319-08970-6_20
12. Magnusson, P.C., Weisshaar, A., Tripathi, V.K., Alexander, G.C.: Transmission Lines and Wave Propagation. CRC Press (2017)
13. OCaml: https://ocaml.org/ (2023)
14. Saadat, H.: Power System Analysis. McGraw-Hill (1999)
15. Zelby, L.W., Mathes, J.B., Shawver, J.W.: Transmission Line Design for a Power Distribution System at 20 KHz for Aircraft. Tech. rep, NASA (1986)

Certification of Sorting Algorithms Using *Theorema* and Coq

Isabela Drămnesc[1], Tudor Jebelean[2,3], and Sorin Stratulat[4(✉)]

[1] Department of Computer Science, West University of Timişoara, Timişoara, Romania
Isabela.Dramnesc@e-uvt.ro
[2] ICAM, West University of Timişoara, Timişoara, Romania
Tudor.Jebelean@e-uvt.ro
[3] RISC, Johannes Kepler University, Linz, Austria
[4] Université de Lorraine, CNRS, LORIA, Metz 57000, France
sorin.stratulat@univ-lorraine.fr

Abstract. Sorting is an operation that has very important practical applications, in particular for instance in the storage and analysis of data related to the environment, climat change, etc.

We describe experiments of automated certification of various sorting algorithms by using the *Theorema* as well as Coq and we compare the two techniques.

The sorting algorithms are: *Quick–Sort*, *Patience–Sort*, *Min–Sort*, *Max–Sort*, and *Min–Max–Sort*. In both systems we construct the appropriate underlying theory, we define the algorithms in functional style, we run them on examples and we produce the proof of their correctness together with proofs of various lemmas that are necessary.

In *Theorema* the proofs are almost completely automatic, are presented in natural style, and the underlying theory uses multisets in order to express the fact that the input and the output have the same elements. Moreover the proofs use a generalized induction scheme based on the well-founded ordering on lists defined by strict inclusion of multisets.

In Coq the proofs are based on scripts, they require more additional lemmas, and they use element counts to compare the contents of the list. However, both the algorithm definitions as well as the proofs are absolutely rigurous as Coq cannot accept any elements that are not theoretically correct.

1 Introduction

Sorting algorithms play a fundamental role in various computational tasks, serving as the backbone for a wide range of applications across diverse domains, in particular in the ones related to environment, climate change, etc., due to the huge size of the data that has to be indexed and processed. As the volume and complexity of data continue to grow exponentially, the efficiency and correctness of sorting algorithms becomes imperative due to various reasons such as: data integrity and accuracy, performance optimization, security, and algorithmic transparency.

S. M. Watt and T. Ida (Eds.): SCSS 2024, LNAI 14991, pp. 38–56, 2024.
https://doi.org/10.1007/978-3-031-69042-6_3

We focus on the automation of the verification process of sorting algorithms and of the auxiliary sub-algorithms. We develop proof–based techniques in the *Theorema* system for algorithm certification, we use the Coq interactive theorem prover for the verification of the same algorithms, and finally we compare the two approaches.

The *Theorema* system [8,9,37] is a complex framework implemented in *Mathematica*[1]. The system allows to define mathematical theories, including definition of algorithms by logical formulae, to experiment by running the algorithms, and to develop and use automatic provers. The system facilitates the verification of algorithms because their implementation in *Theorema* does not use a programming language, but they are defined directly in predicate logic together with their specification, thus there is no need to generate verification conditions. A main feature of the *Theorema* system is to generate proofs in natural style: both the inference rules and the presentation of the proofs imitate the human style.

The Coq system [4,35] is a state-of-the-art proof assistant that can be used to formalize algorithms and, the same time, to define and prove properties about them, by using a higher-order language called Calculus of Inductive Constructions. Based on the Curry-Howard isomorphism [23], the properties to be proved are *types* and the proofs are *terms* having as types the properties they prove. A crucial specificity of Coq is its *kernel* that implements an algorithm which checks whether a proof term has as type the property it proves. Thanks to this type-checking algorithm, the Coq proofs are reputed to be correct and Coq is widely used to certify algorithms.

Related Work. Formal certification environments like Coq [4] and Isabelle/HOL [28] have been used to certify classical algorithms on arrays/lists [5,10,19, 29,30,34,36,38]. Other approaches use Krakatoa [27] in [36], SPARK* [22] in [2], PVS [33] in [12], KeY [1] in [6], and ACL2 [25] in [32].

Concerning the differences between the various approaches, the definitions of the algorithms and the definitions of sortedness are basically syntactic versions of the same functions and predicates expressed in functional style, while some other presentations [3,21,31] use imperative constructs. However the definition of the concept "have the same elements" (the input list vs. the sorted list) has several realizations: [7] uses a function that deletes the first occurrence of an element, [24] uses indices in arrays and the existence of a bijection, [11] counts elements, [20] compares the lists obtained by filtering individual elements, and finally only [10] uses multisets. These differences have a significant impact on the corresponding proofs, and these are typically more complex than the proofs related to sortedness.

Furthermore the proofs differ in the choice of the inference rules and proof strategies, as well as in the number of the necessary auxiliary notions and lemmas, which influences the length of the full proving process, its degree of automation, naturalness, understandability, etc. Therefore the research in this area is

[1] www.wolfram.com/mathematica.

continuing to improve various aspects of mechanical verification, and the present paper aims to contribute to this trend.

Natural style (namely the approach in which the formulae, the inference steps, and the proof text are similar to the ones used by humans) is addressed in relatively few works: ours on verification and synthesis [13,15], as well as [7]. Also, there is no previous work in Coq on the verification of the algorithms presented here, see e.g. [19]. Similar work has been done by the authors on sorting algorithms for binary trees [14,16,18].

The novelty of this paper consists in:

- computer based certification of some important sorting algorithms;
- systematic comparison of the certification process in two systems that are quite different in their approach;
- development in *Theorema* of proof techniques that allow to produce relatively short proofs that are also in natural style;
- the use in *Theorema* of multisets and of inference rules that are relevant to them and to lists;
- generation and certification in Coq of additional properties about the sorting algorithms and auxiliary functions.

2 Context and Notations

The correctness of a sorting algorithm consists of two conditions on the output list: (a) it is sorted and (b) has the same elements as the input list. In *Theorema*, (b) is expressed using multisets, and in Coq using the number of occurrences.

Notations in *Theorema*. We consider multisets and lists over a totally ordered domain. We use uppercase roman letters like U, V, T for lists. A list is either empty $\langle\rangle$, or of the form head–tail denoted by $a \smile U$, (a is the head and U is the tail of the list – which is always a list). The elements of a list or a multiset are objects from a totally ordered domain (notation $<$ and $\leq$), and are denoted by lowercase roman letters like a, b, c, x. $\frown$ adds an element at the end of a list ($U \frown a$). For multisets we use the notations: $\emptyset$ for the empty set, $\{\{a\}\}$ for the multiset containing the element a occurring once, and $\mathcal{M}[U]$ for the multiset of the list U. The additive union of multisets is denoted by $\uplus$ (keeps the multiplicity of elements), like in [26]. The total ordering is extended to *element–list* (*element* is smaller than each member of *list*), *list–element* (each member of *list* is smaller than *element*), and *list*$_1$–*list*$_2$ (each member of *list*$_1$ is smaller than each element of *list*$_2$).

The type of the objects is not used explicitly, but it is automatically detected by the prover according to the notation conventions mentioned above.

In *Theorema*, function and predicate applications use squared brackets (e.g., $F[x], P[x]$). The quantified variables are written under the quantifier (e.g. $\underset{X}{\forall}$ "for all X", $\underset{X}{\exists}$ "exists X"), and Skolem constants have integer indices (e.g., U_0, a_0).

Notations in Coq. We represent the multisets of naturals as lists, typed **list nat**, and the In and count functions for defining the permutation relation between them. The constructors for **list** (resp., **nat**) are nil and :: (the notation for cons) (resp., 0 and S (the successor function)).

The recursive functions, as count, should be total and terminating. They are based on the `match` construct that defines different cases according to the constructors of the type of the function argument given as matching expression. Coq automatically checks the totality property by analysing the `match` cases and how they cover all the possible values the matching expression can take. Checking the termination property may be more intricate, requiring that some function argument should decrease after each recursive call w.r.t. some well-founded order. The `Fixpoint` keyword is used for defining the recursive functions for which Coq automatically identifies the recursive function argument and the well-founded order, otherwise the keyword `Function` is used. For the last case, the argument for recursion and the well-founded order are explicitly defined using the `wf` keyword, and the user has to provide the proofs for the termination conditions. The predicates are defined inductively, using the `Inductive` keyword and in terms of *axioms* that play the role of *constructors*.

3 The Algorithms

We certify the following sorting algorithms (that were synthesized in [15]):

1. *Quick–Sort* with auxiliary functions: *Concat[U, V]* (U concatenated with V), *LoE[U,a]* (the elements of U that are smaller than or equal to a), *High[U,a]* (the elements of U that are strictly greater than a);
2. *Patience–Sort* with auxiliary: *SelSort[U]*, *SelRest[U]* (split U in two lists: one list that is already sorted, and the other list containing the remaining elements), and *Merge[U, V]* (merge two sorted lists into a sorted one);
3. *Min-Sort*, with auxiliary: *min[U]* (the minimum of U), and *Trimmin[U]* (remove the minimum from U);
4. *Max-Sort*, with auxiliary: *max[U]* and *Trimmax[U]* – uses maximum.
5. *Min-Max-Sort*, auxiliary: *min[U]*, *max[U]*, and *TrimMM[U]* (remove the minimum and the maximum of U).

We present now the definition of the algorithm *Min-Max-Sort* and its auxiliary functions in the *Theorema* system.

Definition 3.1. *Min-Max-Sort.*

$$\underset{a,b,U}{\forall}\left(\begin{array}{c} MMS[\langle\rangle] = \langle\rangle \\ MMS[a \smile \langle\rangle] = a \smile \langle\rangle \\ MMS[a \smile (b \smile U)] = min[a \smile (b \smile U)] \smile (MMS[TrimMM[a \smile (b \smile U)]]) \\ \frown max[a \smile (b \smile U)] \end{array}\right)$$

Note that in the *Theorema* system one abbreviates several universal quantifiers by a single one containing several variables, and one can also indicate some simple condition on these variables in a second line under the quantifier. Furthermore such a quantifier can prefix a conjunction of several formulas that are listed vertically without the conjunction symbol.

The above definition of *Min-Max-Sort* returns the sorted version of the input list. It places the minimum of the input list at the beginning of the output and the maximum at the end of the it, and then applies recursively to the list of the remaining elements, selected by the function *TrimMM* shown below.

Definition 3.2. *TrimMM.*

$$\left(\begin{array}{l}\underset{\substack{a,b,U\\ a\leq b}}{\forall}\left(\mathit{TrimMM}[a\smile(b\smile U)]=\mathit{TrimMmA}[a,b,U]\right)\\ \underset{\substack{a,b,U\\ b<a}}{\forall}\left(\mathit{TrimMM}[a\smile(b\smile U)]=\mathit{TrimMmA}[b,a,U]\right)\end{array}\right)$$

TrimMM calls the auxiliary function *TrimMmA* that returns the list without the minimum and the maximum elements from the input list.

Definition 3.3. *TrimMmA.*

$$\left(\begin{array}{c}\underset{a,b}{\forall}\left(\mathit{TrimMmA}[a,b,\langle\rangle]=\langle\rangle\right)\\ \underset{\substack{a,b,c,U\\ c<a}}{\forall}\left(\mathit{TrimMmA}[a,b,c\smile U]=a\smile\mathit{TrimMmA}[c,b,U]\right)\\ \underset{\substack{a,b,c,U\\ (a\leq c\wedge c\leq b)}}{\forall}\left(\mathit{TrimMmA}[a,b,c\smile U]=c\smile\mathit{TrimMmA}[a,b,U]\right)\\ \underset{\substack{a,b,c,U\\ b<c}}{\forall}\left(\mathit{TrimMmA}[a,b,c\smile U]=b\smile\mathit{TrimMmA}[a,c,U]\right)\end{array}\right)$$

Definition 3.4. *min.*

$$\left(\underset{a,U}{\forall}\left(\mathit{min}[a\smile U]=\mathit{minA}[a,U]\right)\right)$$

The above function calls the following tail recursive function that gives the minimum element from a list.

Definition 3.5. *minA.*

$$\left(\begin{array}{c}\underset{a}{\forall}\left(\mathit{minA}[a,\langle\rangle]=a\right)\\ \underset{\substack{a,b,U\\ a\leq b}}{\forall}\left(\mathit{minA}[a,b\smile U]=\mathit{minA}[a,U]\right)\\ \underset{\substack{a,b,U\\ b<a}}{\forall}\left(\mathit{minA}[a,b\smile U]=\mathit{minA}[b,U]\right)\end{array}\right)$$

Definition 3.6. *max.*

$$\left(\underset{a,U}{\forall}\left(\mathit{max}[a\smile U]=\mathit{maxA}[a,U]\right)\right)$$

The above function calls the following tail recursive function that gives the maximum element from a list.

Definition 3.7. *maxA*.

$$\left(\begin{array}{c}\underset{a}{\forall}(maxA[a,\langle\rangle]=a)\\ \underset{\substack{a,b,U\\ a\leq b}}{\forall}(maxA[a,b\smile U]=maxA[b,U])\\ \underset{\substack{a,b,U\\ b<a}}{\forall}(maxA[a,b\smile U]=maxA[a,U])\end{array}\right)$$

4 Certification in *Theorema*

4.1 Basic Definitions.

The predicate *IsSorted* defined below returns true iff the input list is sorted.

Definition 4.1. $\underset{a,U}{\forall}\left(\begin{array}{c}IsSorted[\langle\rangle]\\ IsSorted[a\smile U]\Longleftrightarrow(a\leq U\wedge IsSorted[U])\end{array}\right)$

The function $\mathcal{M}$ defined below retuns the multiset of a list.

Definition 4.2. $\underset{a,U}{\forall}\left(\begin{array}{c}\mathcal{M}[\langle\rangle]=\emptyset\\ \mathcal{M}[a\smile U]=\{\{a\}\}\uplus\mathcal{M}[U]\end{array}\right)$

4.2 Special Inference Rules and Strategies

The *Theorema* proofs use general inference rules from basic logic, but also certain special inference rules specific to the domain of lists and multisets.

The general rules are classical inference rules similar to those of sequent calculus, and other straightforward natural rules like applying properties of equality, using definitions, replacement by equal terms, etc. We list below the more important general rules, which are specific to our prover.

G1: *Generalized induction.* When proving the goal $\varphi[X]$, we may assume $\varphi[Y]$ for any Y strictly smaller than X with respect to strict inclusion of multisets $(X \subset Y)$.

G2: *Cascading.* When the proof fails, construct a conjecture from the current proof state and prove it separately. This step requires the intervention of a human because it is not completely automated.

G3: *Contracting.* Reduce repeating composite constant term to constant.

G4: *Equality reduction.* Delete identical terms that occur on both sides of an equality goal.

Below are the most important inference rules that are specific to the domains of lists and multisets.

S1: *List expansion.* When it is assumed that a list X is nonempty, it is replaced by $a \smile Y$, where a and Y are new Skolem constants, and similarly for lists containing at least two elements.

S2: *Multiset expansion.* The term $\mathcal{M}[T]$ where T is a composite term representing a list can be expanded into several $\mathcal{M}$ terms by using multiset union. This is used mostly in conjunction with the rule **G4**.

S3: *Inequality reduction.* When the goal is an inequality (with respect to the order used for sorting) between lists, a term T representing a list whose multiset is known to be included in the multiset of another list X can be replaced by X.

Some of these rules have been used in [17] for verification of *Merge-Sort* and *Insert–Sort*, namely **G1**, **G2** and **G4**.

4.3 The Certification of *Min-Max-Sort*.

For the certification of *Min-Max-Sort* algorithm we have to prove the two properties: that the algorithm preserves multisets and that the output is sorted. The proofs are summarized in the next subsections.

***Min-Max-Sort* preserves multisets.**

Conjecture 4.3. $\underset{X}{\forall}\Big(\mathcal{M}[X] = \mathcal{M}[MMS[X]]\Big)$

For proving this conjecture, it is necessary to use the following two properties (which were generated by cascading and were proved – the proofs are detailed later in the paper):

Proposition 4.4. $\underset{U\neq\langle\rangle}{\forall}(\mathcal{M}[U] = \{\{min[U]\}\} \uplus \mathcal{M}[TrimMM[U]] \uplus \{\{max[U]\}\})$

Proposition 4.5. $\underset{U\neq\langle\rangle}{\forall}(\mathcal{M}[TrimMM[U]] \subset \mathcal{M}[U])$

Proof. Prove Conjecture 4.3 by cases using Definition 3.1.
Case 1. $X = \langle\rangle, MMS[\langle\rangle] = \langle\rangle$ trivial.
Case 2. $X = a_0 \smile \langle\rangle, MMS[a_0 \smile \langle\rangle] = a_0 \smile \langle\rangle$ trivial.
Case 3. $X = a_0 \smile (b_0 \smile U_0), MMS[a_0 \smile (b_0 \smile U_0)] = min[a_0 \smile (b_0 \smile U_0)] \smile MMS[TrimMM[a_0 \smile (b_0 \smile U_0)]] \frown max[a_0 \smile (b_0 \smile U_0)]$

Prove

$$\begin{gathered}\mathcal{M}[a_0 \smile (b_0 \smile U_0)] = \mathcal{M}[min[a_0 \smile (b_0 \smile U_0)] \smile \\ MMS[TrimMM[a_0 \smile (b_0 \smile U_0)]] \frown max[a_0 \smile (b_0 \smile U_0)]].\end{gathered} \tag{1}$$

By Definition 4.2 the goal becomes:

$$\begin{gathered}\{\{a_0\}\} \uplus \{\{b_0\}\} \uplus \mathcal{M}[U_0] = \{\{min[a_0 \smile (b_0 \smile U_0)]\}\}\uplus \\ \mathcal{M}[MMS[TrimMM[a_0 \smile (b_0 \smile U_0)]]] \uplus \{\{max[a_0 \smile (b_0 \smile U_0)]\}\}\end{gathered} \tag{2}$$

By Proposition 4.5 and by **G1** the goal becomes:

$$\begin{gathered}\{\{a_0\}\} \uplus \{\{b_0\}\} \uplus \mathcal{M}[U_0] = \{\{min[a_0 \smile (b_0 \smile U_0)]\}\}\uplus \\ \mathcal{M}[TrimMM[a_0 \smile (b_0 \smile U_0)]] \uplus \{\{max[a_0 \smile (b_0 \smile U_0)]\}\}\end{gathered} \tag{3}$$

By Proposition 4.4 the goal is proved.

The proof of Proposition 4.4 is done by cases using Definition 3.2.

Proof. Case 1: $U_0 = a_0 \smile (b_0 \smile \langle\rangle)$ (the list has exactly two elements) is straightforward without induction, because in this case *TrimMM* reduces to the empty set.

Case 2: $U_0 = a_0 \smile (b_0 \smile (c_0 \smile V_0))$ (the list has more than two elements)

Using Definitions 3.4, Definition 3.6, and Definition 3.3 the following goal is proved by cases

$$\begin{aligned}\{\{a_0\}\} \uplus \{\{b_0\}\} \uplus \{\{c_0\}\} \uplus \mathcal{M}[V_0] = \{\{min[a_0 \smile (b_0 \smile (c_0 \smile V_0))]\}\}\uplus \\ \mathcal{M}[TrimMM[a_0 \smile (b_0 \smile (c_0 \smile V_0))]] \uplus \{\{max[a_0 \smile (b_0 \smile (c_0 \smile V_0))]\}\}\end{aligned} \tag{4}$$

Case 2.1.: $a_0 \leq b_0$

The goal (4) is

$$\begin{aligned}\{\{a_0\}\} \uplus \{\{b_0\}\} \uplus \{\{c_0\}\} \uplus \mathcal{M}[V_0] = \{\{minA[a_0, c_0 \smile V_0]\}\}\uplus \\ \mathcal{M}[TrimMmA[a_0, b_0, c_0, V_0]] \uplus \{\{max[b_0, c_0 \smile V_0]\}\}\end{aligned} \tag{5}$$

Using Definition 3.3 we prove by cases: *Case 2.1.1.* $V_0 = \langle\rangle$
Case 2.1.1.1 $c_0 < a_0$ the goal is:

$$\{\{a_0\}\} \uplus \{\{b_0\}\} \uplus \{\{c_0\}\} \uplus \emptyset = \{\{c_0\}\} \uplus \mathcal{M}[a_0 \smile TrimMmA[c_0, b_0, \langle\rangle]] \uplus \{\{b_0\}\} \tag{6}$$

which is

$$\{\{a_0\}\} \uplus \{\{b_0\}\} \uplus \{\{c_0\}\} \uplus \emptyset = \{\{c_0\}\} \uplus \{\{a_0\}\} \uplus \emptyset \uplus \{\{b_0\}\} \tag{7}$$

This is true by commutativity of multiset union.

For the following two cases, namely, *Case 2.1.1.2* $a_0 \leq c_0 \wedge c_0 \leq b_0$ and *Case 2.1.1.3* $b_0 < c_0$ the proofs are similar to *Case 2.1.1.1*.

Case 2.1.2. $c_0 < a_0$ From the assumptions, by transitivity, we know

$$c_0 < b_0 \tag{8}$$

The goal (5) becomes:

$$\begin{aligned}\{\{a_0\}\} \uplus \{\{b_0\}\} \uplus \{\{c_0\}\} \uplus \mathcal{M}[V_0] = \{\{minA[c_0, V_0]\}\}\uplus \\ \{\{a_0\}\} \uplus \mathcal{M}[TrimMmA[b_0, c_0, V_0]] \uplus \{\{maxA[b_0, V_0]\}\}\end{aligned} \tag{9}$$

By **G4** the goal becomes:

$$\begin{aligned}\{\{b_0\}\} \uplus \{\{c_0\}\} \uplus \mathcal{M}[V_0] = \{\{minA[c_0, V_0]\}\}\uplus \\ \mathcal{M}[TrimMmA[b_0, c_0, V_0]] \uplus \{\{maxA[b_0, V_0]\}\}\end{aligned} \tag{10}$$

This is true by **G1** because $b_0 \smile (c_0 \smile V_0)$ is strictly included in $a_0 \smile (b_0 \smile (c_0 \smile V_0))$.

For the following two cases, namely *Case 2.1.3.* $a_0 \leq c_0 \wedge c_0 \leq b_0$ and *Case 2.1.4.* $b_0 < c_0$, the proofs are similar to *Case 2.1.2.*.

Case 2.2.: $b_0 < a_0$ As in *Case 2.1* four main cases are generated, namely *Case 2.2.1.* $V_0 = \langle\rangle$, *Case 2.2.2.* $c_0 < b_0$, *Case 2.2.3.* $b_0 \leq c_0 \wedge c_0 \leq a_0$ and *Case 2.2.4.* $a_0 < c_0$. The proofs in these cases are similar to the previous cases shown.

The proof of Proposition 4.5 is done by cases using Definition 3.2.

Proof. Using **S1**, the goal is

$$\mathcal{M}[\mathit{TrimMM}[a_0 \smile (b_0 \smile V_0)]] \subset \mathcal{M}[a_0 \smile (b_0 \smile V_0)]) \tag{11}$$

By Definition 3.2 we have two cases:

Case 1: $a_0 \leq b_0$, $\mathit{TrimMM}[a_0 \smile (b_0 \smile V_0)] = \mathit{TrimMmA}[a_0, b_0, V_0]$. And four more cases are generated using Definition 3.3, namely *Case 1.1.* $V_0 = \langle\rangle$, *Case 1.2.* $V_0 = c_0 \smile W_0, c_0 < a_0$, *Case 1.3.* $V_0 = c_0 \smile W_0, a_0 \leq c_0 \wedge c_0 \leq b_0$ and *Case 1.4.* $V_0 = c_0 \smile W_0, b_0 < c_0$. The proofs are similar in all cases. We summarize for *Case 1.4.*. By transitivity we know $a_0 < c_0$. By Definition 4.2, Definition 3.3 the goal becomes:

$$\{\{b_0\}\} \uplus \mathcal{M}[\mathit{TrimMmA}[a_0, c_0, W_0]] \subset \{\{a_0\}\} \uplus \{\{b_0\}\} \uplus \{\{c_0\}\} \uplus \mathcal{M}[W_0]) \tag{12}$$

By **G4** the goal becomes:

$$\mathcal{M}[\mathit{TrimMmA}[a_0, c_0, W_0]] \subset \{\{a_0\}\} \uplus \{\{c_0\}\} \uplus \mathcal{M}[W_0]) \tag{13}$$

which is true by **G1** because $a_0 \smile (b_0 \smile W_0)$ is strictly included in $a_0 \smile (b_0 \smile (c_0 \smile W_0))$.

Case 2: $b_0 < a_0$, $\mathit{TrimMM}[a_0 \smile (b_0 \smile V_0)] = \mathit{TrimMmA}[b_0, a_0, V_0]$. Similarly, four more cases are generated using Definition 3.3, namely *Case 2.1.* $V_0 = \langle\rangle$, *Case 2.2.* $V_0 = c_0 \smile W_0, c_0 < b_0$, *Case 2.3.* $V_0 = c_0 \smile W_0, b_0 \leq c_0 \wedge c_0 \leq a_0$ and *Case 2.4.* $V_0 = c_0 \smile W_0, a_0 < c_0$. The proofs for all these cases are similar to the ones shown before.

Min-Max-Sort sorted output.

Conjecture 4.6. $\underset{X}{\forall}\left(\mathit{IsSorted}[\mathit{MMS}[X]]\right)$

For proving this conjecture it is necessary to use the following properties:

Proposition 4.7. $\underset{X}{\forall}(\mathit{min}[X] \leq X)$

Proposition 4.8. $\underset{X}{\forall}(X \leq \mathit{max}[X])$

Proposition 4.9. $\underset{X}{\forall}(\mathit{min}[X] \leq \mathit{max}[X])$

Proposition 4.10. $\underset{a,X}{\forall}(\mathit{IsSorted}[X \frown a] \Longleftrightarrow \mathit{IsSorted}[X] \wedge X \leq a)$

Proposition 4.11.
$\underset{X}{\forall}((\mathit{min}[X] \leq X \wedge \mathit{min}[X] \leq \mathit{max}[X]) \Longrightarrow \mathit{min}[X] \leq X \frown \mathit{max}[X]))$

Proof. Case 1. $X_0 = \langle\rangle$ trivial. *Case 2.* $X_0 = a_0 \smile \langle\rangle$ trivial.

Case 3. $X_0 = a_0 \smile (b_0 \smile U_0)$ The goal is:

$$IsSorted[min[X_0] \smile MMS[TrimMM[X_0]] \frown max[X_0]] \tag{14}$$

By Definition 4.1 the goal reduces to:

$$\begin{gathered} min[X_0] \leq MMS[TrimMM[X_0]] \frown max[X_0] \wedge \\ IsSorted[MMS[TrimMM[X_0]] \frown max[X_0]] \end{gathered} \tag{15}$$

By Proposition 4.11 the goal reduces to

$$\begin{gathered} min[X_0] \leq MMS[TrimMM[X_0]] \wedge min[X_0] \leq max[X_0] \wedge \\ IsSorted[MMS[TrimMM[X_0]] \frown max[X_0]] \end{gathered} \tag{16}$$

By Proposition 4.4 (*TrimMM* preserves multisets) and **S3** the goal reduces to:

$$\begin{gathered} min[X_0] \leq TrimMM[X_0] \wedge min[X_0] \leq max[X_0] \wedge \\ IsSorted[MMS[TrimMM[X_0]] \frown max[X_0]] \end{gathered} \tag{17}$$

By Proposition 4.5 and **S3** the goal reduces to:

$$\begin{gathered} min[X_0] \leq X_0 \wedge min[X_0] \leq max[X_0] \wedge \\ IsSorted[MMS[TrimMM[X_0]] \frown max[X_0]] \end{gathered} \tag{18}$$

By Proposition 4.7 the goal reduces to:

$$min[X_0] \leq max[X_0] \wedge IsSorted[MMS[TrimMM[X_0]] \frown max[X_0]] \tag{19}$$

By Proposition 4.9 the goal reduces to:

$$IsSorted[MMS[TrimMM[X_0]] \frown max[X_0]] \tag{20}$$

By Proposition 4.10 the goal reduces to:

$$IsSorted[MMS[TrimMM[X_0]]] \wedge MMS[TrimMM[X_0]] \leq max[X_0] \tag{21}$$

By Proposition 4.5 and **G1** the goal reduces to:

$$MMS[TrimMM[X_0]] \leq max[X_0] \tag{22}$$

By Conjecture 4.3 (*Min-Max-Sort* preserves multisets) and **S3** the goal reduces to:

$$TrimMM[X_0] \leq max[X_0] \tag{23}$$

By Proposition 4.5 and and **S3** the goal reduces to:

$$X_0 \leq max[X_0] \tag{24}$$

This holds by Proposition 4.8.

For space reasons we cannot describe in detail the proofs of the other sorting algorithms (*Quick–Sort, Patience–Sort, Min–Sort,* and *Max–Sort*), but in fact the proof presented here is the most complex. The other proofs have a similar structure: two main theorems that ensure sortedness and the permutation property, and the lemmas that express the corresponding properties of the auxiliary algorithms.

5 Certification in Coq

We have used Coq to certify the algorithms from Sect. 3. Generally speaking, for each algorithms, we proved that they are *sorting* algorithms, i.e., the output list is a permutation of the input list that is also sorted (in this paper, in increasing order). Due to the lack of space, we will detail the certification process only for *Min-Max-Sort.*

The output list is checked to be sorted by the **sorted** inductive predicate:

```
Inductive sorted : list nat → Prop :=
  snil : sorted nil
| s1 : ∀ x, sorted (x::nil)
| s2 : ∀ x y l, sorted (y::l) → x ≤ y → sorted (x::y::l).
```

The permutation relation is defined using the recursive function count, for counting the number of occurrences of an element in a list, the boolean equality =? and the builtin membership predicate In:

```
Fixpoint count x l :=
  match l with
    nil ⇒ 0
  | hd :: tl ⇒ if x =? hd then S (count x tl) else count x tl
  end.
Definition permutation l l' := ∀ x, (In x l ↔ In x l') ∧ count x l = count x l'.
Definition is_a_sorting_algorithm (f: list nat → list nat) :=
  ∀ l, permutation (f l) l ∧ sorted (f l).
```

The definition of the *Min-Max-Sort* algorithm, as formalized by the MMS function displayed below, is based on the recursive functions maxA, minA and TrimMMA and the builtin functions Nat.lt, Nat.ltb, Nat.leb, length, app, Nat.min and Nat.max standing for, respectively, $<$ on naturals (**nat**) and its boolean version, the boolean $\leq$, the length of a list (**list**), the concatenation of two lists, the minimum and the maximum of two naturals:

```
Fixpoint maxA x l :=
  match l with
    nil ⇒ x
  | hd :: tl ⇒
      if Nat.leb x hd
      then maxA hd tl
      else maxA x tl
end.
```

```
Fixpoint minA x l :=
  match l with
    nil ⇒ x
  | hd :: tl ⇒
      if Nat.leb x hd
      then minA x tl
      else minA hd tl
end.
```

```
Fixpoint TrimMMA a b l :=
  match l with
    nil ⇒ nil
  | c :: tl ⇒
      if Nat.ltb c a
      then a :: (TrimMMA c b tl)
      else
        if Nat.leb c b
         then c :: (TrimMMA a b tl)
         else b :: (TrimMMA a c tl)
  end.
```

```
Function MMS l {
  wf (fun (l1: list nat) (l2: list nat) ⇒
Nat.lt (length l1) (length l2)) l} :=
  match l with
    nil ⇒ nil
  | hd :: tl ⇒
      (match tl with
         nil ⇒ hd :: nil
       | hd' :: tl' ⇒
           app ((minA hd tl) ::
  (MMS (TrimMMA (Nat.min hd hd')
             (Nat.max hd hd') tl')))
       (MMS ((maxA hd tl) :: nil))
       end)
  end.
```

As a proof example in Coq, we give the complete proof script for the lemma sorted_sorted which states that if a non-empty list is sorted then the tail of the list is also sorted:

```
Lemma sorted_sorted: ∀ a l, sorted (a::l) → sorted l.
Proof.
  induction l; simpl; intros.
  - apply snil.
  - inversion H. trivial.
Qed.
```

The proof of sorted_sorted starts by generating the *proof state* which has a *conclusion* represented by the formula to be proved and an empty set of *assumptions*, i.e., formulas that can be used in the proof of the conclusion. Firstly, the application of the `induction` tactic instantiates the variable l using an explicit induction schema issued from the recursive definition of **list** datatype. It produces two new subgoals under the form of logical implications whose conditions are shifted to the set of assumptions by the `intros` tactic. The proofs for each case are preceded by dash (-) symbols. The base case, when l is empty, can be proved by the `apply` tactic as an instance of the snil constructor of the **sorted** definition. The proof of the step case starts by applying the `inversion` tactic on the assumption H[2] which is of the form **sorted** *(a :: a0 :: l)*. Since H can be generated only by the s2 constructor of **sorted**, the condition **sorted** *(a0 :: l)* of s2 should hold and can be added to the set of assumptions. On the other hand, **sorted** *(a0 :: l)* is also the conclusion of the goal, hence the proof can finish by the application of the `assumption` tactic.

Min-Max-Sort is certified if the following lemma is proved:

```
Lemma MMS_is_sound : is_a_sorting_algorithm MMS.
```

[2] this assumption label was generated automatically by the Coq system.

Its proof is based on the two main lemmas:

Lemma MMS_permutation : ∀ l, permutation (MMS l) l.

Lemma MMS_is_sorted : ∀ l, **sorted** (MMS l).

MMS_permutation is based on 6 (resp., 5) lemmas formalising crucial properties of count (resp.,In), as well as 11 lemmas representing properties about minA, maxA, arithmetic and equality reasoning. On the other hand, MMS_is_sorted was based on 12 different lemmas, mostly related to properties of sorted. Most of lemmas have been proved using explicit induction with induction schemas built from the recursive definition of MMS (4 times, using the `Recdef` library and the `Functional Scheme` construction) and of the **list** datatype (21 times, using the `induction` tactic).

The main lemmas used to prove the properties about In are :

Lemma len_TrimMMA : ∀ x y l, Nat.le (length (TrimMMA x y l)) (S (length l)).

Lemma In_TrimMMA : ∀ a b x l, In x (TrimMMA a b l) → $a = x$ ∨ $b = x$ ∨ In x l.

Lemma minMMA_id : ∀ x l, minA x l = x ∨ maxA x l = x ∨ In x (TrimMMA x x l).

Lemma minMMA_id1 : ∀ $a0$ x l, $a0 < x$ → (minA $a0$ l = x ∨ maxA x l = x ∨ In x (TrimMMA $a0$ x l)).

Lemma minMMA_id2 : ∀ b x l, $x < b$ → (minA x l = x ∨ maxA b l = x ∨ In x (TrimMMA x b l)).

Lemma minA_maxA_TrimMMA : ∀ l x a b, In x l → **le** a b → (minA a l = x ∨ maxA b l = x ∨ In x (TrimMMA a b l)).

Lemma In_MMS : ∀ x l, In x l → In x (MMS l).

Lemma minA_In: ∀ a x l, minA a l = x → $a = x$ ∨ In x l.

Lemma maxA_In: ∀ a x l, maxA a l = x → $a = x$ ∨ In x l.

Lemma MMS_In : ∀ x l, In x (MMS l) → In x l.

The main lemmas about count are:

Lemma count_TrimMMA_TT : ∀ x a b l, (x =? minA a l) = true → (x =? maxA b l) = true → $a \leq b$ → S (S (count x (TrimMMA a b l))) = count x (a :: b::l).

Lemma count_TrimMMA_TF: ∀ x a b l, (x =? minA a l) = true → (x =? maxA b l) = false → $a \leq b$ → S (count x (TrimMMA a b l)) = count x (a :: b::l).

Lemma count_TrimMMA_FT: ∀ x a b l, (x =? minA a l) = false → (x =? maxA b l) = true → $a \leq b$ → S (count x (TrimMMA a b l)) = count x (a :: b::l).

Lemma count_TrimMMA_FF: ∀ x a b l, (x =? minA a l) = false → (x =? maxA b l) = false → $a \leq b$ → count x (TrimMMA a b l) = count x (a :: b::l).

Lemma count_MMS : ∀ x l, count x (MMS l) = count x l.

The proofs of the lemmas about count are more complex as they involve arithmetic reasoning. These lemmas are not necessary in the case when the lists characterise sets (lists without repeating elements) for which a simpler permutation relation can be defined as:

`Definition` permutation_sets l l' := $\forall$ x, In x $l \leftrightarrow$ In x l'.

Similarly, the lemmas about In can be ignored if the usual (weaker) definition of permutation on multisets is employed:

`Definition` permutation_multisets l l' := $\forall$ x, count x l = count x l'.

Finally, the lemmas used to prove MMS_is_sorted are:

`Lemma` minA_le_maxA: $\forall$ a b l, $a \leq b \rightarrow$ minA a $l \leq$ maxA b l.

`Lemma` le_maxA : $\forall$ x l, Nat.le x (maxA x l).

`Lemma` MMS_max : $\forall$ x a b l, In x (TrimMMA a b l) $\rightarrow$ Nat.le x (maxA a (b::l)).

`Lemma` le_minA : $\forall$ x l, Nat.le (minA x l) x.

`Lemma` le_minA_In : $\forall$ x y l, In y $l \rightarrow$ Nat.le (minA x l) y.

`Lemma` MMS_min : $\forall$ x a b l, In x (TrimMMA a b l) $\rightarrow$ Nat.le (minA a (b:: l)) x.

`Lemma` maxA_sym : $\forall$ a b l, maxA a (b::l) = maxA b (a::l).

`Lemma` minA_sym : $\forall$ a b l, minA a (b::l) = minA b (a::l).

`Lemma` sorted_sorted_rev: $\forall$ a l, **sorted** $l \rightarrow$ ($\forall$ y, In y $l \rightarrow a \leq y$)
$\rightarrow$ **sorted** (a :: l).

`Lemma` sorted_app : $\forall$ y l, ($\forall$ x, In x $l \rightarrow$ Nat.le x y) $\rightarrow$ **sorted** (l)
$\rightarrow$ **sorted** (l ++ [y]).

6 Conclusions

The main conclusions of this paper are based on the comparison between Coq and *Theorema* specifications and the proofs produced, as detailed below.

Specifications. The types in *Theorema* are not explicitly declared, but they are based on notation conventions. *Theorema* can accept partial functions, such as *Min* and *Max* that are not defined when the argument is an empty list. On the other hand, the Coq specifications are typed and accept only total functions. For the *Min-Max-Sort* example, the translation into Coq was straightforward since the call to these functions (that happens only in the definition of MMS) is done only when their arguments are non-empty lists and allowed us to replace them with the body of their definitions.

On the other hand, the Theorema specification for *Patience-Sort* uses partial functions, like head and *last*, that take lists as arguments. The solution used on the Coq side was to define the return value to be of type **option nat** such that when the arguments are empty lists the returned value is None, otherwise Some x, where x is the body of the partial function when called on non-empty lists. Below, we give the full Coq definitions of these functions, as well as of the auxiliary function *SelSort* that uses them:

```
Function SelSort (l: list nat):=
  match l with
    nil ⇒ Some nil
  | a :: l' ⇒
      match l' with
        nil ⇒ Some [a]
      | _ ⇒
          (match (SelSort (l')) with
              None ⇒ None
            | Some ss ⇒
                (match head (ss) with
                    None ⇒ None
                  | Some hd ⇒ (match last ss with
                                  None ⇒ None
                                | Some lst ⇒ if (a <=? hd) then Some (a :: ss)
                                              else if (lst <=? a)
                                                 Some (ss ++ [a])
                                                 else Some ss
                              end)
                 end
                )
          end)
      end
end.

Definition head (l: list nat):=
  match l with
  | nil ⇒ None
  | hd :: tl ⇒ Some hd
  end.

Function last (l: list nat) :=
  match l with
  | nil ⇒ None
  | hd :: tl ⇒ match tl with
                  nil ⇒ Some hd
                | _ ⇒ last tl
                end
  end.
```

Another important difference between systems is the following: in Coq one can only define terminating functions, while in *Theorema* this is not necessary.

Proofs. The proofs in both Coq and *Theorema* systems have been built using the *cascading* proof strategy: when a proof fails on some subgoal s, s is converted to a lemma whose proof may be based on other lemmas that are expected to be simpler to prove or are already proved. In Coq some lemmas can be directly accessed from the standard library that comes with the system, however, many necessary lemmas had to be created by the user. In *Theorema* for the certification process we do not need to use a specific domain of ordered elements, but we use inference rules which are based on the natural properties of total order (e.g. transitivity). The theory necessary for the proofs is not imported from libraries, but is constructed ad-hoc for the purpose of definition and certification of algorithms. However, we can also run the algorithms in *Theorema* and for this purpose we use numbers with the ordering provided by the *Mathematica* libraries.

During the design of the Coq proofs, we have used some lemmas from the List and Arith standard libraries, for example the Nat.lt_le_incl lemma that was proved in the file `Nat.v` from Arith. These libraries are not exhaustive and we found convenient to prove additional properties, for example:

Lemma leb_FT_eq : ∀ x a, (x <? a) = false → (x <=? a) = true → x = a.

Lemma leb_TT_eq : ∀ x a, (x <=? a) = true → (a <=? x) = true → x = a.

The *Theorema* proofs are automatically generated in natural style, are easy to read as they are similar to human proofs. In contrast, in Coq the user needs the computer to run the proof scripts step by step which displays the current state of the proof. The generation of Coq scripts was highly interactive. However, Coq gives the opportunity to the user to automate the proof process by using tactics, script-generators and solvers for decision problems.

In Coq, once the proofs are finished, they are certified by the kernel of the system using the Curry-Howard isomorphism, therefore the proofs are automatically ensured to be logically correct. In contrast, in *Theorema* it is possible to introduce inference rules that are not logically correct, therefore we took much care when designing them.

The *Theorema* certification of all the algorithms described in Sect. 3, as well as the Coq scripts can be found at https://members.loria.fr/SStratulat/files/SCSS2024.zip.

Future Work. One important direction to proceed towards more efficient generation of such proofs is the automatic generation of the necessary lemmas in the cascading step.

This work constitutes a good basis for a possible integration of the two systems by translating the *Theorema* proofs into Coq scripts in order to be rigorously verified. Thus, we would have natural style proofs that use high-level inference rules and strategies, but can also be completely trusted because they are certified by a safe system.

Another interesting followup of this work in *Theorema* is the study of the duality between certification proofs and synthesis proofs.

Acknowledgements. This work is co-funded by the European Union, Erasmus+ project AiRobo: Artificial Intelligence based Robotics, 2023-1-RO01-KA220-HED-000152418.

References

1. Ahrendt, W., Beckert, B., Bubel, R., Hähnle, R., Schmitt, P., Ulbrich, M.: Deductive Software Verification. The KeY Book: From Theory to Practice. Springer, Cham (2016). https://doi.org/10.1007/978-3-319-49812-6
2. Baity, R., Humphrey, L.R., Hopkinson, K.: Formal verification of a merge sort algorithm in SPARK. In: AIAA SciTech Forum, American Institute of Aeronautics and Astronautics (2024/02/01) (2021). https://doi.org/10.2514/6.2021-0039
3. Beckert, B., Schiffl, J., Schmitt, P.H., Ulbrich, M.: Proving JDK's dual pivot quicksort correct. In: Paskevich, A., Wies, T. (eds.) Verified Software. Theories, Tools, and Experiments, pp. 35–48. Springer International Publishing, Cham (2017). https://doi.org/10.1007/978-3-319-72308-2_3
4. Bertot, Y., Casteran, P.: Interactive Theorem Proving and Program Development Coq'Art: The Calculus of Inductive Constructions, Texts in Theoretical Computer Science, vol. Springer, XXV (2004)
5. Bockenek, J., Lammich, P., Nemouchi, Y., Wolff, B.: Using Isabelle/UTP for the verification of sorting algorithms: A case study. EasyChair Preprint no. 944 (2019). https://doi.org/10.29007/ddqm
6. Bove, A., Coquand, T.: Formalising bitonic sort in type theory. In: Filliâtre, J.-C., Paulin-Mohring, C., Werner, B. (eds.) Types for Proofs and Programs, pp. 82–97. Springer Berlin Heidelberg, Berlin, Heidelberg (2006). https://doi.org/10.1007/11617990_6
7. Buchberger, B.: Algorithm invention and verification by lazy thinking. In: Analele Universitatii de Vest, Timisoara, Ser. Matematica - Informatica. vol. XLI, pp. 41–70 (2003)
8. Buchberger, B., Jebelean, T., Kriftner, F., Marin, M., Tomuta, E., Vasaru, D.: A survey on the Theorema project. In: International Symposium on Symbolic and Algebraic Computation, pp. 384–391. ACM Press (1997)
9. Buchberger, B., Jebelean, T., Kutsia, T., Maletzky, A., Windsteiger, W.: Theorema 2.0: Computer-assisted natural-style mathematics. J. Formalized Reason. **9**(1), 149–185 (2016).https://doi.org/10.6092/issn.1972-5787/4568
10. Burgos, M.P.F.: Formalization of sorting algorithms in Isabelle/HOL. Master's thesis, Vrije Universiteit Amsterdam (2019)
11. Certezeanu, R., Drossopoulou, S., Egelund-Muller, B., Leino, K.R.M., Sivarajan, S., Wheelhouse, M.: Quicksort revisited: Verifying alternative versions of quicksort. Theory and Practice of Formal Methods: Essays Dedicated to Frank de Boer on the Occasion of His 60th Birthday, pp. 407–426 (2016)
12. Couturier, R.: Formal engineering of the bitonic sort using PVS. In: Proceedings of the 2nd Irish Conference on Formal Methods (IW-FM'98), pp. 16–34. BCS Learning & Development Ltd., Swindon, GBR (1998)
13. Dramnesc, I., Jebelean, T.: Synthesis of list algorithms by mechanical proving. J. Symb. Comput. **68**, 61–92 (2015). https://doi.org/10.1016/j.jsc.2014.09.030
14. Drămnesc, I., Jebelean, T.: Automatic synthesis of merging and inserting algorithms on binary trees using multisets in Theorema. In: Slamanig, D., Tsigaridas, E., Zafeirakopoulos, Z. (eds.) Mathematical Aspects of Computer and Information Sciences: 8th International Conference, MACIS 2019, Gebze, Turkey, November 13–15, 2019, Revised Selected Papers, pp. 153–168. Springer International Publishing, Cham (2020). https://doi.org/10.1007/978-3-030-43120-4_13

15. Dramnesc, I., Jebelean, T.: Synthesis of sorting algorithms using multisets in Theorema. J. Logical Algebraic Methods Programm. **119**, 100635 (2020). https://doi.org/10.1016/j.jlamp.2020.100635
16. Drămnesc, I., Jebelean, T.: AlConsâĂŕ: deductive synthesis of sorting algorithms in Theorema. In: Cerone, A., Ölveczky, P.C. (eds.) Theoretical Aspects of Computing – ICTAC 2021: 18th International Colloquium, Virtual Event, Nur-Sultan, Kazakhstan, September 8–10, 2021, Proceedings, pp. 314–333. Springer International Publishing, Cham (2021). https://doi.org/10.1007/978-3-030-85315-0_18
17. Dramnesc, I., Jebelean, T.: Mechanical verification of insert-sort and merge-sort using multisets in Theorema. In: IEEE 21st International Symposium on Intelligent Systems and Informatics (SISY 2023), pp. 55–60. IEEE Xplore (2023)
18. Dramnesc, I., Jebelean, T., Stratulat, S.: Mechanical synthesis of sorting algorithms for binary trees by logic and combinatorial techniques. J. Symb. Comput. **90**, 3–41 (2019)
19. Filliâtre, J.C., Magaud, N.: Certification of sorting algorithms in the system Coq. In: Theorem Proving in Higher Order Logics: Emerging Trends (1999)
20. Georgiou, P., Hajdu, M., Kovacs, L.: Saturating sorting without sorts. In: Proceedings of 25th Conference on Logic for Programming, Artificial Intelligence and Reasoning (LPAR 2024). EPiC Series in Computing, vol. 100, pp. 88–105. EasyChair (2024).https://doi.org/10.29007/rg9z, https://easychair.org/publications/paper/qbDc
21. de Gouw, S., de Boer, F.S., Rot, J.: Verification of counting sort and radix sort. Deductive Software Verification–The KeY Book: From Theory to Practice, pp. 609–618 (2016)
22. Hoang, D., Moy, Y., Wallenburg, A., Chapman, R.: Spark 2014 and GNATprove. Int. J. Softw. Tools Technol. Transfer **17**(6), 695–707 (2015). https://doi.org/10.1007/s10009-014-0322-5
23. Howard, W.A.: The formulas-as-types notion of construction. In: To H. B. Curry: Essays on Combinatory Logic, Lambda Calculus, and Formalism, pp. 479–490. Academic Press (1980), reprint of 1969 article
24. Jiang, D., Zhou, M.: A comparative study of insertion sorting algorithm verification. In: 2017 IEEE 2nd Information Technology, Networking, Electronic and Automation Control Conference (ITNEC), pp. 321–325 (2017). https://doi.org/10.1109/ITNEC.2017.8284998
25. Kaufmann, M., Moore, J.S.: ACL2 Version 8.3 - The User's Manual (1999)
26. Knuth, D.E.: The Art of Computer Programming, Volume 3: Sorting and Searching, 2nd edn. Addison Wesley (1998)
27. Marché, C., Paulin-Mohring, C., Urbain, X.: The KRAKATOA tool for certification of JAVA/JAVACARD programs annotated in JML. J. Logic Algebraic Programm. **58**(1-2), 89–106 (2004). https://doi.org/10.1016/j.jlap.2003.07.006, https://hal.science/hal-01984932
28. Nipkow, T., Wenzel, M., Paulson, L.C. (eds.): Isabelle/HOL. Springer Berlin Heidelberg, Berlin, Heidelberg (2002)
29. Petrovic, D.: Verification of selection and heap sort using locales. Arch. Formal Proofs (2014). https://www.isa-afp.org/entries/Selection_Heap_Sort.shtml
30. Quarfot Orrevall, S., Gengelbach, A.: Implementation and verification of sorting algorithms with the interactive theorem prover HOL. Student thesis, Department of Information Technology, Mathematics and Computer Science, Disciplinary Domain of Science and Technology, Uppsala University (2020). http://urn.kb.se/resolve?urn=urn:nbn:se:uu:diva-424295

31. Safari, M., Huisman, M.: A generic approach to the verification of the permutation property of sequential and parallel swap-based sorting algorithms. In: Dongol, B., Troubitsyna, E. (eds.) Integrated Formal Methods: 16th International Conference, IFM 2020, Lugano, Switzerland, November 16–20, 2020, Proceedings, pp. 257–275. Springer International Publishing, Cham (2020). https://doi.org/10.1007/978-3-030-63461-2_14
32. Sandip, R., Sumners, R.W.: Verification of an in-place quicksort in ACL2. In: Proceedings of the 3rd International Workshop on the ACL2 Theorem Prover and Its Applications (2002). https://api.semanticscholar.org/CorpusID:264243016
33. Shankar, N., Owre, S., Rushby, J.M., Stringer-Calvert, D.W.J.: PVS prover guide - version 7.1. SRI International (2020)
34. Sternagel, C.: Proof pearl - a mechanized proof of GHCs mergesort. J. Autom. Reason. **51**(4), 357–370 (2013)
35. The Coq development team: The Coq Reference Manual. INRIA (2020). http://coq.inria.fr/doc
36. Tushkanova, E., Giorgetti, A., Kouchnarenko, O.: Specifying and proving a sorting algorithm. Tech. rep., Laboratoire d'Informatique de l'Université de Franche-Comte (2009)
37. Windsteiger, W.: Theorema 2.0: A system for mathematical theory exploration. In: ICMS 2014. LNCS, vol. 8592, pp. 49–52 (2014). https://doi.org/10.1007/978-3-662-44199-2_9
38. Zhang, Y., Zhao, Y., Sanan, D.: A verified timsort C implementation in Isabelle/HOL. arXiv preprint arXiv:1812.03318 (2018)

A Method to Prove Japanese Theorems and Others Appeared in Wasan Using Maxima

Setsuo Takato[1,2](✉) and Hideyo Makishita[2]

[1] KeTCindy Center, Kiyomidai-higashi, Kisarazu 2920041, Chiba, Japan
setsuotakato@gmail.com, hideyo@shibaura-it.ac.jp
[2] College of Engineering, Shibaura Institute of Technology, Tokyo, Japan

Abstract. Many plane geometry problems in Wasan, Japanese mathematics, have beautiful results but are difficult to prove, and simple methods fail when trying with computer algebra. We found that by using certain parameters, all quantities of a triangle can be expressed by their rational expressions. We call this method the MNR method and have implemented this method as a package in Maxima. A considerable number of problems, including well-known Japanese theorems, can be solved using this method.

Keywords: KeTCindy · KeTCindyJS · Cinderella2 · CindyJS · Maxima · MNR method

1 Introduction

Many people learned and studied Wasan, which was mathematics unique to Japan, during the Edo period (1603–1867)[1]. Some of them solved difficult problems or proved new theorems in Euclidean geometry. These people put the results in the book they wrote or drew figures of problems on wooden boards called Sangaku and hung them up at shrines and temples. Figure 1 is an example of Sangaku [4].

The problem on the right is called Japanese Theorem II by Uegaki [6,7]. The letters are written vertically from right to left, and the question, answer, and solution are written in that order. Here, we will explain them. However, the question sentences are paraphrased.

[1] During the Edo period, Japan was isolated from Europe and mathematics also developed independently.

H. Makishita—Contributing author.

S. M. Watt and T. Ida (Eds.): SCSS 2024, LNAI 14991, pp. 57–78, 2024.
https://doi.org/10.1007/978-3-031-69042-6_4

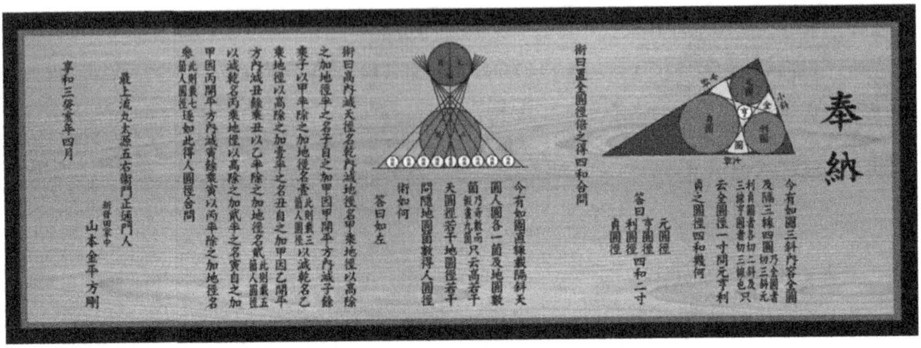

Fig. 1. Sangaku Lost from the Hakusan Shrine (Reconstruction)

Question Let the radius of the inscribed circle of the large triangle be R, the radius of the inscribed circle, the radii of the three circumscribed circles of the small triangle be r, r_1, r_2, r_3. Express the sum $r + r_1 + r_2 + r_3$ by R.

Answer The sum of r, r_1, r_2, r_3 is twice R.

Solution Multiply R by 2 to get the answer.

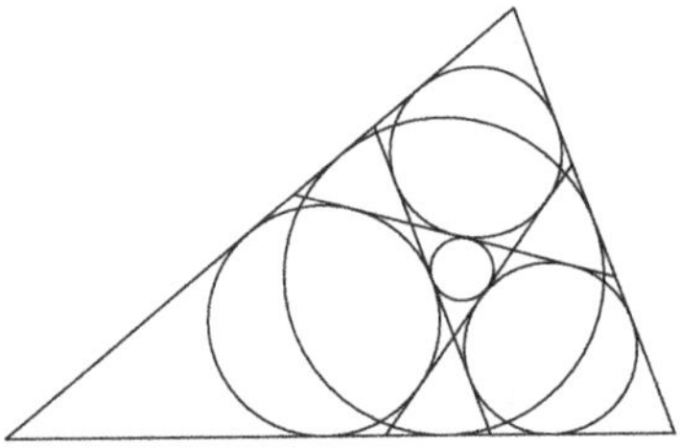

Fig. 2. Japanese Theorem II

Note that the solution is short and almost the same as the answer. Solving these problems in Wasan by hand would require long calculations. Also, when using some computer algebra, the equations will be mixed with radicals and will fail in most cases. Therefore, we came up with the MNR method, which expresses various quantities as rational expressions using half of the two base angles of a triangle and the radius of the inscribed circle. In Sect. 2, we will first explain the MNR method and MNR package for Maxima named `mnr.max` . Next, in Sects. 3 and 4, we will discuss the flow of solutions for the Japanese Theorems and others.

2 Development of MNR Package for Maxima

For the MNR method, the half-angle tangent is important. Take a triangle ABC with the radius of the inscribed circle being r as Fig. 3, and put $m = \tan\frac{B}{2}$[2], $n = \tan\frac{C}{2}$. Then all quantities of the triangle can be expressed as rational expressions of m, n, and r as follows.

[2] In Japanese mathematics textbooks, the slope of a line is often written as m.

1. Sides

$$\text{edgB}(BC) = \frac{r}{m} + \frac{r}{n}, \ \text{edgR}(CA) = \frac{r(1+n^2)}{n(1-nm)}, \ \text{edgL}(AB) = \frac{r(1+m^2)}{m(1-nm)}$$

2. Vertices

$$\text{vtxL}(B) = [-\frac{r}{m}, -r], \ \text{vtxR}(C) = [\frac{r}{n}, -r], \text{vtxT}(A) = [\frac{r(n-m)}{1-mn}, \frac{r(1+m*n)}{1-m*n}]$$

3. Incenter

$$\text{inC} = [0,0], \ \text{inR} = r$$

4. Circumcenter

$$\text{cirC} = [\frac{r(m-n)}{2mn}, \frac{(m^2+3m^2n^2+n^2-1}{4mn(1-mn)}], \text{cirR} = \frac{r(m^2+1)(n^2+1)}{4mn(1-mn)}$$

5. Eccentric center

$$\text{exCa} = [\frac{r(m-n}{mn)}, -\frac{r(mn+1}{mn}], \ \text{exRa} = \frac{r}{mn}$$

$$\text{exCb} = [-\frac{r(1+m^2)}{m(1-mn)}, \frac{rn(1+m^2}{m(1-mn)}], \text{exRb} = \frac{r(m+n)}{m(1-mn)}$$

$$\text{exCc} = [\frac{r(1+n^2)}{n(1-mn)}, \frac{rm(1+n^2)}{n(1-mn)}], \text{exRc} = \frac{r(m+n)}{n(1-mn)}$$

6. Orthocenter and Centroid

$$\text{ortC} = [\frac{r(n-m)}{1-mn}, \frac{r(3m^2n^2-m^2-2mn-n^2+1)}{2mn(1-mn)}]$$

$$\text{barC} = [\frac{r(2mn-1)(n-m)}{3mn(1-mn)}, \frac{r(3mn-1)}{3(1-mn)}]$$

In the MNR method, these values are defined as global variables.

The main reason these quantities can be expressed as rational expressions in m, n, and r is that trigonometric functions such as sin B are expressed in this way.

$$\sin B = 2\sin\frac{B}{2}\cos\frac{B}{2} = \frac{2m}{1+m^2}$$

$$\cos B = 2\cos^2\frac{B}{2} - 1 = \frac{1-m^2}{1+m^2}$$

$$\tan\frac{A}{2} = \tan\frac{\pi-B-C}{2} = \cot\frac{B+C}{2} = \frac{1-mn}{m+n}$$

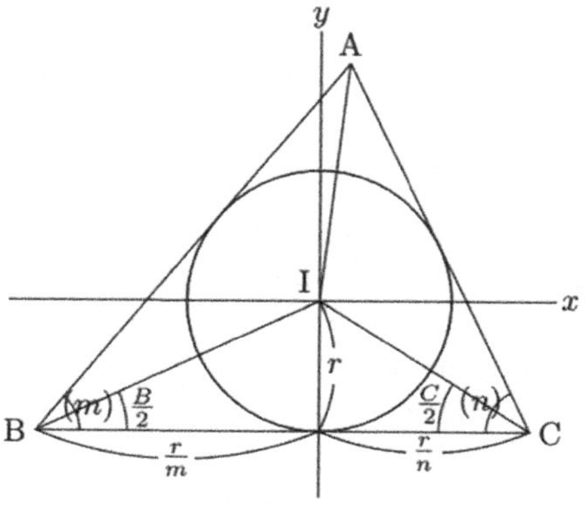

Fig. 3. Definition of m, n, r

The following three functions are the core of the MNR method:

putT(m,n,r) Used to place a triangle as Fig 3.
Specifically, it assigns values to all global variables.

slideT(p1,p2) Used to translate the triangle so that p1 becomes p2.
Specifically, it changes values of global variables such as vtxL to vtxL+(p2-p1).

rotateT(m,pt) Used to rotate around pt.
Specifically, it rotates global variables such as vtxL by angle $2\tan^{-1} m$ around pt.

Hereafter, for a positive number m, we express angle α such that $m = \tan\frac{\alpha}{2}$ as (m). For example, $(1), (\sqrt{3})$ represent angles $\frac{\pi}{2}, \frac{2\pi}{3}$ respectively.

The supplementary angle of (t) is expressed as $(\frac{1}{t})$, since $\tan\frac{\pi-\alpha}{2} = \cot\frac{\alpha}{2} = \frac{1}{t}$, and the complementary angle as $(\frac{1-t}{1+t})$.

We included the following functions in `mnr.max`.

supA(t):=1/t
comA(t):=(1-t)/(1+t)
plusA(t1,t2):=ratsimp((t1+t2)/(1-t1*t2)
minusA(t1,t2):=ratsimp(t1-t2)/(1+t1*t2))

Moreover we also added the following functions to complement Maxima.

numer(f):=factor(num(ratsimp(f)))
denomf(f):=factor(denom(ratsimp(f)))
frfactor(f):=numer(f)/denomf(f)
ratev(eq,repL):=ratsimp(ev(eq,rep))
frev(eq,repL):=frfactor(ratev(eq,rep))
ratevL(eq,repL):=ratsimp(ev(eq,repL))
frevL(eq,repL):=frfactor(ratevL(eq,repL))
dotProd(v1,v2) dot product
crossProd(v1,v2) cross product
meetLine(pts1,pts2) intersection of two lines pts1,pts2
lenSeg2(p1,[p2]) square of the length of the line segment p1p2
reduceDegree([eq1,eq2],m,step) Elimination of one variable

We have developed KETCindy [3] which is a macro package of the dynamic geometry system Cinderella2 [5] for creating graphs and geometric figures for TEX interactively. KETCindy can also call Maxima and use its calculation results. KETCindy includes the MNR package as a library. Recently, we have incorporated `quickketcindy` into the KETCindy package. It would be convenient when using KETCindy without TEX and only Maxima, or only KETCindy JS. To use quickketcindy/formaxima, follow these steps:

1. Download Maxima from https://sourceforge.net/projects/maxima/files/ and install it.

2. Download Cinderella2 from https://beta.cinderella.de and install it. Note that one should run the installer with administrator privileges in case of Windows.
3. Download KETCindy from https://github.com/ketpic/ketcindy/releases and unzip it. The latest version of KETCindy is currently 4.4.85, so the name of the file is ketcindy-4.4.85. For Windows, change the name to ketcindy4.4.85 and place it directly under C:.
4. Launch a cdy file in ketcindy/quickketcindy/formaxima, say `0comtan.cdy`,

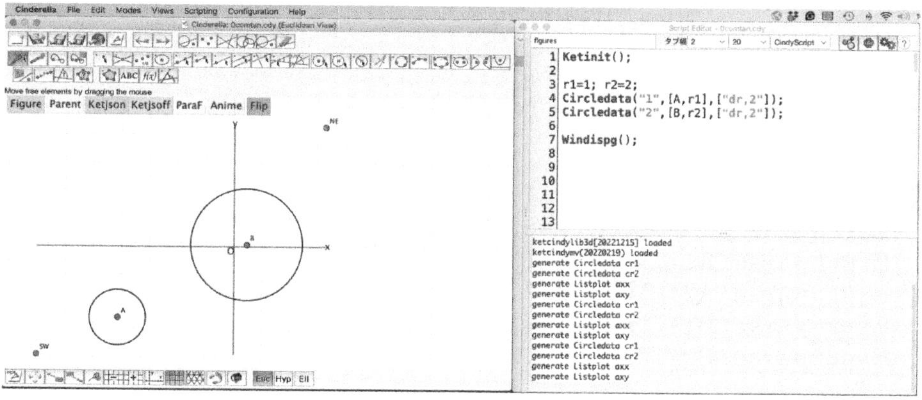

Fig. 4. Windows of Cinderella

Cinderella has two windows, a figure display window and a script window. At start-up, only the figure display window is displayed, but if one select `script/edit scripting` from the menu, the script window will open. The scripts should be written between `Ketinit()` and `Windispg()`.

```
Ketinit();
r1=1; r2=2;
Circledata("1",[A,r1],["dr,2"]); //*1*2
Circledata("2",[B,r2],["dr,2"]);
m=tan(30/2*pi/180); //*3
x1=A.x; y1=A.y; x2=B.x; y2=B.y;
Windispg();
```

*1 `Circledata` draws the circle wirh Center A and radius r1, and assigns the data to cr1. ["dr,2"] is an opton to change the line thickness. Note that commands which start with a capital letter are of ketcindy.
*2 A, B is movable points on the screen called geometric points.
*3 The value `m` will be used when drawing.

As a simple example, let's find the common tangent of two circles, whose result will be used in the proof of Japanese Theorem II. We use the cdy file `0comtan.cdy`. We add the following scripts before Windispg().

```
var1="A1::B1::C1::A2::B2::C2"; *1
cmdL1=concat(Mxbatch("mnr"),[ *2
  "Ca:[x1,y1]", "Cb:[x2,y2]",
  "putT(m,1,r1)", *3
  "slideT([0,0],Ca)", *4
  "A1:vtxT; B1:vtxL; C1:vtxR", *5
  "putT(m,1,r2)", *3
  "slideT([0,0],Cb)", *4
  "A2:vtxT", "B2:vtxL", "C2:vtxR" *5
]);
CalcbyMset(var1,"ans1",cmdL1,[""]); *6
Pos=[3.5,3]; Dy=1; *7
Disptex(1,"B1"); *8
Disptex(0,"A1");
Disptex(0,"B2");
Disptex(0,"A2");
Listplot("1",ParseL([A1,B1,C1,A1])); *9
Listplot("2",ParseL([A2,B2,C2,A2]));
Expr(parse(A1),"n","A_1");
Expr(parse(A2),"n","A_2");
Expr(parse(B1),"sw","B_1");
Expr(parse(B2),"sw","B_2");
```

We add brief explanations.

*1 `var1` is the list of variables returned by Maxima.
*2 `cmdL` is a list of Maxima commands. `Mxbatch` reads all commands defined in `mnr.max` as a list. `concat` is the Cinderella command to join lists.
*3 Place a triangle whose incenter is the origin. Here m is common, and (1) $= \frac{\pi}{2}$.
*4 Shift the triangle so that its incenter is Ca, Cb.
*5 Let the vertices of triangles be [A1,B1,C1] and [A2,B2,C2].
*6 Maxima executes commands and returns the results as a list in variable `ans`. KETCindy assigns each element of `ans` to the variable `var1`. The final optional argument [] allows us to force run(["m"]), read only(["r"]), or automatically determine([""]).
*7 These are the initial position and line width for displaying the expression.
*8 This is a command to display each value of `var1` in TEX format.
*9 `ParseL` is a command that evaluates each element of a list.

Click the gear icon on the top right corner of the script window, then the figure and equation will be displayed on the display window.

Rem. Clicking the cross icon will allow us to move the window left, right, up or down in any direction.

Next, we determine the value of m so that sides B1A1 and B2A2 are on a straight line. To do this, we add the following command sequence cmdL2 to cmdL1 (Figs. 6).

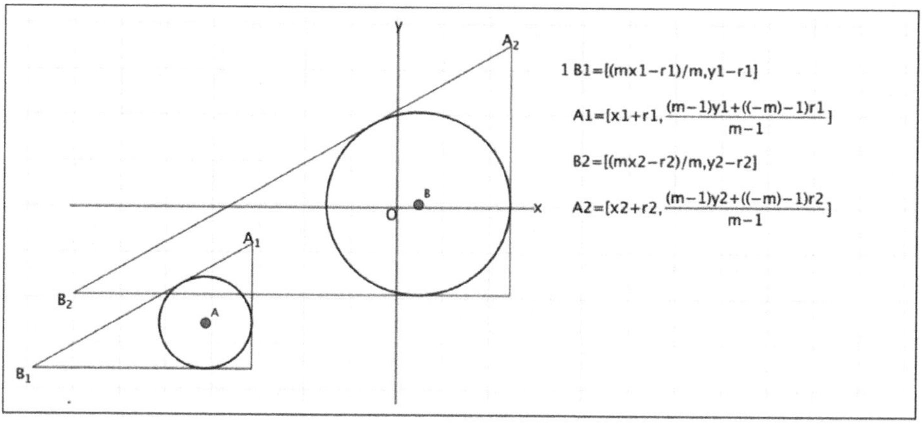

Fig. 5. Figure display window 1

```
var2="eq::A1::B1::C1::A2::B2::C2";
cmdL2=concat(cmdL1,[
  "B1A1:A1-B1",
  "B1B2:B2-B1",
  "eq:crossProd(B1A1,B1B2)",  *1
  "eq:numer(eq)",  *2
  "tmp:solve(eq,m)",
  "sol:tmp[2]",  *3
  "A1:frev(A1,sol)",
  "B1:frev(B1,sol)",
  "C1:frev(C1,sol)",
  "A2:frev(A2,sol)",
  "B2:frev(B2,sol)",
  "C2:frev(C2,sol)"
]);
CalcbyMset(var2,"ans2",cmdL2,[""]);
Pos=[3.5,3]; Dy=1;
Disptex(2,"B1",1);
Disptex(0,"A2");
Disptex(0,"eq");
Mxsetvar(var2,ans2);
Listplot("a",ParseL([A1,B1,C1,A1]));
Listplot("b",ParseL([A2,B2,C2,A2]));
```

*1 The condition is $\overrightarrow{B1A1} \times \overrightarrow{B1B2} = 0$

*2 We take only the numerator of the fraction and simplify it.

*3 `eq` is a quadratic equation. Choose one of the solutions.

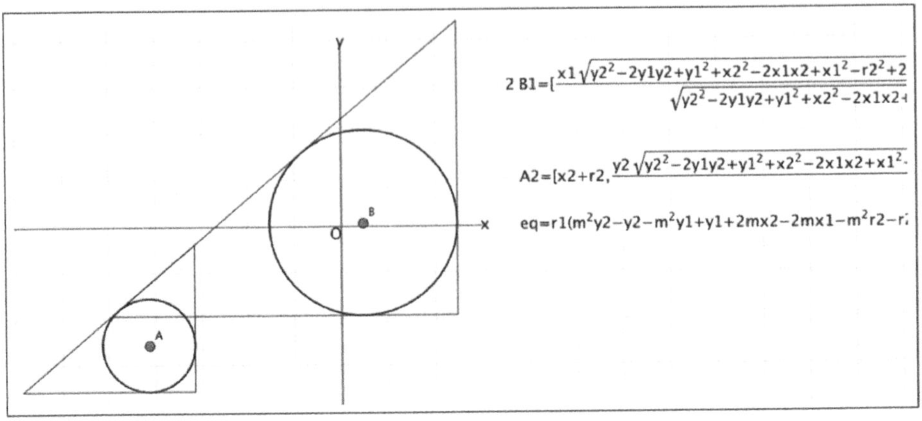

Fig. 6. Common tangent of two circles

We added 4 commands `comTan1`, `comTan2`, `comTanC1`, and `comTanC2` to `mnr.max`. For example, `comTan` is defined as follows:

```
comTan(C1,r1,C2,r2,ch):=block(
  [mL,x1,y1,x2,y2,pA1,pB1,pC1,pA2,pB2,pC2,v1,v2,
   eq,sol,sol1,sol2,tmp,tmp1,out],
  x1:C1[1], y1:C1[2], x2:C2[1], y2:C2[2],
  putT(mL,1,r1), slideT([0,0],C1),
  pA1:vtxT, pB1:vtxL, pC1:vtxR,
  putT(mL,1,r2), slideTriangle([0,0],C2),
  pA2:vtxT, pB2:vtxL, pC2:vtxR,
  v1:ratsimp(pA1-pB1), v2:ratsimp(pA2-pB1),
  tmp:crossProd(v1,v2), eq:numer(tmp),
  sol:solve(eq,mL), tmp:sol[ch],
  pA1:ratev(pA1,tmp), pB1:ratev(pB1,tmp), out:[pA1,pB1],
  out
)$
comTan1(C1,r1,C2,r2):=commonTan(C1,r1,C2,r2,1)$
comTan2(C1,r1,C2,r2):=commonTan(C1,r1,C2,r2,2)$
```

Fig. 7. Command of common tangent lines

3 Proof of Japanese Theorem II

Now that we are ready, let's prove the Japanese Theorem II (**Fig.** 2).

Step 1. Set the incircle and three circumscribed circles of the small triangle.

```
var1="pA::pB::pC::pI::rI"+
   "::Ca::Ra::Cb::Rb::Cc::Rc";
cmdL1=concat(Mxbatch("mnr"),[
  "putT(m,n,r)",
  "pI:inC", "rI:inR",
  "pA:vtxT","pB:vtxL","pC:vtxR",
  "Ca:exCa","Ra:exRa","Cb:exCb",
  "Rb:exRb","Cc:exCc","Rc:exRc"
]);
CalcbyMset(var1,"ans1",cmdL1,[""]);
m=tan(66/2*pi/180);
n=tan(57/2*pi/180);
r=0.4;
Listplot("1",ParseL([pA,pB,pC,pA]));
Circledata("1",ParseL([pI,r]));
Circledata("1a",ParseL([Ca,Ra]));
Circledata("1b",ParseL([Cb,Rb]));
Circledata("1c",ParseL([Cc,Rc]));
```

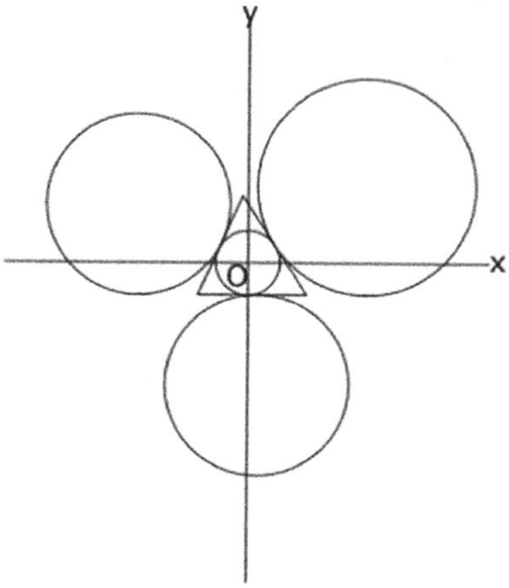

Fig. 8. Step 1

Step 2. Find the vertices D, E, F of the triangle formed by the common tangent.

```
var2=var1+"D::E::F";
cmdL2=concat(cmdL1,[
  "out:comTan1(Ca,Ra,Cb,Rb)",
  "pts1:[out[1],out[2]]",
  "out:comTan1(Cc,Rc,Ca,Ra)",
  "pts2:[out[1],out[2]]",
  "out:comTan1(Cb,Rb,Cc,Rc)",
  "pts3:[out[1],out[2]]",
  "D:meetLine(pts1,pts2)",
  "E:meetLine(pts2,pts3)",
  "F:meetLine(pts3,pts1)"
 ]);
 CalcbyMset(var2,"ans2",cmdL2,[]);
   Listplot("1",ParseL([pA,pB,pC,pA]));
   Circledata("1",ParseL([pI,r]));
   Circledata("1a",ParseL([Ca,Ra]));
   Circledata("1b",ParseL([Cb,Rb]));
   Circledata("4",ParseL([Cc,Rc]));
   Listplot("2",ParseL([D,E,F,D]));
   Letter(parse(D),"s","D");
   Letter(parse(E),"e","E");
   Letter(parse(F),"w","F");
```

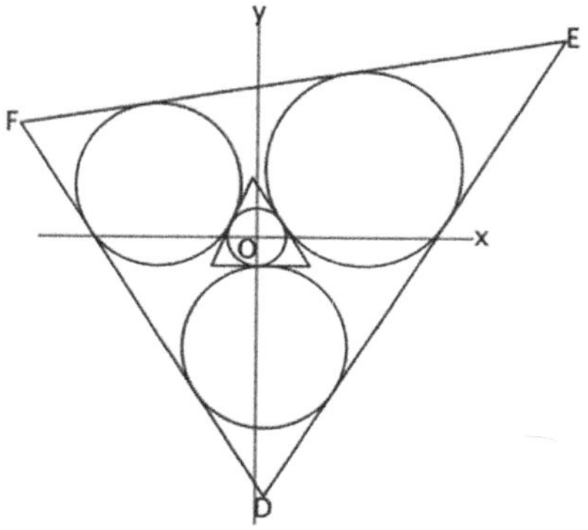

Fig. 9. Step 2

Step 3. Find the radius R of the outer triangle and $r + Ra + Rb + Rc$.

```
var3=var2+"::DE::EF::FD::s::S::R::sum::CR";
cmdL3=concat(cmdL2,[
  "tmp1:frfactor(lenSeg2(D,E))",
  "tmp2:frfactor(lenSeg2(E,F))",
  "tmp3:frfactor(lenSeg2(F,D))",
  "assume(m>0,n>0,m<1,n<1,m*n-1<0)",*1
  "assume((m+1)*n+m-1>0)", *2
  "DE:frfactor(sqrt(tmp1))",
  "EF:frfactor(sqrt(tmp2))",
  "FD:frfactor(sqrt(tmp3))",
  "s:frfactor((DE+EF+FD)/2)",
  "vDF:frfactor(F-D)",
  "vDE:frfactor(E-D)",
  "S:frfactor(1/2*crossProd(vDF,vDE))",
  "R:frfactor(S/s)",
  "sum:frfactor(r+Ra+Rb+Rc)",
  "CR:frfactor((DE*F+EF*D+FD*E)/(2*s))" *3
];
CalcbyMset(var3,"ans3",cmdL3,[""]);
Disptex(0,"DE"); Disptex(0,"EF"); Disptex(0,"FD");
Disptex(0,"s"); Disptex(0,"S"); Disptex(0,"R");
Disptex(0,"sum");
Circledata("C",ParseL([CR,R]));
```

*1 Maxima command **assume** sets conditions for simplifying radicals.
*2 When apex angle A is acute,
$\tan(A/2) = \cot(B/2 + C/2) = (1 - mn)/(m + n) < 1$
*3 CR is the incenter of the triangle DEF.

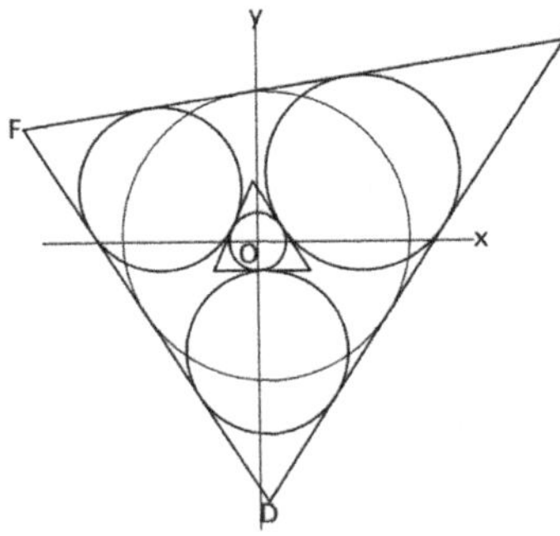

$$DE=\frac{(m^2+1)^2(m^2n^2-n^2-2mn-m^2-1)r}{(m-1)m(m+1)(mn-1)(mn-n-m-1)(mn+n+m-1)}$$

$$EF=-\frac{(n+m)(m^2n^2-n^2-2mn-m^2-1)r}{(m-1)m(m+1)(n-1)n(n+1)}$$

$$FD=\frac{(n^2+1)^2(m^2n^2-n^2-2mn-m^2-1)r}{(n-1)n(n+1)(mn-1)(mn-n-m-1)(mn+n+m-1)}$$

$$s=\frac{4(n+m)(m^2n^2-n^2-2mn-m^2-1)r}{(m-1)(m+1)(n-1)(n+1)(mn-n-m-1)(mn+n+m-1)}$$

$$S=-\frac{2(n+m)(m^2n^2-n^2-2mn-m^2-1)^2r^2}{(m-1)m(m+1)(n-1)n(n+1)(mn-1)(mn-n-m-1)(mn+n+m-1)}$$

$$R=-\frac{(m^2n^2-n^2-2mn-m^2-1)r}{2mn(mn-1)}$$

$$sum=\frac{(m^2n^2-n^2-2mn-m^2-1)r}{mn(mn-1)}$$

Fig. 10. Proof of $R = r + Ra + Rb + Rc$

The results are as follows, and $2R = r + Ra + Rb + Rc$ holds.

$$R = \frac{(m^2n^2 - n^2 - 2\,mn - m^2 - 1)r}{2\,mn(mn-1)}$$

$$r + Ra + Rb + Rc = \frac{(m^2n^2 - n^2 - 2\,mn - m^2 - 1)r}{mn(mn-1)}$$

4 Proof of Japanese Theorem I

Let P_n be a convex n-polygon inscribed in a circle, and consider the polygon triangulation of P_n. The Japanese theorem I claims that the sum of the radii of all inscribed circles is independent of the method of division [1]. One might understand the meaning more by moving the figure interactively, so we created the HTML with KETCindy JS. Go to `ketcindy samples`:

https://s-takato.github.io/ketcindysample/misc/offline/jpntheoremv3jsoffL.html.

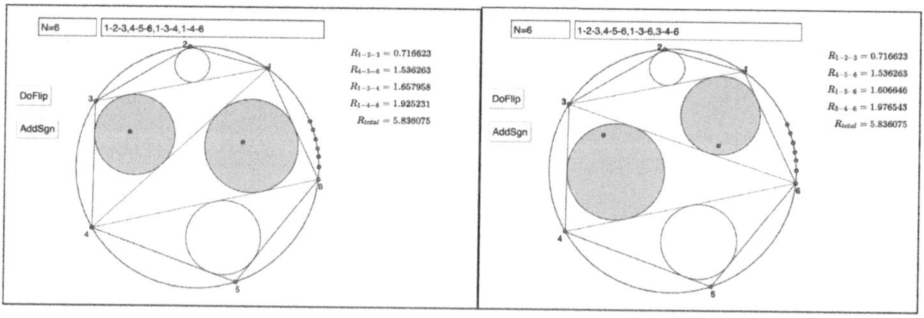

Fig. 11. Japanese theorem I and Flip operation

Place a red point in each of the two circles that are tangent to an edge, and click the button `Doflip`, then the edge, circles will change. However, the sum of the radii remains unchanged. Also, flipping is an operation performed on quadrilaterals, so we only need to show the case where $n = 4$. Now, we start to prove this theorem with the MNR method.

Step 1. Put $pA(0,0), pB(a,0)$. Set $\angle DAB = (m), \angle ABC = (n), \angle ABD = (n1)$. Note that $\angle ADC = \mathrm{supA}(n)$ and $\angle BCD = \mathrm{supA}(m)$ since the P_4 is inscribed in the circle.

```
var1="pA::pB::pC::pD::AD::BD::BC"
    + "::iC1::r1::iC2::r2::cC::R";
cmdL1=concat(Mxbatch("mnr"),[
 "pA:[0,0]","pB:[a,0]",
 "putT(m,n1,r1)","slideT(vtxL,pA)",
 "pD:vtxT","BD:edgR","AD:edgL","AB:edgB",
 "iC1:inC","cC:cirC","R:cirR",
 "eq:numer(AB-a)",
 "sol1:solve(eq,r1)",
 "tmp:supA(plusA(m,n1))",
 "tmp1:minusA(supA(n),tmp)",
 "tmp2:minusA(n,n1)",
 "putT(tmp1,tmp2,r2)",
 "slideT(vtxR,pB)",
 "rotateT(-n1,pB)",
 "pC:vtxT","BC:edgR","BD1:edgB",
 "iC2:inCenter",
 "eq:numer(BD-BD1)",
 "sol2:solve(eq,r2)",
 "solL:[sol2,sol1]",
 "r1:frevL(r1,solL)", "r2:frevL(r2,solL)",
 "pD:frevL(pD,solL)", "AD:frevL(AD,solL)",
 "BD:frevL(BD,solL)",
 "iC1:frevL(iC1,solL)",
 "cC:frevL(cC,solL)",
 "R:frevL(R,solL)",
 "pC:frevL(pC,solL)",
 "iC2:frevL(iC2,solL)",
 "BC:frevL(BC,solL)"
]);
CalcbyMset(var1,"ans1",cmdL1,[""]);
```

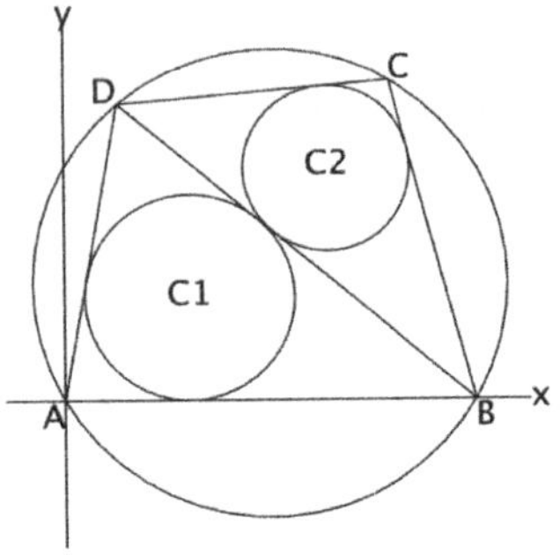

Fig. 12. Step 1

Rem. One can draw the triangle CDB according to the following flow.

(1) Place the triangle C_1D_1B using the fact that
$\angle CDB = (\pi - \angle ABC) - (\pi - \angle DAB - \angle ABD)$
$\angle CBD = \angle ABC - \angle ABD$.
(2) Rotate C_1D_1B around B by $-\angle ABD$ to create the triangle C_2D_2B.
(3) Find the radius r_2 so that point D_2 coincides with point D.

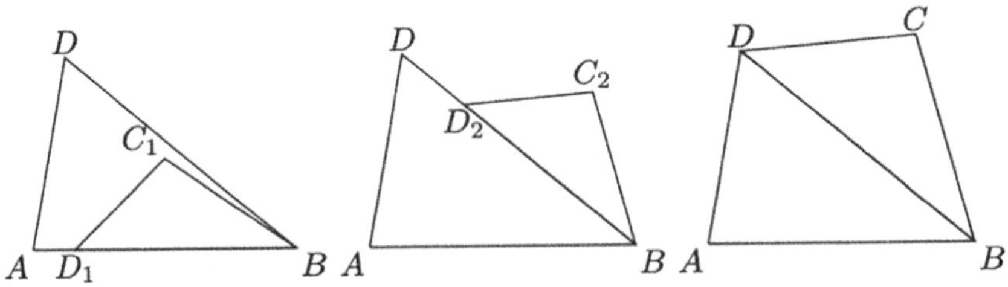

Fig. 13. Steps for drawing the triangle CDB

```
var2=var1+
"::r3a::r3b::iC3a::iC3b::m1a::m1b";
cmdL2=concat(cmdL1,[
"BC:"+BC,
"putT(m1,n,r3)","slideT(vtxL,pA)",
"iC3:inCenter",
"eq1:numer(edgB-a)",
"eq2:numer(edgR-BC)",
"sol:algsys([eq1,eq2],[m1,r3])",  *1
"m1a:frev(m1,sol[1])",
"r3a:frev(r3,sol[1])",
"iC3a:frev(iC3,sol[1])",
"m1b:frev(m1,sol[2])",
"r3b:frev(r3,sol[2])","iC3b:frev(iC3,sol[2])"
]);
CalcbyMset(var2,"ans2",cmdL2,[]);
```

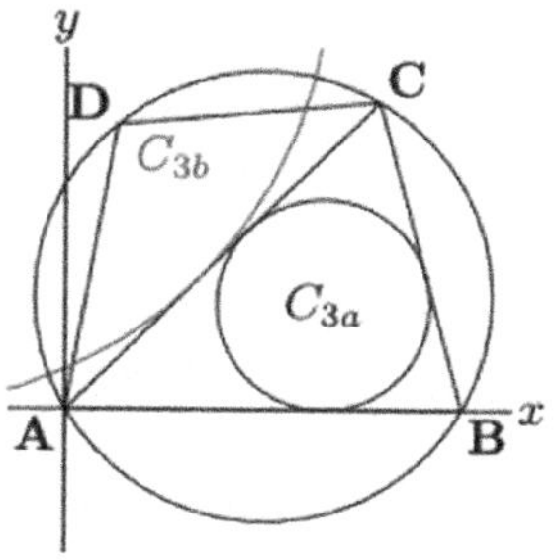

Fig. 14. Step 2

Step 2. Find $(m1) = \angle CAB$ and the radius of the inscribed circle of triangle CAB.

*1 This is a Maxima command to solve simultaneous equations. Here, the unknowns are m1 and r3. The Maxima library of Gröbner bases is also available, but in this case, the command `algsys` is faster.

Rem. Draw the figure on the display window like Fig. 13 and choose the appropriate one(sol[1]).

Step 3. Finally, the theorem is proven by calculating `r1+r2` and `r3+r4`.

```
var3=var2+"::iC4::r4::sum12::sum34";
cmdL3=concat(cmdL2,[
"m1:m1b","C3:C3b","r3:r3b",
"tmp1:minusA(m,m1)",
"tmp2:supA(plusA(m1,n))",
"tmp2:minusA(supA(m),tmp2)",
"putT(tmp1,tmp2,r4)",
"slideT(vtxL,pA)",
"rotateT(m1,pA)",
"iC4:inCenter",
"eq:numer(edgL-AD)",
"solr4:solve(eq,r4)",
"iC4:frevL(iC4,solr4)",
"r4:frevL(r4,solr4)",
"sum12:frfactor(r1+r2)",
"sum34:frev(r3+r4,sol)"
]);
CalcbyMset(var3,"ans3",cmdL3,[""]);
Pos=NE.xy+[0,-0.5]; Dy=2;
Disptex(0,"sum12"); Disptex(0,"sum34");
```

From Fig. 14, one can confirm that $sum12 = sum34$.

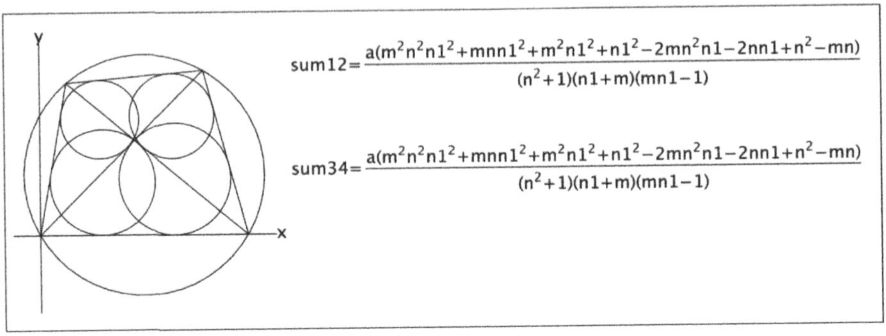

Fig. 15. Screenshot of window showing the figure and formula

5 Chain Circles

Many Japanese mathematicians during the Edo period studied chained circles, known as Steiner chains in Europe. Among them, Naoen Ajima and Sadakazu Ikeda are famous. In Fig. 15, let the centers and radii of circles O and C be $(0,0)$, r and $(p,0)$, R, respectively. Assume that the circle C_0, r_0 touches both O and C, and C_1 is tangent to O, C, C_0. To use the MNR method, let

$$\angle OC_0C = (m_0), \angle OC_1C = (m_1).$$

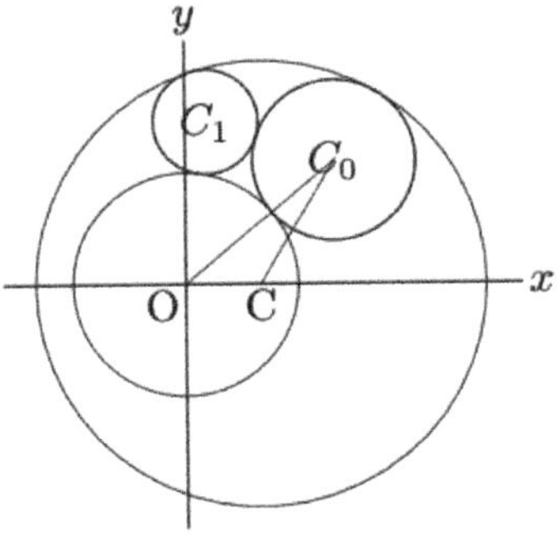

Fig. 16. Two circles in the chain

In the next subsection, 5.1, we show that m_1 can be expressed as a linear fraction of m_0, and therefore a general formula of m_k can be obtained (Figs. 16, 17, 18, 19 and 20).

5.1 General Formula for Chain Circles

We derive a general formula for m_k in the following steps:

1. To derive the formula for r_k in terms of m_k.
2. To find the recurrence formula $m_1 = f(m_0)$.
3. To simplify f to a linear fraction.
4. To derive the general formula $m_k = g(m_0)$

Step 1. First, we will find a formula to express r_0 in terms of $m = m_0$. The formula holds exactly the same for r_1, m_1.

```
var1="C0::n0::r0";
cmdL1=concat(Mxbatch("mnr"),[
  "O:[0,0]",
  "putT(m,n0,i0)",
  "slideT(vtxL,O)",*2
  "eq:vtxR[1]-p",*3
  "sol:solve(eq,i0)",
  "C0:frev(vtxT,sol)",
  "OC0:frev(edgL,sol)",
  "CC0:frev(edgR,sol)",
  "eq1:Numer(OC0-r0-r)",
  "eq2:Numer(CC0+r0-R)",
  "sol:algsys([eq1,eq2],[n0,r0])",
  "C0:frev(C0,sol)",
  "n0:frev(n0,sol)",
  "r0:frev(r0,sol)"
]);
CalcbyMset(var1,"ans1",cmdL1,[""]);
```

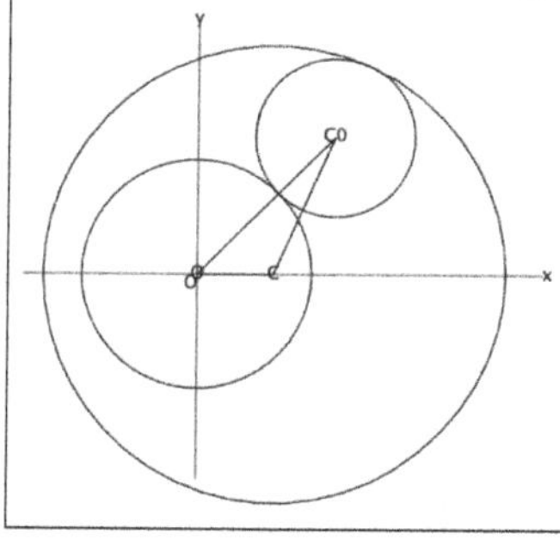

$$C0=\left[-\frac{(m-1)(m+1)(r-p+R)(r+p+R)}{2(m^2r+r+m^2p-p+Rm^2+R)}, \frac{m(r-p+R)(r+p+R)}{m^2r+r+m^2p-p+Rm^2+R}\right]$$

$$n0=\frac{r-p+R}{m(r+p+R)}$$

$$r0=-\frac{m^2r^2+r^2+2m^2pr-2pr+m^2p^2+p^2-R^2m^2-R^2}{2(m^2r+r+m^2p-p+Rm^2+R)}$$

Fig. 17. Circle C_0 tangent to O and C

Step 2. We will find the recurrence formula for m_0 and m_1.

```
var2=var1+"::sol::m1::C1::n1::r1::m1num::m1den";
cmdL2=concat(cmdL1,[
  "C1:frev(C0,m=m1)",
  "r1:frev(r0,m=m1)",
  "eq:lenSeg2(C0,C1)-(r0+r1)^2",    // |C1-C0|=r0+r1
  "sol:solve(eq,m1)",
  "sol:sol[2]", //positive direction
  "m1:frev(m1,sol)",
  "C1:frev(C1,sol)",
  "n1:frev(n1,sol)",
  "r1:frev(r1,sol)",
  "m1num:num(m1)",
  "m1den:denom(m1)"
]);
CalcbyMset(var2,"ans2",cmdL2,[""]);
```

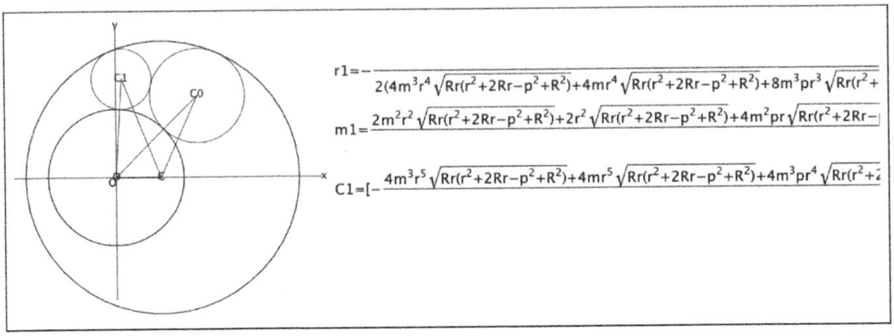

Fig. 18. Recurrence formula for C_0 and C_1

Step 3. Since the above formula is too long to calculate the general terms using symbolic calculations. The steps below are operations that simplify it[3].

3.1 Take out the expression in the radical in the numerator and factorize it.

```
CalcbyMset(var2,"ans2",cmdL2,[""]);
```

[3] Prof. Takuya Kitamoto of Yamaguchi University obtained the first-order fractional formula using Gröbner basis as follows:
"load(grobner)",
"eq1:f-m1d",
"eq2:d^2-d2",
"gb:poly_reduced_grobner([eq1,eq2],[m,p,r,R,d,f])",
"solf:gb[length(gb)-1]". .

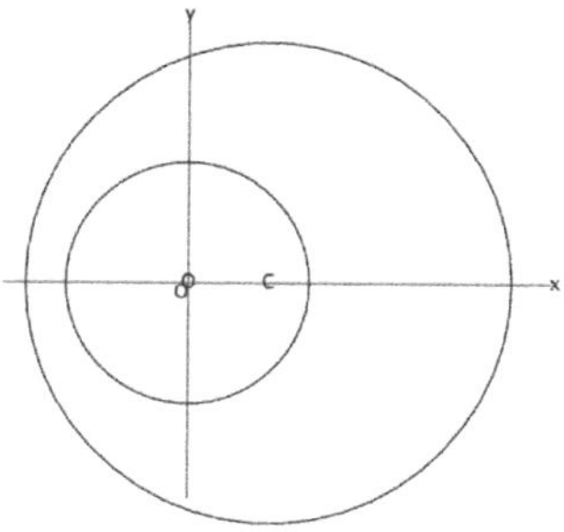

$$m1=-\frac{mr^4+4Rmr^3-2mp^2r^2-2dm^2r^2+6R^2mr^2-2dr^2-4Rmp^2r-4dm^2pr+4dpr+}{(r+p+R)(m^2r^3+3m^2pr^2-Rm^2r^2-4Rr^2+3m^2p^2r-2Rm^2pr+4R}$$

$$m1n=-(mr^4+4Rmr^3-2mp^2r^2-2dm^2r^2+6R^2mr^2-2dr^2-4Rmp^2r-4dm^2pr+4dpr$$

$$m1d=(r+p+R)(m^2r^3+3m^2pr^2-Rm^2r^2-4Rr^2+3m^2p^2r-2Rm^2pr+4Rpr-R^2m^2r-4R$$

$$d2=Rr(r-p+R)(r+p+R)$$

Fig. 19. Recurrence formula(2) for C_0 and C_1.

```
d2=Mxfactor(m1num,1);
m1d=replace(m1,d2,"d^2");
  //Execute the above three lines in advance:
var3="m1n::m1d::m1::d2";
cmdL3=concat(Mxbatch("mnr"),[
 "assume(d>0)",
 "d2:"+d2,
 "m1:"+m1d,
 "m1:frfactor(m1)",
 "m1n:numer(m1)",
 "m1d:denomf(m1)",
 "d2:factor(d2)"
]);
CalcbyMset(var3,"ans3",cmdL3,[""]);
```

3.2 Replace with the following:

$$r+p+R=s, r-p+R=a, -r-p+R=b$$

```
"m1:"+m1,"eqrpR:[r+p+R=s,r-p+R=a,-r-p+R=b]",
"sab:solve(eqrpR,[r,p,R])",
"sab:sab[1]","m1:frev(m1,sab)",
"m1n:numer(m1)",
"m1d:denomf(m1)","m1d:expand(m1d)"
```

$$m1n=bm^2s\sqrt{a(b+a)s(s-b)}-as\sqrt{a(b+a)s(s-b)}+ab\sqrt{a(b+a)s(s-b)}+a^2\sqrt{}$$
$$m1d=b^2m^2s^2-abs^2-a^2s^2+ab^2s+a^2bs$$

Furthermore, replace the radical part of m1n with d and write it as m1nd. Along with that, put m1dd=m1d.

3.3 Both m1nd and m1dd are quadratic expressions of m[4].

```
"m1nd:"+m1nd,
"m1dd:"+m1dd,
"Dn: disc(m1nd,m)", *1
"Dd: disc(m1dd,m)",
```

$Dn=as(a^3s^3-4bd^2s-4b^2d^2+4abd^2)$

$Dd=-4ab^2(b-a)s^3(s+b)$

*1 `disc` is the function of `mnr` to calculate the discriminant.

3.4 By using `d^2=a*(b+a)*s*(s-b))` and then factorizing it, Dn and Dd are transformed as follows:

```
 d2=Mxfactor(m1n,2); //KeTCindy executes this line
 Dn=replace(Dn,"d^2",d2); //Same as above
"Dn:"+Dn,
"Dd:"+Dd,
"d2:"+d2,
"rat:frfactor(Dd/d2)",
"Dd:rat*d^2",
"Dn1:factor(Dn)",
"Dd1:factor(Dd)"
```

$Dn1=a^2s^2(2bs-as+2b^2-2ab)^2$

$Dd1=4b^2d^2s^2$

3.5 Calculate $sqn = \sqrt{Dn1}$, $sqd = \sqrt{Dd1}$.

```
"assume(a>0,b>0,d>0,s>0)",
"m1nd:"+m1nd,"m1dd:"+m1dd,
"Dn1:"+Dn1,"Dd1:"+Dd1,
"sqn:frfactor(sqrt(Dn1))",
"sqd:frfactor(sqrt(Dd1))"
```

$sqn=as((2b-a)s+2b^2-2ab)$

$sqd=2bds$

[4] Kitamoto suggested that we use 'poly_normal_form' as an alternative way to derive the formula in 3.7.

3.6 Find two solutions for each of equations m1nd=0, m1dd=0.

```
"sqn:"+sqn ,"sqd:"+sqd ,
"d2:"+d2 ,
"an: coeff(m1nd,m,2)" ,
"bn: coeff(m1nd,m,1)" ,
"cn: coeff(m1nd,m,0)" ,
"ad: coeff(m1dd,m,2)" ,
"bd: coeff(m1dd,m,1)" ,
"cd: coeff(m1dd,m,0)" ,
"ans1n: frfactor((-bn+sqn)/(2*an))" ,
"ans2n: frfactor((-bn-sqn)/(2*an))" ,
"ans1d: frfactor((-bd+sqd)/(2*ad))" ,
"ans2d: frfactor((-bd-sqd)/(2*ad))" ,
"rat: ans2n/d2" ,
"ans2n: frfactor(rat*d^2)" ,
```

```
ans1n=-(a(s+b-a))/d

ans2n=-d/(bs)

ans1d=d/(bs)

ans2d=-d/(bs)
```

3.7 Factor m1, m2 using the solution of ansn, ansd. Furthermore, reduce the common factor of the numerator and denominator. This is the recurrence formula for m of two adjacent circles, and the key point is that m1 is a first-order fractional expression.

```
"ans1n:"+ans1n ,"ans2n:"+ans2n ,
"ans1d:"+ans1d ,"ans2d:"+ans2d ,
"ans1n: frfactor(ans1n)" ,
"an:"+an ,"bn:"+bn ,
"ad:"+ad ,."bd:"+bd ,
"tmp1: an*(m-(ans1n))*(m-(ans2n))" ,
"tmp2: ad*(m-(ans1d))*(m-(ans2d))" ,
"m1: frfactor(tmp1/tmp2)"
```

$$m1 = -\frac{as+dm+ab-a^2}{bms-d}$$

Set $s + b - a = c$, then $m1$ will be

$$\boxed{m1 = -\frac{dm + ac}{bsm - d}}.$$

Step 4. We derive the general term of m_k.

4.1 Let A be the adjoint matrix of $m1$:

$$M = \begin{pmatrix} -d & -ac \\ bs & -d \end{pmatrix}.$$

The eigenvalues and eigenvectors of matrix M can be calculated with Maxima.

```
"assume(s>0,a>0,b>0,c>0)",
"m1f:"+m1f,
"m1f:frfactor(m1f)",
"m1n:expand(num(m1f))",
"m1d:expand(denom(m1f))",
"an:coeff(m1n,m,1)",
"bn:coeff(m1n,m,0)",
"ad:coeff(m1d,m,1)",
"bd:coeff(m1d,m,0)",
"M:matrix([an,bn],[ad,bd])",
"eL:eigenvalues(mM)",
"evL:eigenvectors(mM)",
"t1:eL[1][1]","t2:eL[1][2]",
"p1:evL[2][1][1]","p2:evL[2][2][1]"
```

$$t1=(-\%i\sqrt{a}\sqrt{b}\sqrt{c}\sqrt{s})-d$$
$$t2=\%i\sqrt{a}\sqrt{b}\sqrt{c}\sqrt{s}-d$$
$$p1=[1,\frac{\%i\sqrt{b}\sqrt{s}}{\sqrt{a}\sqrt{c}}]$$
$$p2=[1,-\frac{\%i\sqrt{b}\sqrt{s}}{\sqrt{a}\sqrt{c}}]$$

4.2 We find the polar form by transforming the real and imaginary parts.

```
"assume(s>0,a>0,b>0,c>0,d>0)",
"t1:"+t1,"rp:realpart(t1)",
"ip:imagpart(t1)",
"at2:rp^2+ip^2","at2:factor(at2)",
 at2=Assign(at2,["d^2","("+d2str+")","c","("+cstr+")"]);
   //KeTCindy executes the above line
"at:sqrt(at2)",
"tt:ip/rp"
```

$$at=as$$
$$tt=(\sqrt{a}\sqrt{b}\sqrt{c}\sqrt{s})/d$$

4.3 From this, we get $t_1 = ase^{i\theta}, t_2 = ase^{-i\theta}$, here, $\tan\theta = \frac{\sqrt{abcs}}{d}$. Also, if we set $P = \begin{pmatrix} \sqrt{ac} & \sqrt{ac} \\ i\sqrt{bs} & -i\sqrt{bs} \end{pmatrix}$ from p_1 and p_2, M is diagonalized by P:

$$D = P^{-1}MP = as\begin{pmatrix} e^{i\theta} & 0 \\ 0 & e^{-i\theta} \end{pmatrix},$$

$$M^k = PD^kP^{-1} = P(as)^k \begin{pmatrix} e^{ik\theta} & 0 \\ 0 & e^{-ik\theta} \end{pmatrix} P^{-1}$$

$$= \frac{(as)^k}{\sqrt{abcs}} \begin{pmatrix} \sqrt{abcs}\cos k\theta & ac\sin k\theta \\ -bs\sin k\theta & \sqrt{abcs}\cos k\theta \end{pmatrix}.$$

4.4 Therefore, the general term m_k is

$$m_k = \frac{m\sqrt{abcs}\cos k\theta + ac\sin k\theta}{-mbs\sin k\theta + \sqrt{abcs}\cos k\theta} = \frac{m\sqrt{abcs} + ac\tan k\theta}{-mbs\tan k\theta + \sqrt{abcs}}$$

We can calculate C_k and r_k from m_k using the following formula:

$$\boxed{\begin{aligned} C_k &= \left[-\frac{a(m_k-1)(m_k+1)s}{2({m_k}^2 s+a)}, \frac{asm_k}{s{m_k}^2+a}\right] \\ r_k &= \frac{bs{m_k}^2+ac}{2(s{m_k}^2+a)} \end{aligned}}.$$

5.2 Ring Circles

When all chain circles touch each other, they are called ring circles. We find the condition for N circles C_0, C_1, $\cdots$, C_{N-1} to be ring circles.

```
"mk:(m*sqrt(a*b*c*s)+a*c*tan(k*theta))/
    (-m*b*s*tan(k*theta)+sqrt(a*b*c*s))",
                                          from (4.4)
"eq:numer(mk-m)"
```

The results are as follows:

$$m_k = \frac{\tan^{-1} k\theta - m\sqrt{abcs}}{\sqrt{abcs} - bms\tan k\theta}$$
$$eq = (bm^2\,s + ac)\tan(k\theta)$$

From this, the condition for creating a ring is

$$N\theta = \pi, \tan\theta = \tan\frac{\pi}{N} = \frac{\sqrt{abcs}}{d} = \sqrt{\frac{(R-r)^2-p^2}{4Rr}}.$$

This is called Steiner's condition. Hereafter, assume that N is an even number, and set $N = 2n$. We will prove the so-called Ikeda's theorem which claims the sum of the reciprocals of the radii of two opposing circles is constant. Since $n\theta = \frac{\pi}{2}$, m_n, r_0 and r_n becomes as follows:

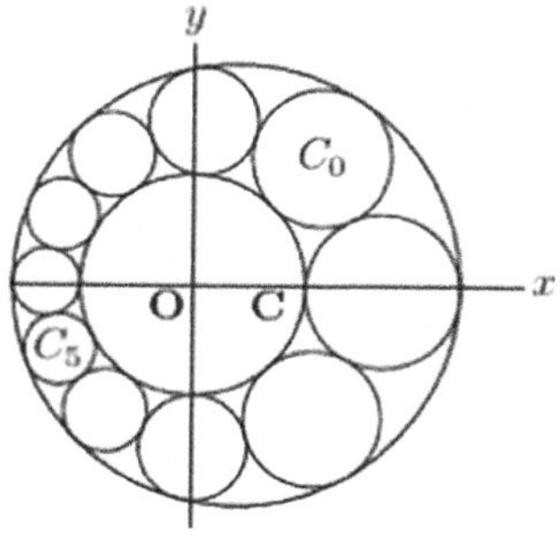

Fig. 20. Ring circles

$$m_n = \frac{ac}{bms},\ r_0 = \frac{bm^2\,s+ac}{2(m^2\,s+a)},$$
$$r_n = \frac{bc(bm^2\,s+ac)}{2(b^2\,m^2\,s+ac^2)}.$$

From these formulas, we get the following formula:

$$\frac{1}{r_0} + \frac{1}{r_n} = \frac{2(c+b)}{bc},$$

which does not include m, so the theorem has been proved.

6 Conclusion

Many geometry problems in Wasan required extensive calculations, and Wasan scholars used their superior calculation and intuition skills to solve them. Even when trying to solve these problems using computer algebra, appropriate measures are required, and the MNR method is one of them. It is expected that the use of modern tools by students and mathematics educators to prove theorems or to solve problems will stimulate their motivation and interest.

References

1. Oshima, T.: Japanese Theorem (2022). https://www.ms.u-tokyo.ac.jp/~oshima/lecture/sangaku0.pdf. (in Japanese)
2. Hirata, K., Shinomiya, M.: An extension of Ikeda's theorem, bulletin of the faculty of education. Ehime University, vol. 65, pp. 137–141 (2018). (in Japanese)
3. Takato, S.: What is and how to use KeTCindy-linkage between dynamic geometry software and graphics capabilities -. In: ICMS, pp. 371–379 (2016)
4. Wakuta, K., Togawa, K.: The Sangaku Lost from the Hakusan Shrine in Niigata, Research Reports of National Institute of Technology KOSEN) Nagaoka College, vol. 47, pp. 7–16 (2011). (in Japanese)
5. Gebert, J., Kortenkamp, U.: The Cinderella.2 Manual. Springer (2006). https://doi.org/10.1007/978-3-540-34926-6
6. Ahuja, A., Uegaki, W., Matsushita, K.: Japanese Theorem: a little known theorem with many proofs, PART I, II. Missouri J. Math. Sci. **16**, 72–80, 149–158 (2004)
7. Uegaki, W.: On the Origin and History of the Japanese Theorem, BULLETIN of the Faculty of Education in Mie University(Natural Science), vol. 52, pp. 23–45 (2001). (in Japanese)
8. Fukagawa, H., Pedoe, D.: Japanese Temple Geometry Problems, Winnipeg. The Charles Babbage Research Centre, Canada (1989)

Foundations of Haskell's Rewrite Rules Based on Higher-Kinded Polymorphic Rewrite Systems

Makoto Hamana(✉)

Department of Computer Science and Networks, Kyushu Institute of Technology, Iizuka, Japan
hamana@csn.kyutech.ac.jp

Abstract. The aim of this paper is to establish theoretical foundations of GHC's rewrite rules. The Glasgow Haskell Compiler (GHC) has the feature of rewrite rules to specify optimising transformations. Rewrite rules have been widely used in many libraries. However, there has been no theory to formalise the rules and establish their correctness. We present System $\mathrm{F_{RE}}$—the polymorphic λ-calculus System F_ω extended with higher-order term rewriting and equational reasoning to model GHC's rewrite rules. We develop a theory and methods for verifying correctness of rewrite rules. The key to our method is to guarantee the rewriting properties of local confluence and strong normalisation. We prove the Rule Meaning Preservation Theorem that gives a simple criterion for establishing correctness of rewrite rules, which is suited for mechanical checking.

1 Introduction

The Glasgow Haskell Compiler (GHC) is an open source compiler for the Haskell functional language [10]. It has the feature of *rewrite rules* to specify optimising transformations [15]. Rewrite rules have been widely used in many libraries.

But there has been no formal theory that formalises the rules and establishes their correctness. In this paper we present System $\mathrm{F_{RE}}$, a variant of the polymorphic λ-calculus extended with rewrite rules and equations. By giving a rewriting semantics of Haskell, we show that rewrite rules and the functional programming language based on the polymorphic λ-calculus are modeled uniformly in a single framework, which allows us to verify the rewrite rules. The aim of this paper is to establish theoretical foundations of GHC's rewrite rules.

Rewrite Rules in GHC. To illustrate a problem concerning the correctness of a rule, we consider the Haskell program `Diverge.hs` involving a rewrite rule as shown in Fig. 1. The code inside the `{-# ... #-}` is called a *pragma*. Inside the `RULES` pragma there is a rule called `"one"` which tells GHC to rewrite an expression "`f` t" to "1". But in the program the function f is defined to always return 0. What is the output of `main`?

S. M. Watt and T. Ida (Eds.): SCSS 2024, LNAI 14991, pp. 79–95, 2024.
https://doi.org/10.1007/978-3-031-69042-6_5

```
-- Diverge.hs
f :: Int -> Int
f x = 0

{-# RULES
"one" forall x.f x = 1
 #-}
main = print (f 2)
```

```
-- Loop.hs
{-# RULES
"loop" forall x y.
          f x y = f y x
 #-}

e = f 0 1
```

```
> ghc -O Loop.hs
   -ddump-rule-firings
..
Rule fired: loop (Loop)
Rule fired: loop (Loop)
Rule fired: loop (Loop)
..
Simplifier ticks exhausted
```

Fig. 1. Are these rules correct?

Calling GHC with `-fenable-rewrite-rules` applies the rewrite rule before compilation, so the output is `1`. This shows that the rewrite rule inadvertently changes the meaning of the original program. Namely, the rule is considered to be wrong. Since the rule feature was introduced as an optimisation tool, it should not change the meaning of the original program.

More than 20 years have passed since rewrite rules were first proposed for GHC [15]. Observations have shown that it is useful in very many libraries[1], whose efficiency often depends crucially on rewrite rules. For example, GHC's own base library contains more than 100 rules. However, GHC does not currently attempt to check the correctness of rules in a program. Even the concept of "correctness" has not been rigorously formulated, so it remains unclear what the criteria should be. First we clarify two correctness properties of rewrite rules.

Termination. Termination is the most important property to ensure in the situation of GHC. If there is a non-terminating rewrite rule, the compilation fails at the simplification phase as shown as `Loop.hs` in Fig. 1.

Therefore, we need to clarify termination or non-termination of rewrite rules. Note that termination is known to be an undecidable property, i.e., there is no algorithm to judge whether given rewrite rules are terminating or not *in general*. However, for particular classes of problems, we can have an algorithm to decide termination. In this paper, we give a theoretical criterion, called the Polymorphic General Schema. This is a syntactic criterion to judge strong normalisation of rewrite rules, which is suitable for automation.

Finite Meaning Preservation. We need also to check that rewrite rules do not change the original meaning of a program. In the case of `Diverge.hs` in Fig. 1, the rewrite rule `"one"` does not preserve the original meaning. We formulate the notion of finite meaning preservation as follows.

We say that a set $\mathcal{R}$ of rewrite rules is *finite meaning-preserving* w.r.t. a program $\mathcal{P}$ if for each rule $l \Rightarrow r \in \mathcal{R}$, instances of l and r instantiated by finite and total values have the same finite and total values evaluated by the

[1] https://www.aosabook.org/en/ghc.html.

```
-- Fact.hs
fact 0 = 1
fact n = n * fact (n-1)
```

```
{-# RULES
"fact10" fact 10 = 120
#-}
```

Fig. 2. Factorial function with a special case

```
-- Append.hs
(++) :: [a] -> [a] -> [a]
[]     ++ ys = ys
(x:xs) ++ ys = x : (xs ++ ys)

{-# RULES
"assoc" forall xs ys zs. (xs ++ ys) ++ zs = xs ++ (ys ++ zs)
#-}
```

Fig. 3. Append program with the associativity rule

program $\mathcal{P}$. (We will give a more precise rewriting theoretic definition of the meaning-preserving in Sect. 5, Definition 4).

For example, given the program `Fact.hs` in Fig. 2, the rule `"fact10"` is finite meaning-preserving w.r.t. the program because the lhs of the rule is evaluated to the value 120 and so is the rhs, therefore they have the same finite meaning.

As another example, given the program `Append.hs` in Fig. 3, the rule `"assoc"` is finite meaning-preserving w.r.t the program. We will discuss it in more details in Sect. 2.

How to Ensure the Finite Meaning Preservation of Rules. Consider again the example of append function with the associativity rule in Fig. 3. To say that the rule `"assoc"` is meaning-preserving w.r.t. the program is to ***prove*** that this equation holds for arbitrary lists under the program. As is well-known in the *Algebra of Programming* methodology [2,3,9], proving this requires structural induction on lists. Proving by induction involves appropriate applications of the induction hypothesis, and sometimes requires non-trivial lemmas. A clever prover may be able to prove such properties automatically on inductive types. However, since Haskell is a higher-order polymorphic functional programming language, programs and rules can also involve higher-order polymorphic functions. To prove equations involving higher-order functions, one may need to use more sophisticated proof principles. How to mechanize such proofs is not obvious and may be difficult.

Equational Logic Approach. To discuss the finite meaning preservation of a rewrite rule in a formal setting, we need a suitable framework for dealing with meaning and equality. One way is to use denotational semantics and insist that a rule $l \Rightarrow r$ preserves finite meaning as $[\![l]\!] = [\![r]\!]$. However, this is not easy for mechanization because it requires the formalisation of various mathematical structures, such as complete partial orders. Moreover, it is unclear how automatic proofs are possible for this purpose. Instead, we use a logical approach to reason about equations. We use equational logic [8] with an appropriate higher-order and polymorphic typed extension. A rule can be thought of as an oriented equation. Therefore we formalise "a rule $l \Rightarrow r$ is finite meaning-preserving w.r.t. a program $\mathcal{P}$" as "an equation $l = r$ is provable under the assumption $\mathcal{P}$".

For example, we consider again the example of append in Fig. 2. We regard the program as a set of equational axioms

$$\mathcal{P} = \left\{ \begin{array}{lll} \forall ys :: [a]. & [] \mathbin{++} ys & = ys \\ \forall x :: a.\ xs, ys :: [a]. & (x : xs) \mathbin{++} ys & = x : (xs \mathbin{++} ys) \end{array} \right\}$$

Then we can formulate the meaning preservation of an equation $l = r$ as the provability of it from $\mathcal{P}$. The inference rules of the ordinary first-order many-sorted equational logic EL_1 consist of reflexivity, transitivity, symmetry, congruence, substitution, and axiom rules [1,8,17] (Sec.3.1). We denote by $\mathcal{P} \vdash_{\mathsf{EL}_1} s = t$ the deducibility of $s = t$ from the axioms of $\mathcal{P}$ by EL_1 and call $s = t$ an *equational theorem* of $\mathcal{P}$.

It is important to note that in EL_1 the general associativity is not deducible from $\mathcal{P}$:

$$\mathcal{P} \nvdash_{\mathsf{EL}_1} \forall xs, ys, zs :: [a].\, (xs \mathbin{++} ys) \mathbin{++} zs = xs \mathbin{++} (ys \mathbin{++} zs) \tag{1}$$

Which form of associativity is deducible from $\mathcal{P}$ in EL_1? All of its ground instances

$$\mathcal{P} \quad \vdash_{\mathsf{EL}_1} \quad (xs\theta \mathbin{++} ys\theta) \mathbin{++} zs\theta = xs\theta \mathbin{++} (ys\theta \mathbin{++} zs\theta) \tag{2}$$

are deducible, where θ is an arbitrary substitution that assigns a ground list (i.e. a list containing no variable) to each variable. The notation $xs\theta$ denotes a term obtained by the application of θ to xs.

To see why (2) is deducible in EL_1, consider the substitution $\theta : xs, ys, zs \mapsto []$. Then $([] \mathbin{++} []) \mathbin{++} [] = [] = [] \mathbin{++} ([] \mathbin{++} [])$ is formally provable (by constructing a proof tree) from $\mathcal{P}$ in EL_1 by using the axiom instantiation of the first equation in $\mathcal{P}$, congruence, symmetry, and transitivity.

For the case of substitution $\theta : xs \mapsto (n : ns)$, etc., where $n : ns$ is a ground list, the associativity is similarly proved using a previously deduced associativity for the list ns. This is nothing but a proof by structural induction on lists using an induction hypothesis. This kind of theorems (such as (2)) is known as ***inductive theorems*** [1] (Definition 3.5.10), [17] (Sec. 3.2.4) in theory of term rewriting and universal algebra. In summary, under the axioms $\mathcal{P}$, $\forall xs, ys, zs :: [a].\, (xs \mathbin{++} ys) \mathbin{++} zs = xs \mathbin{++} (ys \mathbin{++} zs)$ is not an equational theorem of $\mathcal{P}$, but an inductive theorem of $\mathcal{P}$. Every equational theorem is an inductive theorem, but not vice versa.

For this reason, we formulate the finite meaning preservation of $l \Rightarrow r$ w.r.t. $\mathcal{P}$ as a property whether $l = r$ is an *inductive theorem* of $\mathcal{P}$ (Definition 3).

Rewriting Approach to Inductive Equational Reasoning. For mechanical rule checking, we need an algorithm to decide whether an equation is an inductive theorem or not. Ordinary equational theories can be decided if the given axioms are expressed as terminating and confluent rules. This is a well-known rewriting approach, as Knuth and Bendix solved the word problem for groups by constructing such axioms using the completion technique. But now we need to prove all the *ground instances of an equation* (such as (2)), which requires structural induction. This is different from proving a universally quantified equation (such as (1)) in EL_1. Structural induction could be taken as an additional inference rule of EL_1. But [14] proved that equational logic with structural induction is not complete. It follows that inductive theorems on natural numbers are not recursively enumerable [4]. In this paper we take a different approach, which establishes the following new theorem for deciding inductive theorems.

The Rule Meaning Preservation Theorem. Let $\mathcal{P}$ be a total Haskell program and $l \Rightarrow r$ a rewrite rule. Suppose that

(i) $\mathcal{P} \cup \{l \Rightarrow r\}$ is locally confluent, and
(ii) $\mathcal{P} \cup \{l \Rightarrow r\}$ is strongly normalising.

Then $l = r$ is an inductive theorem of $\mathcal{P}$, therefore, $l \Rightarrow r$ is meaning-preserving with respect to $\mathcal{P}$.

This theorem, later formally proved as a finer version (Theorem 7), provides a simple algorithm for deciding inductive theorems by checking (i) and (ii). Namely, if we have automatic local confluence and termination (i.e. strong normalisation) checkers, then we can decide the correctness automatically. A remarkable point is that these conditions do not use structural induction. This theorem is simple in form, but powerful. In fact, we can use it to prove the correctness of the associativity of append, the map fusion law, and the Maybe monad laws (see Sect. 2,2,6). This theorem requires checking the termination and local confluence of the union of a program and a rewrite rule. Therefore, we will develop methods to verify local confluence and termination of rewrite systems for Haskell, which are suited for mechanical checking.

Organisation and Contributions. We make the following contributions.

(i) System F_{RE}: We develop a formal system for rewriting and equational reasoning that extends the polymorphic λ-calculus System F_ω (Sect. 4). We give rewrite rule specifications of Haskell programs (Sect. 4).
(ii) The Rule Meaning Preservation Theorem (Sect. 1, Theorem 7): We establish a rewriting theoretical criterion to ensure the finite meaning preservation of the rewrite rules. (Sect. 5).
(iii) Critical pair analysis: We present a method for checking local confluence that extends Knuth and Bendix's method [11] to higher-order polymorphic rules.

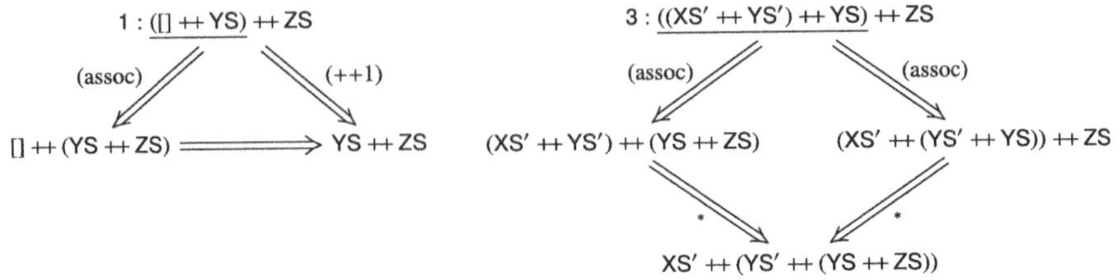

Fig. 4. Critical pairs of append (excerpt)

We use the notation $\overline{A}$ for a sequence $A_1, \cdots, A_n$, and $|\overline{A}|$ for its length. We use the abbreviations "lhs" and "rhs" to mean left-hand side and right-hand side, respectively.

2 Introductory Examples

Example: Meaning Preservation of the Associativity of Append. We illustrate how to use the Rule Meaning Preservation Theorem. We first consider the example of append in Fig. 3. A set $\mathcal{P}$ of rewrite rules obtained from the Haskell program, called *a rewrite rule specification*, is given by

```
(++1)  []      ++ YS ⇒ YS
(++2)  (X:XS)  ++ YS ⇒ X : (XS ++ YS)
```

Now a set $\mathcal{R}$ of rewrite rule to be checked is

```
(assoc) (XS ++ YS) ++ ZS ⇒ XS ++ (YS ++ ZS)
```

To apply the Rule Meaning Preservation Theorem, we need to show local confluence of $\mathcal{P} \cup \mathcal{R}$. *Local confluence* (LCR) is a property of the reduction relation, stating that any two divergent computation paths are finally joinable, as shown in the right diagram. The proof requires an analysis of all possible situations that admit two ways of reductions, and also to check their convergence. In this case of the append function with associativity, careful inspection of the rules reveals that it has, in all, three patterns of such situations, as depicted in Fig. 4. Next it is apparent that all of these patterns are convergent. Importantly, this finite number of checks is sufficient to infer that all the other infinite numbers of instances of the divergent situations are convergent.

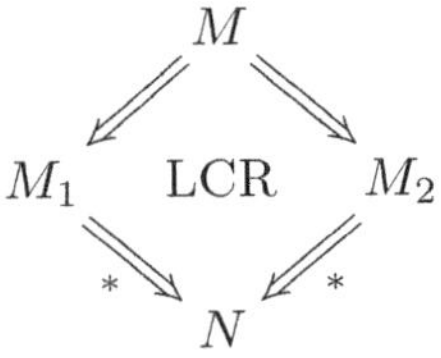

This proof method is known as Knuth and Bendix's critical pair analysis [11]. The divergent terms in Fig. 4 are designated as *critical pairs* because these show critical situations that may break confluence. A critical pair is obtained by an *overlap* between two rules, which is computed using unification (in general *higher-order pattern unification* [13]). For instance, an overlap exists between the rules `(assoc)` and `(++2)` because a subterm of `(assoc)` and the whole lhs of `(++2)`

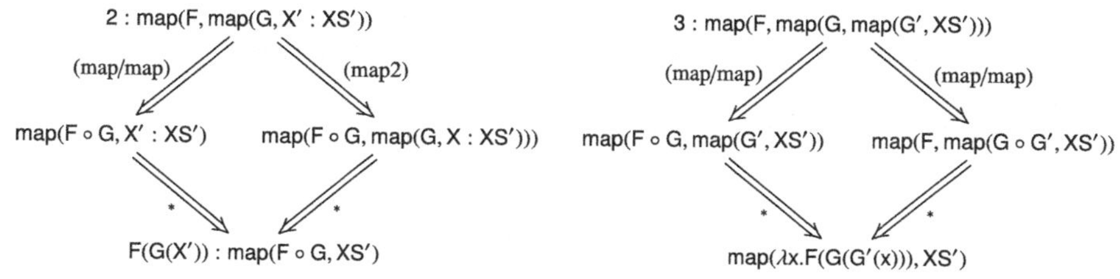

Fig. 5. Critical pairs of map (excerpt)

$$\texttt{XS ++ YS} \stackrel{?}{=} \texttt{(X':XS') ++ YS'}$$

are unifiable by a unifier $\theta = \{\texttt{XS} \mapsto \texttt{X':XS'},\ \texttt{YS'} \mapsto \texttt{YS}\}$. The instantiated term `((X':XS') ++ Y) ++ Z` by θ is the source of the divergence (2 :) in Fig. 4, which admits reductions by the two rules `(assoc)`,`(++2)`. The divergent terms are joinable by further rewriting. All three critical pairs are successfully joinable as shown in Fig. 4, which concludes the local confluence of the rules.

Next we need to prove strong normalisation of the rules. This is not difficult because $\mathcal{P}$ is defined by structural recursion on lists and `(assoc)` simply moves the brackets to the right. So we conclude the meaning preservation of the rule `"assoc"`. Note that in this checking, we have not used explicit induction on lists.

Example: Meaning Preservation of Map/Map Fusion. We consider an example of higher-order polymorphic programs, i.e., the familiar `map` and composition functions, and a rewrite rule `"map/map"`, which translates the composition of two `map`s to a single `map` in Fig. 6. The rhs of `"map/map"` is more efficient than the lhs because it traverses a list once rather than twice in the lhs. Therefore, this is an optimisation rule. This is the first example of "Playing by the Rule" [15]; it is also used in several libraries such as `Data.Text`. We prove the correctness of this rule by the Rule Correctness Theorem. This example involves a higher-order polymorphic function `map`. The program and rules in Fig. 6 are formally formulated as rewrite systems in System $\mathrm{F_{RE}}$. For the sake of readability, type judgments are simplified here by omitting environments and types, and we present only the rewriting rules. A set $\mathcal{P}$ of rewrite rules obtained from the Haskell program, called *a rewrite rule specification*, is given by

```
(map1)  map f []     ⇒ []
(map2)  map f (x:xs) ⇒ f x : map f xs
(o)     (.) f g x ⇒ f (g x)
```

Now a set $\mathcal{R}$ of rewrite rules to be checked is

```
(map/map)  map f (map g xs) ⇒ map (f . g) xs
```

To apply the Rule Meaning Preservation Theorem, we need to check local confluence of $\mathcal{P} \cup \mathcal{R}$. In this case, there are three critical pairs and all of them

```
-- Map.hs                              (.) :: (b -> c) -> (a -> b) -> (a -> c)
map :: (a -> b) -> [a] -> [b]          (.) f g x = f (g x)
map f []     = []                      {-# RULES
map f (x:xs) = f x : map f xs          "map/map" forall f g xs.
                                         map f (map g xs) = map (f . g) xs #-}
```

Fig. 6. Example: map function with map/map fusion

are successfully joinable as shown in Fig. 5. This shows local confluence of the computation rules.

The intuitive reason of strong normalisation is that (map1)(map2) are defined by structural recursion on lists, and in (map/map), the number of `map` is decreasing. To show that (o) is strongly normalising is more difficult, which is the same reason that the β-reduction in the typed λ-calculus terminates.

Since all the conditions of the Rule Meaning Preservation Theorem are satisfied, we conclude that meaning preservation of the rule `(map/map)`.

3 GHC and Rewrite Rules

GHC. The compilation process of a Haskell program consists of three big steps: *front-end*, *optimizer*, and *back-end*. The front-end consists of parsing, type checking and transformation into the GHC's intermediate language called *Core* implementing System F_C [12,18]. The optimizer optimizes the Core program through various transformations. The optimization of a Core program is divided into a series of Core-to-Core translations. The *simplifier* is one of them, which also uses *rewrite rules* specified in the program.

GHC Rewrite Rules. The syntax of *rewrite rules* is:

```
{-# RULES
"name" [<phase>] forall <var>...<var>. f <expr> = <expr>
... #-}
```

All variables in the rule must be listed in the `forall`-quantification. The lhs of a rule must be a function application, where the function `f` should be in the scope. The lhs and rhs must be the same type. The GHC's option `-fenable-rewrite-rules` allows GHC to apply rewrite rules to the source program. The [⟨phase⟩] numbers are used for controlling the order of application of rules. We do not deal with phases in this paper. The rewrite rules are translated to Core at compile-time, and form rules on Core expressions.

Semantics of Rewrite Rules. Formal semantics of the rules have not yet been proposed. Informal semantics of rewrite rules is described in the GHC User's Guide[2] (see also [15] and HaskellWiki[3]).

[2] https://downloads.haskell.org/ghc/latest/docs/users_guide/exts/rewrite_rules.html #rewrite-rules

[3] https://wiki.haskell.org/GHC/Using_rules

There is no mention about how to choose a redex in an expression in the informal semantics. GHC's rewriting does not assume any particular strategy to choose a redex and a rewrite rule. This generality matches the general notion of term rewriting. This observation is the basis of rewriting semantics of Haskell in Sect. 4. The pattern matching mechanism for GHC rules is syntactic matching modulo α-conversion. The lhs of a rule can involve a λ-term.

4 System F_{RE}

In this section, we present System F_{RE}, which is a variant of System F_{ω} [7] extended with **R**ules and **E**quations. We intend to model rules on the GHC's intermediate language Core and to give a formal semantics of GHC's rewrite rules.

System F_{RE} consists of three parts: the higher-order polymorphic λ-calculus, Equational Logic, and rewrite system.

The need of features of System F_{ω} such as higher-kinds and type arguments is exemplified in Example 1.

Higher-Order Polymorphic λ-calculus. First we present the the polymorphic λ-calculus as the basis of System F_{RE}. We give syntax, types and related substitution.

The kinds and types, and the syntax of terms, equations, and rules of System F_{RE} are given in Fig. 7. Types are higher-order polymorphic types as in System F_{ω}, but there is no type level computation. The set $\mathcal{B}$ of *basic types* is given by the set of all well-formed types, which are neither not arrow types nor universally quantified types. We denote by $\mathcal{T}$ the set of all well-kinded types under a typing context Γ, $\mathcal{T}(\Xi)$ the set of all well-kinded types under a kind context Ξ. As usual, the arrow type constructor is right associative. A type $\sigma_1 \to \sigma_2 \to \ldots \to \sigma_n \to \tau$ with $\tau \in \mathcal{B}$ may be denoted by $\sigma_1, \sigma_2, \ldots, \sigma_n \to \tau$. We write $f(t_1, \ldots, t_1)$ for $f\, t_1 \cdots t_n$.

A *type signature* Σ^{ty} is a set of *type constructors* of the forms $T : \kappa_1, \ldots, \kappa_l \to *$, where κ_i's are kinds. When $l = 0$, it is a *base type*. A *(term) signature* Σ is a set of typed function symbols.

A judgment is of the form $\Theta \triangleright \Gamma \vdash t : \tau$ where $\Xi = \alpha_1\, \kappa_1, \ldots, \alpha_n : \kappa_n$ is a *type context*, i.e., a sequence of (type variable, kind)-pairs, $\Gamma = x_1 \sigma_1, \ldots, x_n : \sigma_n$ is a *variable context*, a sequence of (variable, type)-pairs. It is well-formed if $\Xi \vdash \tau_i : \kappa_i$ for each $x_i : \tau_i \in \Gamma$ is derived by the inference rules in Fig. 7 and $\Xi \vdash \tau : *$.

A term, equation, rewrite rule, or rewrite step is well-typed if the corresponding judgment is derived by the **well-typed** rules given in Fig. 7.

We define $\mathrm{T}_{\Sigma}\mathrm{V}$ by the set of all well-typed terms using a term signature Σ, and $\mathrm{T}_{\Sigma}\emptyset$ the set of all well-typed *ground terms*, which are term without free variables. For a set $\Xi = \{\alpha_1, \ldots, \alpha_n\}$ of type variables, a *type substitution* $\rho : \Xi \to \mathcal{T}(\Xi')$ denoted by $\{\alpha_1 \mapsto \sigma_1, \ldots, \alpha_n \mapsto \sigma_n\}$, is a mapping that assigns a type σ_i to each type variable α_i. The notation $\tau\,\rho$, denotes a type by replacing a type variable in $\tau \in S$ with a type using ρ. A *(term) substitution* $\theta = \{x_1 \mapsto s_1, \ldots, x_n \mapsto s_n\}$ is a type preserving mapping that assigns a term s_i to each variable x_i in S. A substitution is *ground* if all s_i are ground terms. The prefix

Kinds, types, and terms.

$\kappa ::= * \mid \kappa_1 \to \kappa_2$

$\tau ::= \alpha \mid T \mid \tau_1 \to \tau_2 \mid \forall\alpha:\kappa.\tau \mid \tau_1\,\tau_2 \qquad e, u, s, t, l, r ::= x \mid f \mid \lambda x:\tau.e \mid e u \mid \Lambda\alpha:\kappa.e \mid e\sigma$

$x, y, z, X, Y, Z, \ldots$ range over variables, α ranges over type variables.

Well-kinded types.

$$\frac{\alpha:\kappa \in \Xi}{\Xi \vdash \alpha:\kappa} \qquad \frac{\Xi \vdash \sigma:* \quad \Xi \vdash \tau:*}{\Xi \vdash \sigma \to \tau:*} \qquad \frac{\Xi, \alpha:\kappa \vdash \tau:*}{\Xi \vdash \forall\alpha:\kappa.\tau:*} \qquad \frac{\Xi \vdash \sigma:\kappa' \to \kappa \quad \Xi \vdash \tau:\kappa'}{\Xi \vdash \sigma\tau:\kappa}$$

$$\frac{T:\kappa_1,\ldots,\kappa_n \to * \in \Sigma^{\mathrm{ty}}}{\Xi \vdash T:\kappa_1,\ldots,\kappa_n \to *}$$

Well-typed terms.

$$\frac{x:\tau \in \Gamma}{\Xi \triangleright \Gamma \vdash x \;:\tau} \qquad \frac{\Xi \triangleright \Gamma, x:\tau \vdash e \;:\tau}{\Xi \triangleright \Gamma \vdash \lambda x:\tau.e \;:\sigma \to \tau} \qquad \frac{\Xi \triangleright \Gamma \vdash e \;:\sigma \to \tau \quad \Xi \triangleright \Gamma \vdash u \;:\sigma}{\Xi \triangleright \Gamma \vdash eu \;:\tau}$$

$$\frac{\Xi, \alpha:\kappa \triangleright \Gamma \vdash e \;:\tau}{\Xi \triangleright \Gamma \vdash \Lambda\alpha:\kappa.e \;:\forall\alpha:\kappa.\tau} \qquad \frac{\Xi \triangleright \Gamma \vdash e \;:\forall\alpha:\kappa.\tau \quad \Xi \vdash \sigma:\kappa}{\Xi \triangleright \Gamma \vdash e\sigma \;:\tau\{\alpha \mapsto \sigma\}} \qquad \frac{f:\tau \in \Sigma}{\Xi \triangleright \Gamma \vdash f \;:\tau}$$

Well-typed equations/rewriting

$$\frac{\Xi \triangleright \Gamma \vdash s \;:\tau \quad \Xi \triangleright \Gamma \vdash t \;:\tau}{\Xi \triangleright \Gamma \vdash s \star t \;:\tau} \quad \star \text{ is either } =, \Rightarrow_{\mathcal{R}}$$

Well-typed rules.

$$\frac{\Xi \triangleright \Gamma \vdash l \;:\tau \quad \Xi \triangleright \Gamma \vdash r \;:\tau}{\Xi \triangleright \Gamma \vdash l \Rightarrow r \;:\tau}$$

Notes.

- l is headed by a function symbol, and is a Miller's higher-order pattern, i.e., a term l in which every occurrence of application is restricted to be the form $M\ x_1\ \ldots\ x_n$, where M is a variable and $x_1, \ldots, x_n$ are distinct bound variables [13].
- Variable occurrence in l must be linear, l and r are long $\beta\eta$-normal forms, and all free variables in r also appear in l.

One-step rewriting.

$$\frac{\Xi \triangleright \Gamma, \overline{x:\sigma} \vdash t \Rightarrow_{\mathcal{R}} t' \;:\tau}{\Xi \triangleright \Gamma \vdash \lambda\overline{x:\sigma}.t \Rightarrow_{\mathcal{R}} \lambda\overline{x:\sigma}.t' \;:\overline{\sigma} \to \tau} \qquad \frac{\begin{array}{c}\Xi \triangleright \Gamma \vdash s_i \;:\sigma_i\xi \quad (1 \le i \le k) \quad \xi:\Xi' \to \mathcal{T}(\Xi) \\ (\Xi' \triangleright M_1:\sigma_1,\ldots,M_k:\sigma_k \vdash \ell \Rightarrow r \;:\tau) \in \mathcal{R}\end{array}}{\Xi \triangleright \Gamma \vdash \ell\xi\{\overline{M \mapsto s}\} \Rightarrow_{\mathcal{R}} r\xi\{\overline{M \mapsto s}\} \;:\tau\xi}$$

$$\frac{\begin{array}{l}f:\forall\overline{\alpha:\kappa}.\overline{\sigma} \to \tau \in \Sigma \quad \xi:\{\overline{\alpha}\} \to \mathcal{T}(\Xi) \quad m = |\overline{\sigma}| \\ \Xi \triangleright \Gamma \vdash t_i \Rightarrow_{\mathcal{R}} t_i' \;:\sigma_i\xi \quad (\text{some single } i) \quad \Xi \triangleright \Gamma \vdash t_j \;:\sigma_j\xi \quad (i \neq j \in \{1,\ldots,m\})\end{array}}{\Xi \triangleright \Gamma \vdash f(\overline{\alpha\xi}, t_1,\ldots,t_i\ldots,t_m) \Rightarrow_{\mathcal{R}} f(\overline{\alpha\xi}, t_1,\ldots,t_i',\ldots,t_m) \;:\tau\xi}$$

$$\frac{\begin{array}{l}(M:\tau_1,\ldots,\tau_m \to \tau) \in \Gamma \\ \Xi \triangleright \Gamma \vdash t_i \Rightarrow_{\mathcal{R}} t_i' \;:\sigma_i \quad (\text{some single } i) \quad \Xi \triangleright \Gamma \vdash t_j \;:\sigma_j \quad (i \neq j \in \{1,\ldots,m\})\end{array}}{\Xi \triangleright \Gamma \vdash M\,t_1 \cdots t_i \cdots t_m \Rightarrow_{\mathcal{R}} M\,t_1 \cdots t_i' \cdots t_m \;:\tau}$$

Fig. 7. System $\mathrm{F_{RE}}$: Syntax and typing rules

notation $\theta(t)$, where θ is a term substitution, denotes ordinary capture avoiding substitution that replaces each variables x_i with a term s_i.

We denote by $\beta\overline{\eta}$-nf(t) the long $\beta\eta$-normal form of a term t. We define the *normalised substitution* by $\$t\theta \triangleq \beta\overline{\eta}\text{-nf}(\theta(t))$ using postfix notation. Henceforth, we will assume that all terms are automatically normalised to long $\beta\eta$-normal forms unless otherwise stated.

Rewrite Systems. The inference rules of the polymorphic equational logic $\mathsf{EL}_\forall$ is a prenex polymorphic version of Polymorphic Equational Logic [5], An equation $s = t$ is an *(equational) theorem* of a set $\mathcal{E}$ of equational axioms, if it is derived from $\mathcal{E}$. A ***rewrite system*** $(\Sigma^{\text{ty}}, \Sigma, \Delta, \mathcal{R})$ consists of a type signature Σ^{ty}, a term signature Σ, a set Δ of constructors and a set $\mathcal{R}$ of well-typed rewrite rules. We often simply write a rewrite system as $(\Sigma, \Delta, \mathcal{R})$, $(\Sigma, \mathcal{R})$ or $\mathcal{R}$ if the signatures are clear from context. We often omit the context and type in a rule and simply write $\ell \Rightarrow r$. A function symbol $f \in \Sigma$ is called *defined* if it occurs at the root of the lhs of a rule in $\mathcal{R}$. We assume that every constructor $c \in \Delta$ must not be a defined function symbol. This matches an assumption of the syntax of GHC's rewrite rules (Sect. 3). Terms constructed from variables and constructors are called *constructor terms.* We design one-step rewriting by $\mathcal{R}$ as an oriented version of equational reasoning of $\mathsf{EL}_\forall$. The inference rules of one-step rewriting by $\mathcal{R}$ is given in Fig. 7, and denoted by $s \Rightarrow_\mathcal{R} t$ if $\Xi \triangleright \Gamma \vdash s \Rightarrow_\mathcal{R} t : \tau$ is derived from $\mathcal{R}$. This defines a binary relation $\Rightarrow_\mathcal{R}$ on the set $\mathrm{T}_\Sigma\mathrm{V}$ of all terms. The (RuleSub) instantiates a rewrite rule $\ell \Rightarrow r$ in $\mathcal{R}$ by using a term substitution $\{\overline{M \mapsto s}\} = \{M_1 \mapsto s_1, \ldots, M_k \mapsto s_k\}$ and a type substitution ξ. Since it uses normalised substitution, in one-step rewriting, the β-reduction may implicitly happen in the substitution process. The (Fun) and (Bind) express that the rewriting step is closed under function symbols and variable binding contexts. By definition, any rewrite step preserves types.

Example 1. The type arguments in rewrite rules are necessary ingredients. For example, the program `Biapplicative.hs` in the `bifunctors` package[4] contains a function `traverseBia` with a rewrite rule:

```
{-# RULES
"traverseBia/list"   forall f t. traverseBia f t = traverseBiaList f t
"traverseBia/Either" forall f t. traverseBia f t = traverseBiaEither f t
 #-}
```

The left-hand sides appear to be overlapped, but the actual intention of these rules is to specialise `traverseBia` with more efficient type specific functions. After parsing in GHC, the rules are elaborated as

```
(traverseBia/list)  traverseBia(%List,p,a,b,c,dT,dB,F,T)  ⇒ traverseBiaList(p,a,b,c,dB,F,T)
(traverseBia/Maybe) traverseBia(%Maybe,p,a,b,c,dT,dB,F,T) ⇒ traverseBiaMaybe(p,a,b,c,dB,F,T)
```

4 https://hackage.haskell.org/package/bifunctors.

```
f []     = 0
f (x:xs) = let z = 2
           in x + z
```

$f = \lambda y.\,\mathsf{case}\ y\ \mathsf{of}$
$\quad [] \to 0$
$\quad (x : xs) \to \mathsf{let}\ z = 2\ \mathsf{in}\ x + z$

$$f([]) \Rightarrow 0$$
$$f(x : xs) \Rightarrow x + z$$
$$z \Rightarrow 2$$

Fig. 8. (1) Haskell program (2) Core def. in System $\mathrm{F_C}$ (3) Rewrite rule specification

Rewrite System Specifications of Haskell Programs. Haskell report [10] does not specify the operational semantics of Haskell. But we need a formal rewriting modeling Haskell's evaluation to apply the Rule Meaning Preservation Theorem. We use an approximation of the operational semantics of GHC by using rewrite systems corresponding to programs, called rewrite system specifications in System $\mathrm{F_{RE}}$.

GHC translates Haskell programs to the language Core [18]. For example, the program (1) in Fig. 8 is translated to (2) the Core's definition (which is slightly simplified where type arguments and some internal symbols are omitted). Core expressions are formulated as λ-terms extended with case and let as formulated in System $\mathrm{F_C}$ [12,18]. A rewrite system specification for it is in (3), and is formally defined as follows.

Definition 2. A *rewrite rule specification* for a Haskell program $\mathcal{H}$ is a rewrite system $(\Sigma^{\mathrm{ty}}, \Sigma, \mathcal{P})$, where Σ^{ty} and Σ are signatures for functions used in $\mathcal{H}$, that satisfies the following conditions:

(i) If a closed term e without let and case is evaluated to a value v by using GHC with $\mathcal{H}$, then we have rewriting $e \Rightarrow^*_{\mathcal{P}} v$ in System $\mathrm{F_{RE}}$.
(ii) The patterns in the lhss of rules in $\mathcal{P}$ corresponding to function definitions and case-expressions are exhaustive.

The condition (i) means that the rewriting by $\mathcal{P}$ is sound w.r.t. the original evaluation. The condition (ii) means that $\mathcal{P}$ gives total functions.

Concretely, a rewrite rule specification is basically the same as the original Haskell program where each program clause is regarded as a rewrite rule. Differences are local let-bindings and case-expressions are lifted as in Fig. 8. These liftings add appropriate free variable arguments to the lifted function corresponding to let-binders and case-branching, in order to preserve the original meaning of Haskell programs. The same approach has also be taken in the preprocessor of the termination checker AProVE [6].

5 Meaning preservation of Rewrite Rules

Definition 3. An equation $s = t$ is an *inductive theorem* of a set $\mathcal{E}$ of equational axioms, if for every ground substitution $\theta : \Gamma \to \mathrm{T}_{\Delta}\emptyset$, $s\theta = t\theta$ is an equational theorem of $\mathcal{E}$.

Every equational theorem is an inductive theorem, but not vice versa. An important thing is that the inference system of $\mathsf{EL}_\forall$ does not suffice to prove all inductive theorems.

We formulate the meaning preservation of rewrite rules in the framework of System $\mathrm{F_{RE}}$ through the notion of inductive theorems. From now on, we suppose a rewrite system $\mathcal{P}$. It is mathematically just a rewrite system, but our intention is that it is a rule specification for a Haskell program.

Definition 4. Let $(\Sigma, \mathcal{P})$ be a rewrite system. A rewrite rule $\Xi \rhd \overline{X:\sigma} \vdash\ l \Rightarrow r\ : \tau$ is ***meaning-preserving*** w.r.t. $\mathcal{P}$ if $l = r$ is an inductive theorem of $\mathcal{P}$. A rewrite system $\mathcal{R}$ is *meaning-preserving* w.r.t. $\mathcal{P}$ if every rule in $\mathcal{R}$ is meaning-preserving w.r.t. $\mathcal{P}$.

Remark 5. If $l \Rightarrow r$ is meaning-preserving, for any type substitution ξ, $l\xi \Rightarrow r\xi$ is also meaning-preserving because inductive theorems are closed under type substitutions.

Lemma 6. *Let $(\Sigma, \Delta, \mathcal{P})$ be a rewrite system and $\Xi \rhd \overline{X:\sigma} \vdash\ l \Rightarrow r\ : b$ a rewrite rule on the signatures Σ and Δ. Define $\widehat{\mathcal{P}} \triangleq \mathcal{P} \cup \{\Xi \rhd \overline{X:\sigma} \vdash\ l \Rightarrow r\ : b\}$. If*

(i) $(\Sigma, \widehat{\mathcal{P}})$ is confluent, and
(ii) $(\Sigma, \mathcal{P})$ is strongly normalising and all the normal forms of ground terms by $\mathcal{P}$ are constructor terms using Δ,

then the rewrite rule $l \Rightarrow r$ is meaning-preserving w.r.t. $\mathcal{P}$.

Proof. Let θ be a ground substitution $\theta : \Gamma \to \mathrm{T}_\Delta\emptyset$. Since $\mathcal{P}$ is SN, we have $l\theta \Rightarrow^*_{\mathcal{P}} d$ and $r\theta \Rightarrow^*_{\mathcal{P}} d'$, where d, d' are normal forms and ground constructor terms. By (RuleSub), we have $l\theta \Rightarrow_{\widehat{\mathcal{P}}} r\theta$ is an equational theorem of $\mathcal{P}$. Since now $\widehat{\mathcal{P}}$ is confluent, we have the joinable diagram shown at the right panel. Note that since all the normal forms of $\mathcal{P}$ are constructor terms, they cannot be rewritten by the rule $l \Rightarrow r$, hence $d = d'$. The diagram shows that $l\theta$ and $r\theta$ are convertible by $\mathcal{P}$, i.e. $l\theta \Leftrightarrow^*_{\mathcal{P}} r\theta$, hence we have $l\theta =_{\mathcal{P}} r\theta$. Therefore, $l = r$ is an inductive theorem of $\mathcal{P}$.

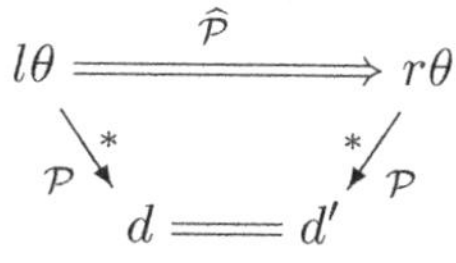

Using this lemma, we prove the main theorem. Before that we prepare the following. Let $(\Sigma, \Delta, \mathcal{R})$ be a rewrite system. To check whether an equation $t = t'$ is an inductive theorem of $\mathcal{P}$, we collect suitable sets of function symbols and rules needed to prove it because not all the function symbols and rules are necessary to check $t = t'$. Let $\mathsf{Fun}(t)$ denote the set of all functions symbols occurring in t. We define

$$\Omega_0^t = \mathsf{Fun}(t) \qquad \Omega_{n+1}^t = \bigcup_{f \in \Omega_n^t} \ \bigcup_{f(\bar{l}) \Rightarrow r \in \mathcal{P}} (\mathsf{Fun}(f(\bar{l})) \cup \mathsf{Fun}(r)) \qquad \Sigma_{\mathcal{R}}^t = \bigcup_{i \in \mathbb{N}} \Omega_i^t \cup \Delta$$

Then the signature $\Sigma_{\mathcal{R}}^t \subseteq \Sigma$ is the set of all function symbols which are reachable by $\mathcal{P}$ from the used function symbols in t.

Theorem 7 (The Rule Meaning Preservation Theorem). *Let* $(\Sigma, \Delta, \mathcal{P})$ *be a rewrite system specification of a Haskell program and* $(\Sigma, \Delta, \mathcal{R})$ *a rewrite system. Define*

$$\Sigma_{\restriction\mathcal{R}} = \bigcup_{l \Rightarrow r \in \mathcal{R}} \Sigma^l_{\mathcal{R}} \cup \Sigma^r_{\mathcal{R}} \qquad \mathcal{P}_{\restriction\mathcal{R}} = \{f(\bar{l}) \Rightarrow r \in \mathcal{P} \mid f \in \Sigma_{\restriction\mathcal{R}}\}$$

Suppose that

(i) $(\Sigma_{\restriction\mathcal{R}}, \mathcal{P}_{\restriction\mathcal{R}} \cup \mathcal{R})$ *is locally confluent, and*
(ii) $(\Sigma_{\restriction\mathcal{R}}, \mathcal{P}_{\restriction\mathcal{R}} \cup \mathcal{R})$ *is strongly normalising.*

Then the rewrite system $\mathcal{R}$ *is meaning-preserving.*

Proof. Suppose the assumptions of the theorem. By Newman's lemma, $(\Sigma_{\restriction\mathcal{R}}, \mathcal{P}_{\restriction\mathcal{R}} \cup \mathcal{R})$ is confluent. Moreover, $(\Sigma_{\restriction\mathcal{R}}, \mathcal{P}_{\restriction\mathcal{R}})$ is strongly normalising. By Definition 2 ii, all the normal forms of ground terms by $\mathcal{P}_{\restriction\mathcal{R}}$ are constructor terms. Hence by Lemma 6, every rule in $\mathcal{R}$ is meaning-preserving w.r.t. $\mathcal{P}_{\restriction\mathcal{R}}$.

Remark 8. Here, $\Sigma_{\restriction\mathcal{R}}$ and $\mathcal{P}_{\restriction\mathcal{R}}$ are restrictions of Σ and $\mathcal{P}$ with respect to the used symbols $\Sigma_{\restriction\mathcal{R}}$ in $\mathcal{R}$. This theorem holds even if we drop the restrictions, i.e., if we replace $\Sigma_{\restriction\mathcal{R}}$ with Σ, and $\mathcal{P}_{\restriction\mathcal{R}}$ with $\mathcal{P}$ as stated in Introduction (Sect. 1), which is simpler in form. Why we add the restrictions is that they increase the applicability of the theorem because SN of $\mathcal{P}_{\restriction\mathcal{R}}$ hold more likely than that of the original $\mathcal{P}$. Moreover, reducing the number of rules $\mathcal{P}_{\restriction\mathcal{R}}$ to be checked than the original $\mathcal{P}$ reduces the computational cost of the check.

Example 9. Consider the map/map example. Suppose that `Map.hs` extended with the definitions `ones = 1:ones` of an infinite list of `1`. In this case, $\mathcal{P}$ (= `Map.hs + ones`) is not SN because `ones` is not strongly normalising. So we cannot conclude the correctness of `map/map` by the unrestricted version of the theorem.

But actually to prove the finite meaning preservation of `map/map`, `ones` is irrelevant. Defining the restrictions w.r.t. $\mathcal{R} = \{$`(map/map)`$\}$, we have $\Sigma_{\restriction\mathcal{R}} = \{$`[], (:), map, (.)`$\}, \Delta = \{$`[], (:)`$\}$ and $\mathcal{P}_{\restriction\mathcal{R}} =$ `Map.hs`, therefore we can apply Theorem 7 as Sect. 2 and conclude that $\mathcal{R}$ is finite meaning-preserving.

Remark 10. The diagram in the proof of Lemma 6 shows why the conditions of this theorem are sufficient to ensure the finite meaning preservation of the rule. Because of strong normalisation, we can ensure the existence of finite values (i.e. normal forms) of the instances of the left and right hand sides $(l\theta, r\theta)$. Because of the confluence of $\mathcal{P}_{\restriction\mathcal{R}} \cup \mathcal{R}$, these values d, d' must be equal. This means that the rewrite rule preserves the meaning $d = d'$.

Note that the meaning preservation of $\mathcal{R}$ is not just a consequence of confluence of $\mathcal{P}_{\restriction\mathcal{R}} \cup \mathcal{R}$. For every rule $l \Rightarrow r$ in $\mathcal{R}$, it is obvious that $\mathcal{P}_{\restriction\mathcal{R}} \cup \mathcal{R} \vdash_{\mathsf{EL}_\forall} l = r$. The theorem ensures more than that, i.e., it ensures the finite meaning preservation of the rule by evaluating both sides of the rule only using $\mathcal{P}_{\restriction\mathcal{R}}$.

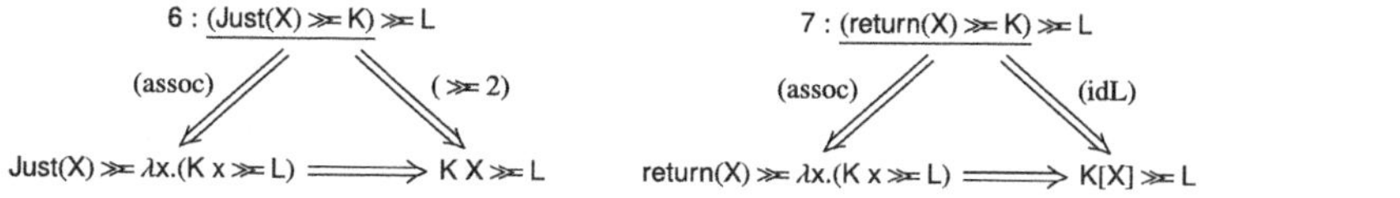

Fig. 9. Critical pairs of the Maybe monad (excerpt)

```
module Maybe where
return :: a -> Maybe a
return x = Just x

(>>=) :: Maybe a
         -> (a -> Maybe b)
         -> Maybe b
Nothing  >>= f = Nothing
(Just x) >>= f = f x
```

```
{-# RULES
"idL" forall x k. return x >>= \y -> k y  = k x
"idR" forall e.    e >>= \y -> return y   = e
"assoc" forall e k l.
  ( e >>=  \x -> k x ) >>= \y -> l y
  = e >>= (\x -> k x   >>= \y -> l y)
 #-}
```

Fig. 10. Example: Maybe monad with monad laws

6 Example

We implemented a prototype analyzer ReCheck to assist the effort of human verification of rewrite rules based on Theorem 7. It consists of about 10000 line Haskell code, implemented as a GHC Core plugin. ReCheck uses GHC's parser and de-sugar preprocessor to parse a Haskell program and obtain the Core program with Core rewrite rules. The analyzer ReCheck assists the following tasks of verifying rewrite rules:

- Generating a candidate rewrite rule specification from a Core program.
- Enumerating critical pairs and trying to check their joinablity for local confluence.
- Applying the Polymorphic General Schema to rules for strong normalisation.

We consider the Maybe monad [16] with the monad laws as the rewrite rules in Fig. 10. We verify that the meaning preservation of the monad laws w.r.t. the Maybe monad defined in Fig. 10. A rewrite rule specification $(\Sigma, \Theta, \mathcal{P})$ consists of a signature Σ

$$\begin{aligned}
&\texttt{return} : \forall a : *.\ a \to \texttt{Maybe}(a),\\
&\texttt{>>=} : \forall a : *, b : *.\ \texttt{Maybe}(a), (a \to \texttt{Maybe}(b))) \to \texttt{Maybe}(b)
\end{aligned}$$

a signature of constructors Θ

$$\texttt{Nothing} : \forall a : *.\ \texttt{Maybe}(a),\ \ \texttt{Just} : \forall a : *.\ a \to \texttt{Maybe}(a)$$

the set of rules translated from the program $\mathcal{P}$

$$\begin{array}{lll}
(\texttt{return}) & \texttt{return}(a, X) & \Rightarrow \texttt{Just}(a, X),\\
(\texttt{>>=1}) & \texttt{>>=}(a, b, \texttt{Nothing}(a), \lambda x.Fx) & \Rightarrow \texttt{Nothing}(b),\\
(\texttt{>>=2}) & \texttt{>>=}(a, b, \texttt{Just}(a, X), \lambda x.Fx) & \Rightarrow FX
\end{array}$$

and the set of rewrite rules $\mathcal{R} = \{(\texttt{idL}), (\texttt{idR}), (\texttt{assoc})\}$. As these show, the type arguments (that are implicit in the source program) are explicit in System $\mathrm{F_{RE}}$. We apply Theorem 7. In this case, the restrictions does not change the rules, i.e. $\Sigma^l_{\mathcal{R}} = \Sigma, \mathcal{P}_{\upharpoonright\mathcal{R}} = \mathcal{P}$.

In this case there are 9 critical pairs shown as excerpt in Fig. 9, and all are joinable, which can be checked by using ReCheck. For brevity, the type arguments are omitted in the figure, but actually considered in unification. We explain two cases. The critical pair (1) in Fig. 9 shows an overlap between the first definition of `>>=` denoted by `(>>=1)` and `"idR"`. Both lhss become the same term `Nothing >>= \x.return x`, which is obtained by applying the unifier $e \mapsto$ `Nothing`, $f \mapsto$ `\x.return x` to lhs. This term is rewritten to `Nothing` by both rules, hence joinable. The critical pair (6) shows an overlap between the second definition of `>>=` denoted by `(>>=2)` and `"assoc"`, and they are joinable. Therefore, $\mathcal{P} \cup \mathcal{R}$ is locally confluent.

We can also show strong normalisation of $\mathcal{P} \cup \mathcal{R}$ by applying the Polymorphic General Schema using ReCheck. By Theorem 7, we conclude that $\mathcal{R}$ is meaning-preserving. As this example shows, it is difficult for humans to enumerate all critical pairs without oversight. ReCheck's assistance reduces this effort. Other monads can be checked to be meaning-preserving in a similar way.

7 Conclusion

We have presented System $\mathrm{F_{RE}}$, a formal system that extends System F_ω with rewriting and equational reasoning, providing a unified framework for modeling and verifying GHC's rewrite rules. We have established the Rule Meaning Preservation Theorem, which gives a simple criterion for ensuring the correctness of rewrite rules, and developed a method for checking local confluence using an extension of Knuth and Bendix's critical pair analysis. We have demonstrated the applicability of our approach on several examples, showing that it enables mechanical rule checking without explicit induction. Our work establishes theoretical foundations and practical methods for verifying optimizing transformations in Haskell and provides a basis for further research on reliable compiler optimizations.

References

1. Baader, F., Nipkow, T.: Term Rewriting and All That. Cambridge University Press, Cambridge (1998)
2. Bird, R., Wadler, P.: An Introduction to Functional Programming. Prentice Hall, New York (1988)
3. Bird, R., Moor, O.D.: Algebra of Programming. Prentice-Hall, New York (1996)
4. Davis, M., Matijasevic, Y., Robinson, J.: Hilbert's tenth problem. diophantine equations: positive aspects of a negative solution. In: Proceedings of Symposia in Pure Math, vol. AMS 28, pp. 323–378 (1978)

5. Fiore, M., Hamana, M.: Multiversal polymorphic algebraic theories: syntax, semantics, translations, and equational logic. In: 28th Annual ACM/IEEE Symposium on Logic in Computer Science, LICS 2013, pp. 520–529 (2013)
6. Giesl, J., Raffelsieper, M., Schneider-Kamp, P., Swiderski, S., Thiemann, R.: Automated termination proofs for Haskell by term rewriting. ACM Trans. Program. Lang. Syst. **33**(2), 1–39 (2011)
7. Girard, J.Y.: Proofs and types. Cambridge University Press (1989), translated and with appendices by Paul Taylor, Yves Lafont
8. Goguen, J., Meseguer, J.: Completeness of many-sorted equational logic. Houst. J. Math. **11**(3), 307–334 (1985)
9. Hutton, G.: Programming in Haskell. Cambridge University Press, Cambridge (2016)
10. Jones, S.P. (ed.): Haskell 98 Language and Libraries: The Revised Report. Cambridge University Press, Cambridge (2003)
11. Knuth, D., Bendix, P.: Simple Word Problems in Universal Algebras. In: Computational Problem in abstract algebra, pp. 263–297. Pergamon Press, Oxford (1970)
12. Martin, S., Manuel, C., Jones, S.P., Kevin, D.: System F with type equality coercions. In: Proceedings of TLDI '07, pp. 53–66 (2007)
13. Miller, D.: A logic programming language with lambda-abstraction, function variables, and simple unification. J. Log. Comput. **1**(4), 497–536 (1991)
14. Nourani, F.: On induction for programming logic: syntax, semantics and inductive closure. Bull. EATCS **13**, 51–64 (1981)
15. Peyton Jone, S., Tolmach, A., Hoare, T.: Playing by the rules: rewriting as a practical optimisation technique in GHC. In: Haskell Workshop 2001 (2001)
16. Wadler, P.: Comprehending monads. In: ACM Conference on Lisp and Functional Programming, pp. 61–78. Nice, France (1990)
17. Wechler, W.: Universal Algebra for Computer Scientists. Springer-Verlag (1992). https://doi.org/10.1007/978-3-642-76771-5
18. Weirich, S., Hsu, J., Eisenberg, R.A.: System FC with explicit kind equality. In: Morrisett, G., Uustalu, T. (eds.) Proceedings of ICFP'13, pp. 275–286. ACM (2013)

Symbolic Graph Query Solving

Dominique Duval and Rachid Echahed(✉)

CNRS and University Grenoble Alpes, Grenoble, France
{dominique.duval,rachid.echahed}@imag.fr

Abstract. Property graphs play an important role in representing data bases in modern graph query languages. In this paper we focus on a particular class of graph queries known as Graph-to-Graph or CONSTRUCT queries. Such queries return graphs instead of tables when applied to actual Property Graphs. We propose a symbolic graph query solving procedure which combines rewriting techniques for goal solving as well as graph transformation techniques. The proposed procedure is proven sound and complete.

Keywords: Operational semantics · Rewrite systems · Graph query languages

1 Introduction

Graph database systems are becoming more and more in demand thanks to their legibility and high flexibility. Several graph query languages have been proposed recently or being developed such as Cypher [8], PGQL[1], GSQL[2] and G-CORE [1], inducing an ISO project to standardize a graph query language. Two separate standards are being issued[3] : GQL and SQL/PGQ.

The aforementioned languages are based on a particular definition of graphs called *property graphs*. These graphs feature nodes and edges that can be typed by means of labels and can also be endowed with finite records. Such graphs provide great flexibility in data representation.

Property graphs are also used to formulate queries. We focus in this paper on a special kind of graph queries, known as graph-to-graph queries or CONSTRUCT queries [1,11], which yield a graph as a result, when applied to a graph data, instead of classical tables. This is by no means a limitation since it is well know that tables can easily be encoded as graphs (see, e.g. [5]).

The semantics of graph queries are based on variables bindings in general [2,8]. Such semantics are not appropriate to handle easily query nesting. Recently, we proposed in [7], in the context of RDF-graphs [12], a kernel query language whose semantics is based on graph homomorphisms. Composition of

Partly supported by the French ANR project VERIGRAPH # ANR-21-CE48-0015.

1 https://pgql-lang.org/.

2 https://www.tigergraph.com/gsql/.

3 https://www.gqlstandards.org/.

S. M. Watt and T. Ida (Eds.): SCSS 2024, LNAI 14991, pp. 96–113, 2024.
https://doi.org/10.1007/978-3-031-69042-6_6

homomorphisms ensures in an obvious way query nesting or more precisely *pattern* nesting. In the present paper we follow such semantics and consider a core query language which allows nesting of patterns in the context of the rich structures of property graphs. We also propose a new symbolic procedure based on a rewriting system which incorporates operators that have been tailored expressly for property graph structures. The proposed procedure, which is proven to be deterministic, terminating, sound and complete, solves queries in a way close to narrowing-based procedures [3], but limited to specific operators over data graphs represented as property graphs.

The paper first defines, in the next section, the data graphs considered in the paper together with some additional definitions. In Sect. 3, the notions of patterns and CONSTRUCT queries are introduced by their syntax and semantics. Then, in Sect. 4, a rewriting system defining a procedure to solve patterns and queries is introduced and the main properties of the procedure are stated. Concluding remarks are provided in Sect. 5.

2 Data Graphs

In this section, we start by fixing some definitions of the data structures used in this paper. We assume given a finite set Lab of labels, a finite set $Prop$ of properties and a possibly infinite set Val of values (integers, booleans, strings, etc.). In the rest of the paper we assume that all expressions are well typed. Let A be a possibly infinite set, we denote by $\widehat{\mathcal{P}}(A)$ the set of finite subsets of A.

Below, we provide the definition of property graphs we consider in this paper.

Definition 1 (Property Graph).
A property graph G is a tuple $G = (N, E, src, tgt, \lambda, \pi)$ where N is a finite set of nodes, E is a finite set of edges such that $N \cap E = \emptyset$. src (resp. tgt) is a function $src : E \rightarrow N$ (resp. $tgt : E \rightarrow N$) defining the source (resp. target) of edges. The function $\lambda : N \cup E \rightarrow \mathcal{P}(Lab)$ specifies, for every node or edge, possible labels in Lab. The function $\pi : N \cup E \rightarrow \widehat{\mathcal{P}}(Prop \times Val)$ specifies, for each node or edge, the possible finite property-value associations.

Example 1. We introduce here a running example of a property graph representing the authorship relation between *persons* and *papers*. The proposed sample graph $G1 = (N_1, E_1, src_1, tgt_1, \lambda_1, \pi_1)$, depicted in Fig. 1, is such that: $N = \{ni \mid 1 \leq i \leq 6\}$, $E_1 = \{ei \mid 1 \leq i \leq 5\}$, $\lambda_1(n1) = \lambda_1(n2) = \lambda_1(n3) = \{\text{person}\}$ and $\lambda_1(n4) = \lambda_1(n5) = \lambda_1(n6) = \{\text{paper}\}$. $\lambda_1(ei) = \{\text{author}\}$ for $1 \leq i \leq 5$. The function π_1 does not assign any data to edges, i.e., $\pi_1(ei) = \emptyset$ for $1 \leq i \leq 5$. However, the definition of π_1 is a bit long to write. It can be deduced easily from Fig. 1. For instance $\pi_1(n1) = \{(name, Paul\ Erdős), (Inst, Univ.Manchester), (Inst, IAS(Princeton))\}$.

The notion of paths plays a significant role in graph queries.

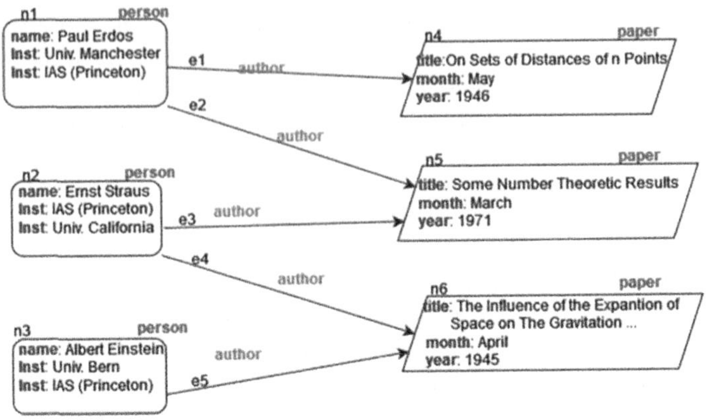

Fig. 1. Sample Property Graph, $G1$, of authors and papers

Definition 2 (Paths).
Let $G = (N, E, src, tgt, \lambda, \pi)$ be a property graph. A path p in G is a string over $N \cup E$ of the form $n_1e_1n_2 \dots n_ke_kn_{k+1}$ for some $k \geq 0$ such that for all j, $1 \leq j \leq k$, $src(e_j) = n_j$ and $tgt(e_j) = n_{j+1}$. We denote by $\mathcal{P}th(G)$ the set of paths of graph G. The source (resp. target) of a path of the form $n_1e_1n_2 \dots n_ke_kn_{k+1}$ is n_1 which is equal to $src(e_1)$ (resp. n_{k+1}, which is equal to $tgt(e_k)$). The concatenation of two paths p_1 and p_2 is written p_1+p_2 and assumes that $src(p_2) = tgt(p_1)$. That is, $(n_1e_1n_2 \dots n_ke_kn_{k+1}) + (n'_1e'_1n'_2 \dots n'_qe'_qn'_{q+1}) = n_1e_1n_2 \dots n_ke_kn'_1e'_1n'_2 \dots n'_qe'_qn'_{q+1}$ if $n_{k+1} = n'_1$.

Definition 3 (Property Graphs with Paths(PGP)).
A property graph with paths (PGP) G is a tuple $G = (N, E, P, src, tgt, \lambda, \pi)$ where $(N, E, src, tgt, \lambda, \pi)$ is a property graph and P is a finite subset of $\mathcal{P}th(G)$.

Notice that we assume the set of paths P to be finite in the definition above only for decidabilty reasons of the operational semantics presented later.

Let $f_i : A_i \to B_i$ for $i \in \{1, 2\}$ be two functions. We say that f_1 and f_2 are joinable if $f_1(x) = f_2(x)$ for all x in $A_1 \cap A_2$. The two following definitions, which are used later, define the union of graphs and graph quotients.

Definition 4 (Graph Union). *Let $G_i = (N_i, E_i, P_i, src_i, tgt_i, \lambda_i, \pi_i)$ for $i \in \{1, 2\}$ be two PGPs such that the functions src_1 and src_2 (resp. tgt_1 and tgt_2) are joinable and $N_i \cap E_j = \emptyset$ for i, j in $\{1, 2\}$. We denote by $G_1 \cup G_2$ the graph $G_1 \cup G_2 = (N_1 \cup N_2, E_1 \cup E_2, P_1 \cup P_2, src_\cup, tgt_\cup, \lambda_\cup, \pi_\cup)$ such that : (i) for all x in $N_1 \cup N_2 \cup E_1 \cup E_2$, $\lambda_\cup(x) = \lambda_1(x) \cup \lambda_2(x)$ and $\pi_\cup(x) = \pi_1(x) \cup \pi_2(x)$, and (ii) for all x in $E_1 \cup E_2$, $src_\cup(x) = src_1(x)$ (resp. $tgt_\cup(x) = tgt_1(x)$) if x in E_1, otherwise $src_\cup(x) = src_2(x)$ (resp. $tgt_\cup(x) = tgt_2(x)$).*

Definition 5 (Graph Equivalence, Quotient Graph).
Let $G = (N, E, P, src, tgt, \lambda, \pi)$. A graph equivalence $\cong$ is a pair $(\cong_n, \cong_e)$ of equivalences on nodes $\cong_n$ and on edges $\cong_e$ such that, for all e_1, e_2 in E, $e_1 \cong_e e_2$

implies that $src(e_1) \cong_n src(e_2)$ *and* $tgt(e_1) \cong_n tgt(e_2)$. *The quotient graph* $G_{\cong} = (N_{\cong_n}, E_{\cong_e}, P_{\cong}, \overline{src}, \overline{tgt}, \bar{\lambda}, \bar{\pi})$ *is such that* $N_{\cong_n}, E_{\cong_e}, P_{\cong}$ *are the intended quotient sets and for all* $\bar{e}$ *in* $E_{\cong_e}$, $\overline{src}(\bar{e}) = \overline{(src(e))}$ *and* $\overline{tgt}(\bar{e}) = \overline{(tgt(e))}$ *where* $\bar{x}$ *denotes the equivalence class of element* x. *For all* $\bar{y} \in (N_{\cong_n} \cup E_{\cong_e})$, $\bar{\lambda}(\bar{y}) = \cup_{i \in \bar{y}} \lambda(i)$ *and* $\bar{\pi}(\bar{y}) = \cup_{i \in \bar{y}} \pi(i)$.

The notion of homomorphism below is quite direct. One just has to deal carefully with all different notions involved in a property graph.

Definition 6 (PGP Graph Homomorphism).
Let $G_i = (N_i, E_i, P_i, src_i, tgt_i, \lambda_i, \pi_i)$ *for* $i \in \{1, 2\}$ *be two PGPs. A graph homomorphism from graph* G_1 *to graph* G_2, *denoted* $m : G_1 \to G_2$, *is defined by two functions* $m_n : N_1 \to N_2$ *and* $m_e : E_1 \to E_2$ *such that:*

1. *For all* a *in* E_1, $src_2(m_e(a)) = m_n(src_1(a))$ *and* $tgt_2(m_e(a)) = m_n(tgt_1(a))$.
2. *For all* b *in* N_1, $\lambda_1(b) \subseteq \lambda_2(m_n(b))$ *and For all* a *in* E_1, $\lambda_1(a) \subseteq \lambda_2(m_e(a))$
3. *For all* b *in* N_1, $\pi_1(b) \subseteq \pi_2(m_n(b))$ *and For all* a *in* E_1, $\pi_1(a) \subseteq \pi_2(m_e(a))$
4. *For all* p *in* P_1, $m_p(p)$ *is in* P_2 *where* m_p *is defined as follows :*
   $m_p(n_1 e_1 n_2 \dots n_k e_k n_{k+1}) = m_n(n_1) m_e(e_1) m_n(n_2) \dots m_n(n_k) m_e(e_k) m_n(n_{k+1})$

Basic graph queries could be expressed by means of PGPs. For that, PGP graphs have to be endowed with variables which can be instantiated while solving graph queries. In the definition of homomorphisms above, elements in N_1 (resp. E_1) may be matched by any element in N_2 (resp. E_2). However, elements in *Lab*, *Prop* and *Val* behave as constants. Therefore, we assume in the sequel given four sets of variables, elements of which can be used in PGPs. These sets of variables are V_v (resp. V_p, V_l and V_{pth}) which represent sets of variables ranging over the set of values *Val* (resp. of properties *Prop*, of labels *Lab* and of paths $\mathcal{P}th(G)$).

We call *path expression* a path which may include variables in V_{pth} and call *open PGP* a PGP including variables.

Definition 7 (Path Expression).
Let G *be a property graph. A* path expression *over* G *and* V_{pth} *is an expression generated by the following grammar where* p *is a path in* $\mathcal{P}th(G)$, x *is a path variable in* V_{pth} *and* $+$ *stands for the concatenation of paths :* $S \to p \mid x \mid S + S$. *A path expression, of the form* $p_1 + p_2$, *resulting of the concatenation of the paths* p_1 *and* p_2 *is such that the target of* p_1 *equals the source of* p_2. *We write* $\mathcal{P}th(G, V_{pth})$ *the set of path expressions over graph* G.

Definition 8 (Open PGP).
A PGP graph $G = (N, E, P, src, tgt, \lambda, \pi)$ *is said to be an* open PGP *if the set* P *can include path expressions (i.e.* $P \subseteq \mathcal{P}th(G, V_{pth})$*) and the target sets of functions* λ *and* π *can include variables. That is* $\lambda : N \cup E \to \mathcal{P}(Lab \cup V_l)$ *and* $\pi : N \cup E \to \widehat{\mathcal{P}}((Prop \cup V_p) \times (Val \cup V_v))$.

Now we are ready to define the notion of match *between open PGPs. A match is a homomorphism based on instantiations of variables. We denote by*

$\mathcal{V}(G)$ the set of all variables appearing in graph G, $\mathcal{V}_{pth}(G) = \mathcal{V}(G) \cap V_{pth}$ the set of path variables occurring in G, $\mathcal{V}_{lab}(G) = \mathcal{V}(G) \cap V_l$, the set of label variables appearing in G, $\mathcal{V}_{prp}(G) = \mathcal{V}(G) \cap V_p$, the set of property variables appearing in G and $\mathcal{V}_{val}(G) = \mathcal{V}(G) \cap V_v$ the set of value variables appearing in G.

Definition 9 (Match).
Let L and G be two open PGP, $L = (N_L, E_L, P_L, src_L, tgt_L, \lambda_L, \pi_L)$ and $G = (N_G, E_G, P_G, src_G, tgt_G, \lambda_G, \pi_G)$. A match $m : L \to G$ is defined by six functions $m_n : N_L \to N_G$, $m_e : E_L \to E_G$, $m_{lab} : \mathcal{V}_{lab}(L) \to Lab \cup \mathcal{V}_{lab}(G)$, $m_{val} : \mathcal{V}_{val}(L) \to Val \cup \mathcal{V}_{val}(G)$, $m_{prp} : \mathcal{V}_{prp}(L) \to Prop \cup \mathcal{V}_{val}(G)$ and $m_{pth} : \mathcal{V}_{pth}(L) \to \mathcal{P}th(G, \mathcal{V}_{pth}(G))$ such that:

1. *For all a in E_L, $src_G(m_e(a)) = m_n(src_L(a))$ and $tgt_G(m_e(a)) = m_n(tgt_L(a))$.*
2. *For all b in N_L, $m(\lambda_L(b)) \subseteq \lambda_G(m_n(b))$ and $m(\pi_L(b)) \subseteq \pi_G(m_n(b))$.*
3. *For all a in E_L, $m(\lambda_L(a)) \subseteq \lambda_G(m_e(a))$ and $m(\pi_L(a)) \subseteq \pi_G(m_e(a))$.*
4. *For all p in P_L, $m(p)$ is in P_G.*

Where

- *$m(F)$, with $F \subseteq (Lab \cup \mathcal{V}_{lab}(L))$, is defined as $m(F) = \{m(f) \mid f \in F\}$ such that $m(f) = f$ if f is a label in Lab and $m(f) = m_{lab}(f)$ if f is a label variable in $\mathcal{V}_{lab}(L)$.*
- *$m(U)$, with $U \subseteq \widehat{\mathcal{P}}((Prop \cup \mathcal{V}_{prp}(L)) \times (Val \cup \mathcal{V}_{val}(L)))$, is defined as $m(U) = \{(m(u_p), m(u_v)) \mid (u_p, u_v) \in U\}$ with $m(u_p) = u_p$ if u_p is a property in $Prop$ and $m(u_p) = m_{prp}(u_p)$ if u_p is a property variable in $\mathcal{V}_{prp}(L)$ and $m(u_v) = u_v$ if u_v is a value in Val and $m(u_v) = m_{val}(u_v)$ if u_v is a value variable in $\mathcal{V}_{val}(L)$.*
- *$m(p)$, with p being a path expression, is defined as follows: $m(p) = m(u) + m(w)$ if p is the concatenation of two paths $p = u+w$; $m(p) = m_{pth}(p)$ if p is a path variable and $m(p) = m_n(n_1)m_e(e_1)m_n(n_2)\ldots m_n(n_k)m_e(e_k)m_n(n_{k+1})$ if p is of the form $n_1e_1n_2\ldots n_ke_kn_{k+1}$.*

In the sequel, we will drop subscripts and simply write $m(t)$ for the application of a match or a homomorphism m on item t when it is clear from the context.

Definition 10 (Compatible Matches). *Two matches $m_1 : L_1 \to G_1$ and $m_2 : L_2 \to G_2$ are* compatible*, written as $m_1 \sim m_2$, if $m_1(x) = m_2(x)$ for each $x \in \mathcal{V}(L_1) \cap \mathcal{V}(L_2)$. Given two compatible matches $m_1 : L_1 \to G_1$ and $m_2 : L_2 \to G_2$, let $m_1 \bowtie m_2 : L_1 \cup L_2 \to G_1 \cup G_2$ denote the unique match such that $m_1 \bowtie m_2 \sim m_1$ and $m_1 \bowtie m_2 \sim m_2$ (which means that $m_1 \bowtie m_2$ coincides with m_1 on L_1 and with m_2 on L_2).*

Definition 11 (Set of Matches). *Let L be an open PGP and G a PGP. A set $\underline{m}$ of matches, all of them from L to G, is denoted $\underline{m} : L \Rightarrow G$.* The image *of L by $\underline{m}$ is the subgraph $\underline{m}(L) = \cup_{m \in \underline{m}}(m(L))$ of G. We denote $Match(L, G) : L \Rightarrow G$ the set of all matches from L to G. When L is the empty graph $\emptyset$, the set*

$Match(\emptyset, G) : \emptyset \Rightarrow G$ has one unique element which is the inclusion of $\emptyset$ into G, then we denote $\underline{i}_G = Match(\emptyset, G) : \emptyset \Rightarrow G$ this one-element set and $\varnothing_G : \emptyset \Rightarrow G$ its empty subset.

Example 2. Let $L1$ be the following open PGP consisting of two nodes x and y of label *person* and one node z of label *paper*, in addition to two edges $x1$ and $y1$ of label *author*.

```
L1 = (x:person)-[x1:author]->(z:paper)
     (y:person)-[y1:author]->(z:paper)
```

The set of matches $\underline{m} = Match(L1, G1)$ from $L1$ to graph $G1$ of Example 1 consists of 9 matches $\underline{m} = \{m_i \mid 1 \leq i \leq 9\}$ whose variable assignments are depicted in the following table.

Table 1. Variable assignements induced by the set $Match(L1, G1)$

	x	y	z	$x1$	$y1$
m_1	n1	n2	n5	e2	e3
m_2	n2	n1	n5	e3	e2
m_3	n2	n3	n6	e4	e5
m_4	n3	n2	n6	e5	e4
m_5	n1	n1	n4	e1	e1
m_6	n1	n1	n5	e2	e2
m_7	n2	n2	n5	e3	e3
m_8	n2	n2	n6	e4	e4
m_9	n3	n3	n6	e5	e5

Definition 12 (Canonical Match and Graph Equivalence).
If $h : L \to G$ is a match and $\cong$ a graph equivalence on G, we write $h_{\cong} : L \to G_{\cong}$ the canonical match obtained from h and $\cong$. If $\underline{h} : L \to G$ is a set of matches. We write $\underline{h}_{\cong} : L \to G_{\cong}$ the set of matches $h_{\cong} : L \to G_{\cong}$ for every match h in $\underline{h}$.

3 Patterns and Queries

In this section we introduce the class of queries we tackle in this paper, namely the CONSTRUCT queries. As said earlier, such queries easily encode SELECT or MATCH queries since tables can be translated into graphs. We start by introducing some basic notions such as *expressions* and some basic operators on graphs that contribute to define the syntax and the semantics of patterns and queries.

3.1 Expressions

Queries can be endowed with classical expressions on integers, strings, booleans etc. which contribute to filtering solutions or computing parts of them such as aggregation operations.

Let $Op_1 = \{-, \text{NOT}, \ldots\}$, $Op_2 = \{+, -, \times, /, =, >, <, \text{AND}, \text{OR}, \ldots\}$ and $Agg = \{\text{MAX}, \text{MIN}, \text{SUM}, \text{AVG}, \text{COUNT}, \text{SHORTEST}, \text{SIMPLE}, \text{TRAIL}, \ldots\}$. be sets of unary operations (resp. binary operations and aggregation operations).

An *Expression* e and its set of variables $\mathcal{V}(e)$ are defined recursively as follows, where $c \in Val$, $x \in \mathcal{V}_{val}$, y is a node, $p \in (Prop \cup \mathcal{V}_{prp})$, $op_1 \in Op_1$, $op_2 \in Op_2$, $agg \in Agg$:

$e ::= c \mid x \mid y.p \mid op_1\ e \mid e\ op_2\ e \mid agg(e_1)$.

$\mathcal{V}(c) = \varnothing$, $\mathcal{V}(x) = \{x\}$, $\mathcal{V}(op_1\ e) = \mathcal{V}(e)$, $\mathcal{V}(e_1\ op_2\ e_2) = \mathcal{V}(e_1) \cup \mathcal{V}(e_2)$, $\mathcal{V}(agg(e)) = \mathcal{V}(e)$, $\mathcal{V}(y.p) = \{y\} \cup (\{p\} \cap \mathcal{V}_{prp})$.

The *value* of an expression with respect to a set of matches $\underline{m}$ (Definition 13) is a family of values $\underline{ev}(\underline{m}, e) = (ev(\underline{m}, e)_m)_{m \in \underline{m}}$ indexed by the set $\underline{m}$. When the expression e is free from any aggregation operator then $ev(\underline{m}, e)_m$ is simply $m(e)$. But in general $ev(\underline{m}, e)_m$ depends on e and m and it may also depend on other matches in $\underline{m}$ when e involves aggregation operators. To each basic operator op is associated a function $[\![op]\!]$ (or simply op) from values to values if op is unary and from pairs of values to values if op is binary. To each aggregation operator agg in Agg is associated a function $[\![agg]\!]$ (or simply agg) from *multisets* of values to values. Note that each family of values determines a multiset of values: for instance a family $\underline{c} = (c_m)_{m \in \underline{m}}$ of values indexed by the elements of a set of matches $\underline{m}$ determines the multiset of values $\{\!|c_m \mid m \in \underline{m}|\!\}$, which is also denoted $\underline{c}$ when there is no ambiguity.

Definition 13 (Evaluation of Expressions). *Let L be a graph, e an expression over L and $\underline{m} : L \Rightarrow G$ a set of matches. The* value *of e with respect to $\underline{m}$ is the family $\underline{ev}(\underline{m}, e) = (ev(\underline{m}, e)_m)_{m \in \underline{m}}$ defined recursively as follows. It is assumed that each $ev(\underline{m}, e)_m$ in this definition is a value (constant).*

- $ev(\underline{m}, c)_m = c$,
- $ev(\underline{m}, x)_m = m(x)$,
- $ev(\underline{m}, y.p)_m = ev(\underline{m}, e_1)_m$ *if* $(m(p), e_1) \in \pi_G(m(y))$,
- $ev(\underline{m}, op\ e_1)_m = [\![op]\!]\ ev(\underline{m}, e_1)_m$,
- $ev(\underline{m}, e_1\ op\ e_2)_m = ev(\underline{m}, e_1)_m\ [\![op]\!]\ ev(\underline{m}, e_2)_m$,
- $ev(\underline{m}, agg(e_1))_m = [\![agg]\!](\underline{ev}(\underline{m}, e_1))$.

3.2 Operations over Data Graphs and Matches

In graph-to-graph queries, one may have to construct new graphs during the resolution process. Below we define the canonical match $Build(m, R) : R \to G \cup H_{m,R}$ which builds, from a match $m : L \to G$, a new match starting from a given graph R by adding, to graph G, the image of R via m, namely $H_{m,R}$. Intuitively, $H_{m,R}$ is obtained from R by renaming the nodes and edges and the variables which are not instantiated by m. $H_{m,R}$ may share nodes and edges with G according to the definition of m.

Definition 14 (Building a Match). *Let $m : L \to G$ be a match and R an open PGP with possible expressions as values such that $\mathcal{V}_{pth}(R) \subseteq \mathcal{V}_{pth}(L)$, $\mathcal{V}_{lab}(R) \subseteq \mathcal{V}_{lab}(L)$ and $\mathcal{V}_{prp}(R) \subseteq \mathcal{V}_{prp}(L)$; that is, the path variables, the label variables and the property variables appearing in R also occur in L. The match $Build(m, R) : R \to G \cup H_{m,R}$ is the unique match (up to variable renaming) based on the following six functions $h_n, h_e, h_{lab}, h_{val}, h_{prp}$ and h_{pth} where $R = (N_R, E_R, P_R, src_R, tgt_R, \lambda_R, \pi_R)$ and $H_{m,R} = (N_H, E_H, P_H, src_H, tgt_H, \lambda_H, \pi_H)$ such that:*

- *$h_n : N_R \to N_H$ such that $h_n(x) = m(x)$ if $x \in N_R \cap N_L$; otherwise $h_n(x) = x'$ where x' is a fresh node.*
- *$h_e : E_R \to E_H$ such that $h_e(x) = m(x)$ if $x \in E_R \cap E_L$; otherwise $h_e(x) = x'$ where x' is a fresh edge with $src_H(x') = h_n(src_R(x))$ and $tgt_H(x') = h_n(tgt_R(x))$*
- *$h_{lab} : \mathcal{V}_{lab}(R) \to Lab \cup \mathcal{V}_{lab}(H_{m,R})$ such that $h_{lab}(x) = m(x)$ if x is a variable label in $\mathcal{V}_{lab}(R)$ (recall that we assume $\mathcal{V}_{lab}(R) \subseteq \mathcal{V}_{lab}(L)$) .*
- *$h_{val} : \mathcal{V}_{val}(R) \to Val \cup \mathcal{V}_{val}(H_{m,R})$ such that $h_{val}(x) = m(x)$ if x is a value variable in $\mathcal{V}_{val}(R) \cap \mathcal{V}_{val}(L)$; otherwise $h_{val}(x) = x'$ where x' is a fresh value variable.*
- *$h_{prp} : \mathcal{V}_{prp}(R) \to Prop \cup \mathcal{V}_{prp}(H_{m,R})$ such that $h_{prp}(x) = m(x)$ if x is a property variable in $\mathcal{V}_{prp}(R)$ (recall that we assume $\mathcal{V}_{prp}(R) \subseteq \mathcal{V}_{prp}(L)$).*
- *$h_{pth} : \mathcal{V}_{pth}(R) \to \mathcal{P}th(H_{m,R}, \mathcal{V}_{pth}(H_{m,R}))$ such that $h_{pth}(x) = m(x)$ (recall that we assume $\mathcal{V}_{pth}(R) \subseteq \mathcal{V}_{pth}(L)$).*
- *$\lambda_H(h_n(x)) = \{h_{lab}(z) \mid x \in N_R$ and $z \in \lambda_R(x)\}$.*
- *$\lambda_H(h_e(x)) = \{h_{lab}(z) \mid x \in E_R$ and $z \in \lambda_R(x)\}$.*
- *$\pi_H(h_n(x)) = \{(m(p), m(e)) \mid x \in N_R$ and $(p, e) \in \pi_R(x)\}$.*
- *$\pi_H(h_e(x)) = \{(m(p), m(e)) \mid x \in E_R$ and $(p, e) \in \pi_R(x)\}$.*

Example 3. Let $m_1 : L1 \to G1$ be the match as defined in Example 2 (cf., the first column of the table) where
`L1 = (x:person)-[x1:author]->(z:paper)<-[y1:author]-(y:person)` and $G1$ the graph defined in Example 1. Let `R3 = (x) -[u:coauthor]-> (y)`.

The match $Build(m_1, R3) : R3 \to G1 \cup H_{m_1,R3}$ is rather straightforward. The graph $G1 \cup H_{m_1,R3}$ is obtained from graph $G1$ by simply adding one edge with label `coauthor` from node $n1$ to node $n2$. Notice that when one considers all the 9 matches of Example 2 and apply $Build(m_i, R3)$ for each match m_i with $1 \leq i \leq 9$, one gets graph $G3$ as illustrated in Example 4.

Notation: Let $G = (N, E, P, src, tgt, \lambda, \pi)$ be a PGP and x an element in $N \cup E$, p a property in $Prop$ and v a value in Val. We denote by $G[x.p \leftarrow v]$ the PGP $(N, E, P, src, tgt, \lambda, \pi')$ such that for all i in $N \cup E$, $\pi'(i) = \pi(i)$ if $i \neq x$ and $\pi'(x) = \pi(x) \cup \{(p, v)\}$.

Hereafter, we define the main operations over graphs and sets of matches that we use in the definition of the semantics of patterns and thus for queries.

Definition 15 (Operations over Graphs and Sets of Matches).

- *For all open PGP graph L and PGP graph G:*
  $Match(L, G) : L \Rightarrow G$ *is the set of all matches from L to G.*
- *For every set of matches* $\underline{m} : L \Rightarrow G$ *and every expression e:*
  $Filter(\underline{m}, e) = \{m \mid m \in \underline{m} \wedge ev(\underline{m}, e)_m = true\} : L \Rightarrow G.$
- *For all sets of matches* $\underline{m} : L_1 \Rightarrow G_1$ *and* $\underline{h} : L_2 \Rightarrow G_2$*:*
  $Join(\underline{m}, \underline{h}) = \{m \bowtie p \mid m \in \underline{m} \wedge p \in \underline{h} \wedge m \sim p\} : L_1 \cup L_2 \Rightarrow G_1 \cup G_2.$
- *For every set of matches* $\underline{m} : L \Rightarrow G$ *from an open PGP graph L to a PGP graph G. For all x, a node or an edge, in L, p a property in* $Prop \cup \mathcal{V}_{prp}(L)$ *and v a value in Val:*
  $Set(\underline{m}, e, x, p) : L \Rightarrow \cup_{m \in \underline{m}} G[m(x).m(p) \leftarrow ev(\underline{m}, e)_m]$
- *For every set of matches* $\underline{m} : L \Rightarrow G$ *from an open PGP graph L to a PGP graph G and every open PGP graph R such that* $\mathcal{V}_{pth}(R) \subseteq \mathcal{V}_{pth}(L)$, $\mathcal{V}_{lab}(R) \subseteq \mathcal{V}_{lab}(L)$ *and* $\mathcal{V}_{prp}(R) \subseteq \mathcal{V}_{prp}(L)$*:*
  $Build(\underline{m}, R) = \{Build(m, R) \mid m \in \underline{m}\} : R \Rightarrow G \cup \cup_{m \in \underline{m}} Build(m, R)(R).$
  Let $\cong$ *be a graph equivalence on* $G \cup \cup_{m \in \underline{m}} Build(m, R)(R)$*. Then*
  $Buildeq(\underline{m}, R, \cong) = Build(m, R)_{\cong} : R \Rightarrow [G \cup \cup_{m \in \underline{m}} Build(m, R)(R)]_{\cong}.$

3.3 Patterns and CONSTRUCT Queries

Patterns are the main building blocks of queries. They can be nested. The semantics of a pattern *Patt* is defined as a set of matches. The source graph of such matches is a graph called *scope graph* of pattern *Patt* and denoted by $[Patt]$.

Definition 16 (Syntax of Patterns). Patterns *Patt and their* scope graphs $[Patt]$ *are defined recursively as follows.*

- *The symbol* $\square$ *is a pattern, called the* empty pattern, *and* $[\square]$ *is the empty graph* $\emptyset$.
- *If L is an open property graph with paths then* $Patt = BASIC(L)$ *is a pattern, called a* basic pattern, *and* $[Patt] = L$.
- *If* P_1 *is a pattern and e a boolean expression such that* $\mathcal{V}(e) \subseteq \mathcal{V}([P_1])$ *then* $Patt = (P_1\ FILTER\ e)$ *is a pattern and* $[Patt] = [P_1]$.
- *If* P_1 *and* P_2 *are patterns then* $Patt = P_1\ JOIN\ P_2$ *is a pattern and* $[Patt] = [P_1] \cup [P_2]$.
- *If* P_1 *is a pattern, e a value expression such that* $\mathcal{V}(e) \subseteq \mathcal{V}([P_1])$*, x a node in* $[P_1]$ *and p is a property (in* $Prop \cup \mathcal{V}_{prp}([P_1])$*) then* $Patt = (P_1\ SET\ x.p = e)$ *is a pattern and* $[Patt] = [P_1]$.
- *If* P_1 *is a pattern, R an open PGP such that* $\mathcal{V}_{pth}(R) \subseteq \mathcal{V}_{pth}(P_1)$, $\mathcal{V}_{lab}(R) \subseteq \mathcal{V}_{lab}(P_1)$ *and* $\mathcal{V}_{prp}(R) \subseteq \mathcal{V}_{prp}(P_1)$*, that is the path variables, the label variables and the property variables appearing in R also occur in* P_1*,* $x \in N_R$ *and p is either a property (*$\in Prop$*) or a star* $\star$*, then*
  $Patt = (P_1\ BUILD\ R\ [GROUP\ x.p]^*)$ *is a pattern and* $[Patt] = R$.

Definition 17 (Evaluation of Patterns, Set of Solutions). *The* set of solutions *or the* value *of a pattern Patt over a PGP, G, is a set of matches*

$[\![Patt]\!]_G : [Patt] \Rightarrow G^{(Patt)}$ *from the scope graph* $[Patt]$ *of* $Patt$ *to a graph* $G^{(Patt)}$ *that contains* G. *This value* $[\![Patt]\!]_G : [Patt] \Rightarrow G^{(Patt)}$ *is defined inductively as follows:*

- $[\![\Box]\!]_G = \varnothing_G : \emptyset \Rightarrow G$.
- $[\![BASIC(L)]\!]_G = Match(L, G) : L \Rightarrow G$.
- $[\![P_1\ FILTER\ e]\!]_G = Filter([\![P_1]\!]_G, e) : [P_1] \Rightarrow G^{(P_1)}$.
- $[\![P_1\ JOIN\ P_2]\!]_G = Join([\![P_1]\!]_G, [\![P_2]\!]_{G^{(P_1)}}) : [P_1] \cup [P_2] \Rightarrow G^{(P_1)^{(P_2)}}$.
- $[\![P_1\ SET\ x.p = e]\!]_G = Set([\![P_1]\!]_G, e, x, p) : [P_1] \Rightarrow \cup_{m \in [\![P_1]\!]_G} G^{(P_1)}[m(x).m(p) \leftarrow ev([\![P_1]\!]_G, e)_m]$.
- $[\![P_1\ BUILD\ R\ [GROUP\ x.p]^*]\!]_G = Buildeq([\![P_1]\!]_G, R, \cong_{[x.p]^*}) : R \Rightarrow [G^{(P_1)} \cup (Build([\![P_1]\!]_G, R)]_{\cong_{[x.p]^*}}$.

The BUILD clause is key in the construction of new data. The evaluation of a pattern of the form P_1 BUILD R with respect to a graph G, generates a new copy of graph R for every match m_i in the set of matches $[\![P_1]\!]_G$. However, there are situations where the generation of new copies of R may go beyond the desired output data mainly due to duplication of nodes(cf. the institution nodes in Example 7). To overcome such a situation, we provide a declarative way to specify graph congruences, the role of which is to make equal some of the nodes which have been generated separately by the BUILD clause. For that we use the GROUP clause, inspired from [1], to specify graph congruences. In a pattern P_1 BUILD R [GROUP $x.p$]*, the optional clause [GROUP $x.p$]* provides the possibility to equate or merge some nodes, image of given nodes x in R, by using an induced graph equivalence, $\cong_{[x.p]^*}$. Two different nodes u and v are $\cong_{[x.p]^*}$ equivalent if u and v are both images of one node x in R via two different matches m_1 and m_2 in $G^{(P_1)}$, say $m_1(x) = u$ and $m_2(x) = v$, such that u and v share a common value for property p. That is, there exists a value c with (p, c) is in $\pi(m_1(x)) \cap \pi(m_2(x))$. Whenever p is a star, all nodes images of a node x in R are equivalent regardless the values associated to the properties. Recall that the equivalence $\cong_{[x.p]^*}$ is such that x represents a node and p a property. Hence, $\cong_{[x.p]^*}$ does not equate edges, i.e., two edges e_1 and e_2 are $\cong_{[x.p]^*}$ equivalent if and only if e_1 and e_2 are identical ($e_1 = e_2$). We do not allow x to be an edge because otherwise the generated equivalence, $\cong_{[x.p]^*}$, would not be a graph equivalence in general (Definition 5), that is, two edges may be equivalent but not their sources or targets.

Example 4. We consider pattern BASIC($L1$) where $L1$ is the graph defined in Example 2 and define two new patterns $L2$ and $L3$. The role of $L2$ is to select only matches that maps different authors, that is the matches which satisfy the condition $x <> y$. These matches $[\![L2]\!]_{G1}$ are $\{m_1, m_2, m_3, m_4\}$ seen in Example 2. Pattern $L3$ constructs the relationship *coauthor* deduced from the evaluation of pattern $L2$ by building graph `R3 = (x) -[u:coauthor]-> (y)`.

```
L2 = BASIC(L1)  FILTER  x <> y
L3 = L2  BUILD  R3
```

The evaluation of pattern L3, $[\![L3]\!]_{G1} : R3 \Rightarrow G3$, transforms graph $G1$ into graph $G3$, depicted in Fig. 2, by adding the coauthor edges.

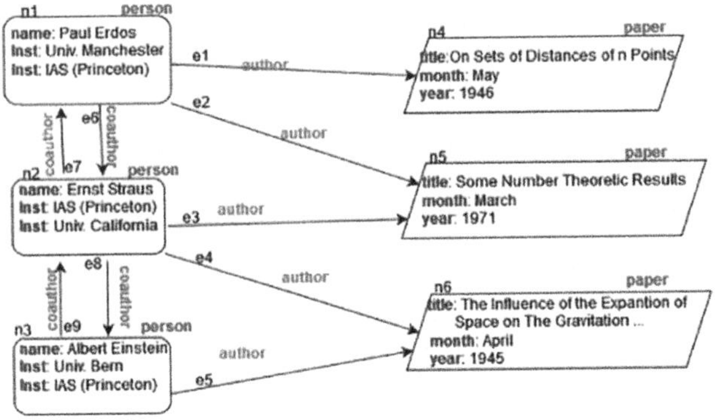

Fig. 2. Property Graph $G3$, target of $[\![L3]\!]_{G1}$

Example 5. To illustrate the use of JOIN operation to build a pattern, we reconsider pattern $L2$ again. $L2$ can be reformulated as a join of two basic patterns before the filter clause.

```
L2bis = (BASIC( (x:person)-[x1:author]->(z:paper)) JOIN
        BASIC((y:person)-[y1:author]->(z:paper)))
        FILTER  x <> y
```

Example 6. We illustrate here the use of aggregation and path variables in a pattern. We define pattern $L4$ which consists of a path variable w. The source of the path variable w is a node of label person, `(x:person)` and its target is the node corresponding to the author P. Erdős, `(y: person)` where `y.name = Paul Erdos`. Two properties are required from path w: (i) to be a trail (no edge can occur twice in w). This condition makes finite the possible paths in the considered graph to match with. (ii) to be shortest. An additional condition over w requires that all edges composing w have labels `coauthor`, written as w : $coauthor^k$. Then, for each author, the length of such path w provides the Erdős number which states the collaboration distance between an author and P. Erdős. We write pattern L4 as follows:

```
L4 =  BASIC((x:person) -[w:<Shortest, Trail> coauthor^k] (y:person))
      WHERE k>=0,  y.name = Paul Erdos
      SET x.Erdos number = length(w)
```

The evaluation of $[\![L4]\!]_{G3}$ is obvious. Its target graph $G4$ is illustrated in Fig. 3 where properties *Erdos number* have been filled.

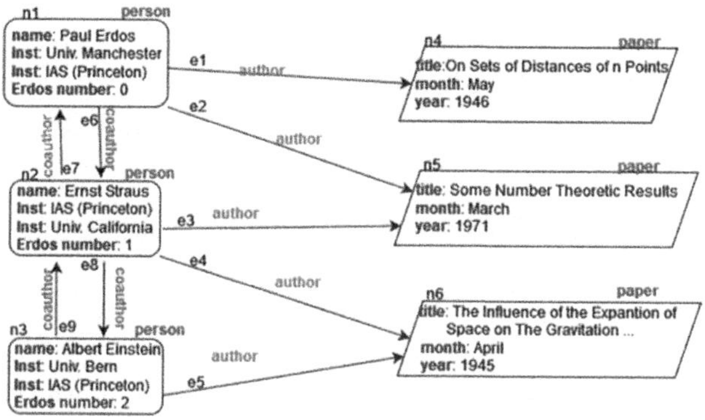

Fig. 3. Graph $G4$ illustrating the computation of Erdős numbers

Example 7. We illustrate here the use of the `GROUP` clause. We define pattern $L5$ which builds, for each author, new nodes corresponding to the institutions the author worked at. Such nodes should be grouped by their names. That is, two nodes representing the same institution should be merged. An edge of label `worked-at` is added between authors and their institutions. Pattern $L5$ can be defined as follows:

```
L5 = BASIC((x:person)) BUILD (x) -[v:worked-at]->(i:institution)
                       SET i.name = x.inst
                       GROUP i.name
```

The evaluation of pattern $L5$ over graph $G4$, $[\![L5]\!]_{G4}$, is a set of matches whose target graph $G5$ is depicted in Fig. 4. Notice that node $n8$ has been generated only once instead of three thanks to the clause `GROUP i.name` which grouped all nodes with the same institution name. The three authors of the running example did work at `IAS (Princeton)`.

Below we define the `CONSTRUCT` queries.

Definition 18 (CONSTRUCT Queries). *Let L be a pattern, R an open PGP, x a node in R and p a property. A CONSTRUCT query, Q,is of the form*

$$CONSTRUCT\ R\ [GROUP\ x.p]^*\ WHERE\ L$$

The GROUP clause is optional. The result *of a query Q over a graph G, denoted $Result_C(Q, G)$, is the subgraph of $G^{(P)}$ image of R by the set of matches $[\![P]\!]_G$ where P is the pattern $P = L\ BUILD\ R\ [GROUP\ x.p]^*$.*

From the definition of CONSTRUCT queries, we notice that a query specifies only the part (graph R) of the target graph to be displayed. Hence, the main important syntactic notion is that of patterns. In the following section, we investigate an operational semantics for patterns and queries.

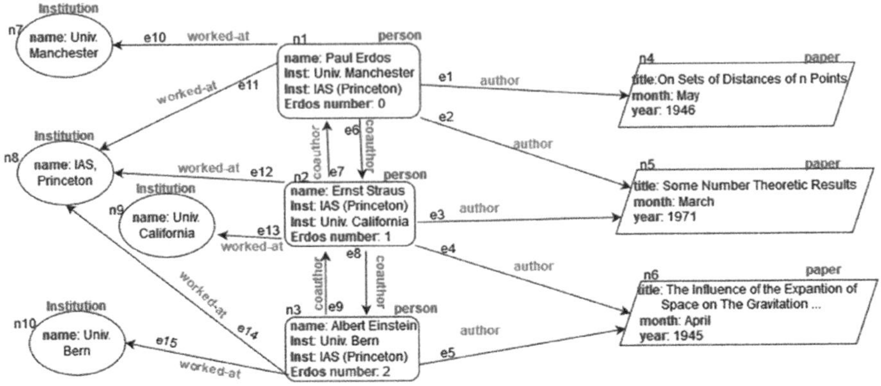

Fig. 4. Graph $G5$ with new institution nodes grouped by names

4 A Rule-Based Operational Semantics

In this section we use rewriting techniques to define an operational semantics to solve patterns and queries. In classical declarative programming languages, goal solving procedures are based on some well known techniques such as narrowing [3] or resolution [9]. Solving a goal g_0 consists in developing derivations of the form

$$g_0 \rightsquigarrow_{[\sigma_0]} g_1 \rightsquigarrow_{[\sigma_1]} g_2 \cdots g_n \rightsquigarrow_{[\sigma_n]} g_{n+1}$$

where g_{n+1} is a "terminal" goal such as the empty clause, unifiable equations or the constant *true*. A solution is obtained by simple composition of local substitutions $\sigma_n \circ \ldots \sigma_1 \circ \sigma_0$ with restriction to variables of the initial goal g_0. In this paper, g_0 is a pattern or a query and the underlying program is a graph (i.e., a database) augmented by a set of rewriting rules defining the behavior of two functions *Solve* (for patterns) and $Solve_Q$ (for queries). Due to the use of aggregation operators in the patterns, one has to compute all solutions simultaneously and thus handle a set of substitutions or matches instead of one substitution at each step as in classical declarative languages. In order to have an easy way to handle such sets of matches, we introduce below the notion of configuration.

Definition 19 (Configuration). *Let* $\underline{m} : L \Rightarrow G$ *be a set of matches from* L *to* G *and* P *a pattern. A configuration is denoted using a mixfix notation as a pair* $[P, \underline{m} : L \Rightarrow G]$ *or simply* $[P, \underline{m}]$. *An* initial *configuration is a configuration of the form* $[P, \underline{i}_G : \emptyset \Rightarrow G]$ *where* $\underline{i}_G = Match(\emptyset, G)$ *is the set with one unique element that is the inclusion of the empty graph,* $\emptyset$*, into* G. *A* terminal *configuration is a configuration of the form* $[\square, \underline{m} : L \Rightarrow G]$.

A configuration $[P, \underline{m} : L \Rightarrow G]$ *represents a state where* P *is a pattern to solve with respect to the current database* G. G *is the target of the current set of matches* $\underline{m} : L \Rightarrow G$. *Finding solutions of a pattern* P *over a graph* G *consists in starting from the term* $Solve([P, \underline{i}_G : \emptyset \Rightarrow G])$ *which applies the function Solve to an initial configuration by performing appropriate rewriting rules to transform configurations until reaching a terminal configuration of the form* $[\square, \underline{m} : L \Rightarrow G']$ *where* $\underline{m} : L \Rightarrow G'$ *represents the expected set of matches (solutions) of* P *over* G *and where* G' *is the graph obtained after solving the pattern* P *over* G*. Notice that* G' *contains* G *but they are not necessarily equal.*

In Fig. 5, we provide a rewriting system, $\mathcal{R}_{gq}^{PG}$, which defines the function *Solve*. This function is defined by structural induction on the first component of configurations, i.e., on patterns. The second argument of configurations, i.e., the sets of matches, in the left-hand sides defining the function *Solve* are always variables of the form $\underline{m} : L \Rightarrow G$ or simply $\underline{m}$ and thus can be handled easily in the pattern-matching process of the left-hand sides of the proposed rules (no need to higher-order pattern-matching nor unification). In the rules of $\mathcal{R}_{gq}^{PG}$, the variable P ranges over *patterns* while variables L, G and R are ranging over PGP *graphs* and $\emptyset$ is the constant denoting the empty graph. Symbol e is a variable over value expressions and x (resp. p) is a variable ranging over nodes (resp. over properties) while $\underline{m}$ and $\underline{h}$ are variables ranging over sets of matches. Some constraints of the rules use operations already introduced in Definition 15, such as *Match*, *Set*, *Filter*, *Buildeq*.

r_0 :	$\mathit{Solve}([\square, \underline{m}])$	$\to$	$[\square, \varnothing_G : \emptyset \Rightarrow G]$
r_1 :	$\mathit{Solve}([\text{BASIC}(L), \underline{m}])$	$\to$	$[\square, \underline{h} : L \Rightarrow G]$ where $\underline{h} = \mathit{Match}(L, G)$
r_2 :	$\mathit{Solve}([P \text{ SET } x.p = e, \underline{m}])$	$\to$	$\mathit{Solve}_{ST}(\mathit{Solve}([P, \underline{m}]), e, x, p)$
r_3 :	$\mathit{Solve}_{ST}([\square, \underline{m}], e, x, p)$	$\to$	$[\square, \underline{h}]$ where $\underline{h} = \mathit{Set}(\underline{m}, e, x, p)$
r_4 :	$\mathit{Solve}([P \text{ FILTER } e, \underline{m}])$	$\to$	$\mathit{Solve}_{FR}(\mathit{Solve}([P, \underline{m}]), e)$
r_5 :	$\mathit{Solve}_{FR}([\square, \underline{m}], e)$	$\to$	$[\square, \underline{h}]$ where $\underline{h} = \mathit{Filter}(\underline{m}, e)$
r_6 :	$\mathit{Solve}([P \text{ BUILD } R\, [\text{ GROUP } x.p]^*, \underline{m}])$	$\to$	$\mathit{Solve}_{BU}(\mathit{Solve}([P, \underline{m}]), R, [x.p]^*)$
r_7 :	$\mathit{Solve}_{BU}([\square, \underline{m}], R, \mathit{cong})$	$\to$	$[\square, \underline{h}]$ where $\underline{h} = \mathit{Buildeq}(\underline{m}, R, \cong_{cong})$
r_8 :	$\mathit{Solve}([P_1 \text{ JOIN } P_2, \underline{m}])$	$\to$	$\mathit{Solve}_{JL}(\mathit{Solve}([P_1, \underline{m}]), P_2)$
r_9 :	$\mathit{Solve}_{JL}([\square, \underline{m}], P)$	$\to$	$\mathit{Solve}_{JR}(\underline{m}, \mathit{Solve}([P, \underline{m}]))$
r_{10} :	$\mathit{Solve}_{JR}(\underline{m}, [\square, \underline{m}'])$	$\to$	$[\square, \underline{h}]$ where $\underline{h} = \mathit{Join}(\underline{m}, \underline{m}')$

Fig. 5. $\mathcal{R}_{gq}^{PG}$: Rewriting rules for patterns

In the sequel, we write $\mathcal{P}_{gq}(\mathcal{X})$ for the term algebra over the set of variables $\mathcal{X}$ generated by the operations occurring in the rewriting system $\mathcal{R}_{gq}^{PG}$.

Rule r_0 considers the degenerated case of the empty pattern $\Box$. In this case there is no solution and the empty set of matches $\varnothing_G$ is computed.

Rule r_1 is key in this system because it considers basic patterns of the form BASIC(L) where L is a PGP graph with possible variables to be instantiated. In this case *Solve*$([\text{BASIC}(L), \underline{m}])$ consists in finding all matches from L to G. These matches instantiate variables in L thanks to the constraint $\underline{h} = \mathit{Match}(L, G)$ of rule r_1. This variable instantiation process is close to the narrowing-based procedures [3]. In this paper, we do not need all the power of narrowing procedures because manipulated data are mostly flat (mainly constants and variables). Thus the unification process used at every step in the narrowing relation is beyond our needs. On the other hand, the classical rewriting relation induced by the above rewriting system is not enough since variables occurring in patterns have to be instantiated and such an instantiation cannot be done by simply rewriting the initial term *Solve*$([P, \underline{i}_G : \emptyset \Rightarrow G])$. Therefore, we propose hereafter a relation induced by the above rewriting system that we call *gq-narrowing*. Before defining this relation, we recall some notations about first-order terms. Readers not familiar with such notations may consult, e.g., [4].

Definition 20 (Position, Subterm Replacement, Substitution, $t{\downarrow_{gq}}$). *A* position *is a sequence of positive integers identifying a subterm in a term. For a term t, the empty sequence, denoted Λ, identifies t itself. When t is of the form $g(t_1, \ldots, t_n)$, the position $i.p$ of t with $1 \leq i \leq n$ and p is a position in t_i, identifies the subterm of t_i at position p. The subterm of t at position p is denoted $t|p$ and the result of replacing the subterm of t at position p with term s is written $t[s]_p$. $t{\downarrow_{gq}}$ is the term obtained from t after evaluation of all expressions (i.e., operations such as Filter, Match, Buileq etc.). A substitution σ is a mapping from variables to terms. When $\sigma(x) = u$ with $u \neq x$, we say that x is in the domain of σ. We write $\sigma(t)$ to denote the extension of the application of σ to a term t which is defined inductively as $\sigma(c) = c$ if c is a constant or c is a variable outside the domain of σ. Otherwise $\sigma(f(t_1, \ldots, t_n)) = f(\sigma(t_1), \ldots, \sigma(t_n))$.*

Definition 21 (gq-narrowing $\rightsquigarrow$). *The rewriting system $\mathcal{R}_{gq}^{PG}$ defines a binary relation $\rightsquigarrow$ over terms in $\mathcal{P}_{gq}(\mathcal{V})$ that we call* gq-narrowing *relation. We write $t \rightsquigarrow_{[u, lhs \to rhs, \sigma]} t'$ or simply $t \rightsquigarrow t'$ and say that t is* gq-narrowable *to t' if there exists a rule $lhs \to rhs$ in the rewriting system $\mathcal{R}_{gq}^{PG}$, a position u in t and a substitution σ such that $\sigma(lhs) = t|_u$ and $t' = t[\sigma(rhs){\downarrow_{gq}}]_u$. Then $\rightsquigarrow^*$ denotes the reflexive and transitive closure of the relation $\rightsquigarrow$.*

Notice that in the definition above of term $t' = t[\sigma(rhs){\downarrow_{gq}}]_u$, the substitution σ is not applied to t as in narrowing $(\sigma(t[rhs]_u {\downarrow_{gq}})$ but only to the right-hand side $(\sigma(rhs))$. This is mainly due to (i) the fact that the unification process is pushed back into rules' constraints and (ii) the fact that aggregations require local instantiations only. Therefore there is no need to propagate variable instantiations. Actually, If we consider again rule r_1, t' would be of the form $t' = t[\Box, (\mathit{Match}(\sigma(L), G) : \sigma(L) \Rightarrow G){\downarrow_{gq}}]_u$ where the evaluation of the Match operation instantiates variables occurring in the pattern (or goal to solve) $BASIC(\sigma(L))$ just like classical narrowing procedures when rules *such as* $f(t_1, \ldots, t_n) \to r$ *are transformed or flattened into* $f(x_1, \ldots, x_n) \to r \mid \bigwedge_1^n Unif(x_i, t_i)$.

Definition 22 (gq-narrowing Derivations). *Let* G *be a graph,* P *a pattern and* $\underline{m}$ *a set of matches. The evaluation of* P *over* G *consists in computing gq-narrowing derivations of the form:*

$$Solve([P, \underline{i}_G : \emptyset \Rightarrow G]) \rightsquigarrow^* [\square, \underline{m}]$$

Notice that $Solve([P, \underline{i}_G : \emptyset \Rightarrow G])$ is intended to find both the solutions (matches) of pattern P over graph G and the graph G' obtained after transforming graph G along the evaluation of the sub-patterns of P.

Example 8. We consider pattern $L3$ as defined in Example 4. $L3 = L2$ BUILD $R3$ where $L2 =$ BASIC($L1$) FILTER $x <> y$.

The expected gq-narrowing derivation over G_1 is as follows:

$$\begin{array}{ll} \multicolumn{2}{l}{Solve([L3, \underline{i}_{G1}])} \\ \rightsquigarrow_{r_6} & Solve_{BU}(Solve([L2, \underline{i}_{G1}]), R3, id) \\ \rightsquigarrow_{r_4} & Solve_{BU}(Solve_{FR}(Solve([BASIC(L1), \underline{i}_{G1}]), x <> y), R3, id) \\ \rightsquigarrow_{r_1} & Solve_{BU}(Solve_{FR}([\square, Match(L1, G1)], x <> y), R3, id) \\ \rightsquigarrow_{r_5} & Solve_{BU}([\square, Filter(Match(L1, G1), x <> y)], R3, id) \\ \rightsquigarrow_{r_7} & [\square, Buildeq(Filter(Match(L1, G1), x <> y), R3, id)] \end{array}$$

The expression $Buildeq(Filter(Match(L1, G1), x <> y), R3, id)$ evaluates to a set of matches whose codomain is exactly the graph displayed in Fig. 2. Notice that when the GROUP clause is empty, the equivalence on nodes is the identity (reflexivity) denoted by the symbol *id* in the third argument of the *Buildeq* operator.

Proposition 1 (Termination). *The relation* $\rightsquigarrow$ *is terminating.*

Proposition 2 (Determinism). *Let* $t_0 \rightsquigarrow t_1 \rightsquigarrow \ldots \rightsquigarrow t_n$ *be a gq-narrowing derivation with* $t_0 = Solve([P, \underline{i}_G])$. *For all* $i \in [0..n]$, *there exists at most one position* u_i *in* t_i *such that* t_i *can be gq-narrowed into* t_{i+1}.

Theorem 1 (Soundness). *Let* G *be a graph,* P *a pattern and* $\underline{m}$ *a set of matches such that* $Solve([P, \underline{i}_G]) \rightsquigarrow^* [\square, \underline{m}]$. *Then for all morphisms* m *in* $\underline{m}$, *there exists a morphism* m' *equals to* m *up to renaming of variables such that* m' *is in* $[\![P]\!]_G$.

Theorem 2 (Completeness). *Let* G_1, G_2 *and* X *be graphs,* P *a pattern and* $h : X \Rightarrow G_2$ *a match in* $[\![P]\!]_{G_1}$. *Then there exist graphs* G_2' *and* X', *a set of matches* $\underline{m} : X' \Rightarrow G_2'$, *a derivation* $Solve([P, \underline{i}_{G_1}] \rightsquigarrow^* [\square, \underline{m}]$ *and a match* $m : X' \Rightarrow G_2'$ *in* $\underline{m}$ *such that* m *and* h *are equal up to variable renaming.*

In Fig. 6, we enrich the rewriting system $\mathcal{R}_{gq}^{PG}$ by means of two additional rules which tackle CONSTRUCT queries. the *result* of a CONSTRUCT query Q over a graph G is a graph $Result_C(Q, G)$. The specification of the display function $Print_C$ is out of the scope of the present paper. The Soundness and completeness of the calculus with respect to CONSTRUCT queries are direct consequences of Theorems 1 and 2.

r_{11} : $\mathit{Solve}_Q(\text{CONSTRUCT } R \text{ [GROUP } x.p]^* \text{ WHERE } P, G) \to \mathit{Display}_C(R, \mathit{Solve}(\, [\, P \text{ BUILD } R \text{ [GROUP } x.p]^*, \underline{i}_G \,]\,))$
r_{12} : $\mathit{Display}_C(R, [\,\square, \underline{m}\,]) \to \mathit{Print}_C(R, \underline{m})$

Fig. 6. $\mathcal{R}_{gq}^{PG}$ (continued): Rewriting rules for queries

5 Conclusion and Related Work

We proposed a symbolic procedure based on rewriting techniques to solve patterns or CONSTRUCT graph queries for a core graph query language. The considered data graphs are represented by the so-called property graphs. The proposed procedure is deterministic, sound and complete. By the nature of the considered graphs, our procedure differs from the one presented for RDF graphs in [7]. The operators on property graphs feature new needs such as SET or GROUP clauses in addition to the way paths play an important role in queries.

The notion of *pattern* present in this paper is close to the syntactic notions of *clauses* in [8] or *graph patterns* in [2]. For such syntactic notions, some authors associate as semantics sets of variables bindings (tables) as in [8,10] or simply graphs as in [1]. In our case, we associate both variable bindings and graphs since we associate sets of graph homomorphisms to patterns. This semantics is borrowed from a first work on formal semantics of graph queries based on category theory [6]. Our semantics allows composition of patterns in a natural way. Such composition of patterns is not easy to catch if the semantics is based only on variable bindings but can be recovered when queries have graph outcomes as in G-CORE [1].

References

1. Angles, R., et al.: G-CORE: a core for future graph query languages. In: Das, G., Jermaine, C.M., Bernstein, P.A. (eds.) Proceedings of the 2018 International Conference on Management of Data, SIGMOD Conference 2018, Houston, TX, USA, 10-15 June 2018, pp. 1421–1432. ACM (2018). https://doi.org/10.1145/3183713.3190654
2. Angles, R., Arenas, M., Barceló, P., Hogan, A., Reutter, J.L., Vrgoc, D.: Foundations of modern query languages for graph databases. ACM Comput. Surv. **50**(5), 68:1–68:40 (2017). https://doi.org/10.1145/3104031
3. Antoy, S., Echahed, R., Hanus, M.: A needed narrowing strategy. J. ACM **47**(4), 776–822 (2000). https://doi.org/10.1145/347476.347484
4. Baader, F., Nipkow, T.: Term Rewriting and All That. Cambridge University Press (1998)
5. Duval, D., Echahed, R., Prost, F.: All you need is CONSTRUCT. CoRR **abs/2010.00843** (2020). https://arxiv.org/abs/2010.00843
6. Duval, D., Echahed, R., Prost, F.: Querying RDF databases with sub-constructs. In: Kutsia, T. (ed.) Proceedings of the 9th International Symposium on Symbolic Computation in Software Science, SCSS 2021, Hagenberg, Austria, 8-10 September 2021. EPTCS, vol. 342, pp. 49–64 (2021). https://doi.org/10.4204/EPTCS.342.5

7. Duval, D., Echahed, R., Prost, F.: A rule-based procedure for graph query solving. In: In: Fernández, M., Poskitt, C.M. (eds.) 16th International Conference on Graph Transformation, ICGT 2023, Held as Part of STAF 2023, Leicester, UK, July 19-20, 2023, Proceedings. Lecture Notes in Computer Science, vol. 13961, pp. 163–183. Springer, Cham (2023). https://doi.org/10.1007/978-3-031-36709-0_9
8. Francis, N., et al.: Cypher: an evolving query language for property graphs. In: SIGMOD Conference, pp. 1433–1445. ACM (2018)
9. Lloyd, J.W.: Foundations of Logic Programming, 2nd edn. Springer (1987). https://doi.org/10.1007/978-3-642-83189-8
10. Pérez, J., Arenas, M., Gutiérrez, C.: Semantics and complexity of SPARQL. ACM Trans. Database Syst. **34**(3), 16:1–16:45 (2009). https://doi.org/10.1145/1567274.1567278
11. SPARQL 1.1 query language. W3C recommendation (March 2013). https://www.w3.org/TR/sparql11-query/
12. RDF 1.1 concepts and abstract syntax. W3C recommendation (February 2014). https://www.w3.org/TR/rdf11-concepts/

Riemann Surfaces, Branch Cuts and Charisma

David J. Jeffrey(✉)

Department of Mathematics, The University of Western Ontario, London, Ontario, Canada N6A 3K7

djeffrey@uwo.ca

Abstract. The plotting of Riemann surfaces by computational software is discussed. The link between the branches of a multi-valued function $g(z)$, which are defined on the *range* of $g(z)$, and a Riemann surface, which is defined on the *domain* of $g(z)$, is emphasized. The connection between the two is clarified by defining a property called *charisma*, which is used to plot the Riemann surface. The charisma is not uniquely defined and the choice can change the appearance of the surface. This approach is used to plot several surfaces using Maple.

Keywords: Riemann surface · Multivalued function · Charisma

1 Introduction

Riemann surfaces of complex functions have been visualized by a number of authors and computer systems, and often they make striking visual images. See [5] for an impressive collection. The traditional way that textbooks introduce Riemann surfaces is through an informal discussion of layered sheets, which are cut and glued together to form a continuous surface [7]. Such an approach does not lend itself to software methods for creating the surfaces. This was discussed in [6], prompted by a demonstration program in Matlab. The methods used in that paper are extended here to strengthen the link between the range and the domain.

Often, Riemann surfaces are used to understand multi-valued functions that are the inverses of 'proper' single-valued functions. Examples include the inverses of the exponential function (namely logarithm), of the trigonometric functions (arc-trigs), and the integral powers (nth-roots). In each case, there is a function $z = f(w)$ which is single valued, and an inverse $w = \check{f}(z)$ which is multivalued. For the multivalued function, an important question is how to separate and access the individual members of the set of multiple values. Two possibilities present themselves: the separation is made either in the range of the function or in its domain.

S. M. Watt and T. Ida (Eds.): SCSS 2024, LNAI 14991, pp. 114–128, 2024.
https://doi.org/10.1007/978-3-031-69042-6_7

2 Labelling the Range

We begin with a common example of a multivalued function: the logarithm. Of the various functions used as examples here, the natural logarithm is the only one for which an explicit notation for its branches has gained some traction. If $z = e^w$, then $w = \ln_z$. Since, for $n \in \mathbb{Z}$, $z = e^{w+2n\pi i} = e^w$, for any complex number z, there are an infinite number of values for the logarithm. The standard treatment defines two logarithm functions. Following the notation of the DLMF [1,4], we write Ln_z to represent the *general logarithm function*, which stands for the infinite collection of values, and $\ln_z$ for the *principal value* or *principal branch*. The principal branch is defined by the condition $-\pi < \Im(\ln_z) \leq \pi$. The general function notation (i.e. Ln_z), however, is frustratingly vague, and leads to statements such as [1]

$$\mathrm{Ln}_z = \ln_z + 2k\pi i \ , \tag{1}$$

where the equation has, on the left, only one variable z, but on the right has two variables z, k.

Therefore, in order to obtain a more precise specification of the values taken by logarithm, the notation

$$\ln_k z = \ln_z + 2k\pi i \ , \tag{2}$$

was introduced in [9]. Geometrically, this coincides with the range of logarithm being partitioned into branches, and each branch being labelled, as can be seen in Fig. 1. We note that $\ln_z$ and $\ln_0 z$ both denote the principal branch. For each separate branch $\ln_k z$, the domain consists of the whole complex plane, with a line of discontinuity, called a branch cut, along the negative real axis. In thinking of branches, it is sometimes helpful to disregard the connections between the branches and think of each branch as a function separate in its own right. For example, the equation $\ln x = 2$ has the solution $x = e^2$, but the equation $\ln_1 x = 2$ has no solution because 2 does not lie in the range of $\ln_1 x$.

The second example of a multivalued function is provided by the cube-root function. We have $z = w^3$, implying the inverse $w = z^{1/3}$. In the complex plane, the cube root always has 3 values. To denote the 3 cube roots, we need a notation which gives us space for a label. The notations $z^{1/3}$ and $\sqrt[3]{z}$ look clumsy with additional labels, and so Beardon [2] has proposed the notation $[z]^{1/3}$ for the set of three values for any particular z. We need here more explicit notation: notation which specifies individual branches. We could modify Beardon's notation to $[z]_k^{1/3}$ to indicate a specific branch, but we here create a separate cube-root function with name: $\mathrm{cbrt}_k\, z$. The range of cbrt is partitioned as shown in Fig. 2, where the branches are defined using the complex phase[1]. With $\mathrm{ph}\, z$ denoting the principal complex phase $-\pi < \mathrm{ph}\, z \leq \pi$, we define the principal branch of cube-root by the requirement $-\pi/3 < \mathrm{ph}(z^{1/3}) \leq \pi/3$. If we denote the primitive root of unity

[1] We use the name complex phase, rather than complex argument, because the word argument will be used for function argument.

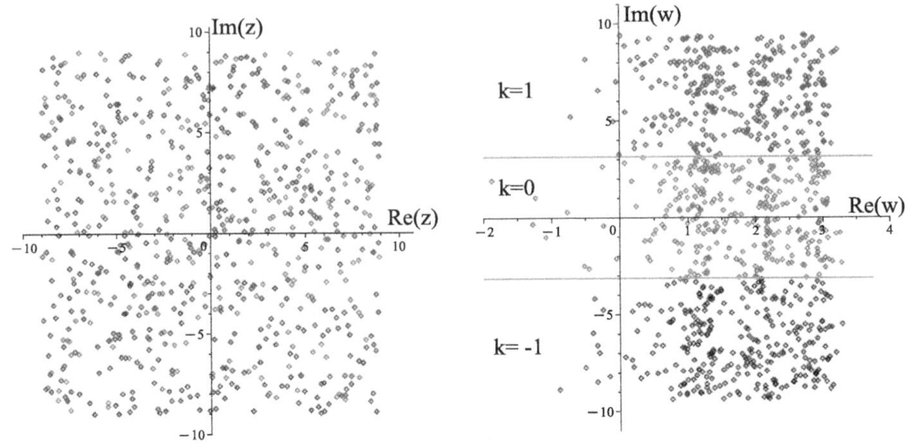

Fig. 1. The domain and range of the multivalued logarithm. The domain, the left set of axes, contains points coloured red, black and blue intermingled. The points are mapped to the range using different branches of logarithm. The black points are mapped with $w = \ln_{-1} z$, red with $w = \ln_z$ and blue with $w = \ln_1 z$. The figure shows only 3 branches, but branches exist for all k. The aim is to separate the points in the domain using a Riemann surface. (Color figure online)

by $\omega = e^{2\pi i/3}$, and $\theta = \operatorname{ph} z$, then the 3 branches are defined by

$$\operatorname{cbrt}_k(z) = \operatorname{cbrt}_k(re^{i\theta}) = \begin{cases} z^{1/3} = r^{1/3}e^{i\theta/3} , & k = 0 , \\ \omega z^{1/3} = r^{1/3}e^{i(\theta+2\pi)/3} , & k = 1 , \\ \overline{\omega} z^{1/3} = r^{1/3}e^{i(\theta-2\pi)/3} , & k = -1 . \end{cases} \tag{3}$$

Note that Maple's `RootOf` notation indexes the branches differently:

$$\texttt{RootOf}(w^3 = re^{i\theta}, w, \text{index} = k) = \begin{cases} r^{1/3}e^{i\theta/3} , & k = 1 , \\ \omega r^{1/3}e^{i\theta/3} , & k = 2 , \\ \overline{\omega} r^{1/3}e^{i\theta/3} , & k = 3 . \end{cases} \tag{4}$$

For each separate branch of $\operatorname{cbrt}_k(z)$, the domain is the whole of the complex plane, with a line of discontinuity (the branch cut) along the negative real axis.

We note as an instructive special case the values of $(-8)^{1/3}$. The three cube roots are $-2, 1 + \sqrt{3}\,i, 1 - \sqrt{3}\,i$. Some readers might be surprised to learn that the principal-branch value of $(-8)^{1/3}$ is not -2. The principal branch value is $\operatorname{cbrt}_0(-8) = 1 + \sqrt{3}\,i$ and the real-value root is branch 1: $\operatorname{cbrt}_1(-8) = -2$. As seen in Fig. 2, the negative real values of the function do not lie in the principal branch.

We can note here that the principal-branch values of both logarithm and cube root are the unique values returned by all major scientific software systems, such as Matlab, Maple and Mathematica. This also applies to other multi-valued functions, such as nth roots and inverse trigonometric functions.

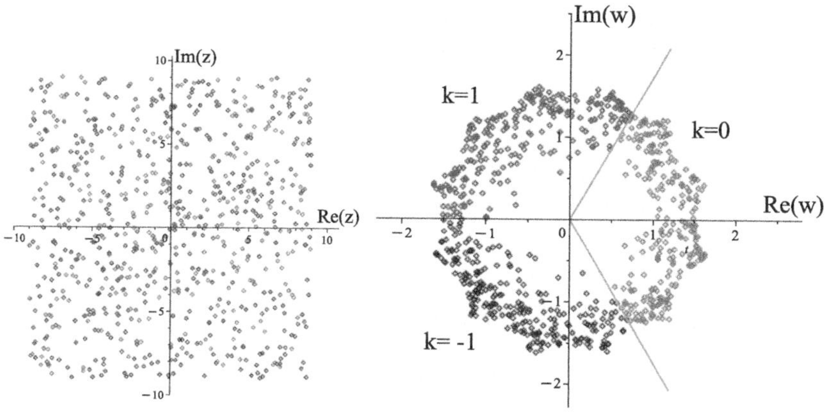

Fig. 2. The range of the cube root partitioned into branches. The domain is the same as used in Fig. 1. As with logarithm, the branches are labelled with colour and by an integer k. In this case there are only 3 branches, separated by the boundaries $re^{\pm i\pi/3}$ and the negative real axis.

3 Labelling the Domain

The main object of this paper is to show how the labelling ideas of the previous section can be transferred from the range of a complex function to its domain, and by doing so we obtain a new perspective on plots of Riemann surfaces. A Riemann surface for a multivalued function is built on the function's domain, but uses information from the range. A typical description of the construction process talks about cutting and joining sheets of the domain. For example, here is a description of a Riemann surface for the square-root function, quoted from [10].

> A Riemann surface for $z^{1/2}$ is obtained by replacing the z plane with a surface made up of two sheets R_0 and R_1, each cut along the positive real axis with R_1 placed in front of R_0. The lower edge of the slit in R_0 is joined to the upper edge of the slit in R_1, and the lower edge of the slit in R_1 is joined to the upper edge of the slit in R_0.

We note in passing that the author specifies the branch cut as being along the positive real axis, whereas standard software practice at present places the cut on the negative axis.

Thus, a Riemann surface for a multivalued function $w = \check{f}(z)$ represents values of z, rather than values of w. The point to understand is that the value of z by itself is not sufficient to determine the value of $\check{f}(z)$, and therefore there must be a property possessed by a particular value of z that decides the value of the function, in conjunction with the complex value of z. This property is not at present visible. We shall call this property *charisma*. A variable z with charisma will be denoted z_C , although at this stage we do not know what charisma is.

In [3], it is pointed out that Riemann surfaces can be understood without embedding them in $\mathbb{R}^3$. While this is true, surfaces in $\mathbb{R}^3$ are a popular way of visualizing Riemann surfaces, so this is the aspect that we study here. We aim to define charisma as a numerical value, which can then serve as an ordinate on an axis perpendicular to the complex plane. We set up 3 axes: real and imaginary axes for locating the complex value of z together with an orthogonal axis representing charisma. The first example will be the cube-root function introduced above.

4 Charisma for Cube Root

We take as a first example the indexed cube root given in (3). We explore four possible choices for the charisma of this function.

4.1 Using Branch Index for Charisma

We have seen that the branch label k is used to assign values in the range of $\mathrm{cbrt}_k(z)$, so we begin by trying the assignment

$$\mathcal{C} = k \ .$$

With the charisma chosen to be the index k, we plot the corresponding surfaces as follows. We create a 3-element plot structure consisting of the real and imaginary parts of a complex number, together with the charisma. The plot of the range (right-hand axes) in Fig. 2 was obtained by assigning each point a branch. This branch value becomes the charisma in the plot structure. The structure is handed to the `plot3d` command in Maple. The results are shown in Fig. 3.

The effect of this choice for the charisma is simply to separate the values of z into three flat planes, stacked and spaced. As a possible Riemann surface, it is unsatisfactory, because the data in the range is contiguous at the boundaries, but separated in the domain. We can understand this plot by placing a point[2] in the *range* of the function. The point now moves around in the range. The image in the domain of the point is found from the mapping $z = w^3$. Each time the point crosses a branch boundary, the branch number jumps discontinuously. This discontinuous change is reflected in the domain by a jump from one sheet to another.

Discontinuous changes in branch label are analogous to driving between states or provinces and crossing a border. The road is continuous, the land is continuous, but suddenly everyone is speaking French and selling fireworks[3].

[2] Or more picturesquely an ant.

[3] At least that is what one sees when driving from Toronto to Montreal.

4.2 A Continuous Charisma

Our aim is to find a charisma that gives a continuous surface in the domain. When searching for a measure of charisma, it is important not to fixate on the domain of z, even though it is the domain where the surface will be located. We are trying to represent the multi-valued nature of the function, and that is defined in the range. In particular, a point circling the origin in the range will see continuous behaviour. Following the implications of this observation suggests that the phase of the cube root could be a better quantity to use for charisma. Thus, given $w = \mathrm{cbrt}_k(z)$, we set

$$\mathcal{C} = \mathrm{ph}(w) \ . \tag{5}$$

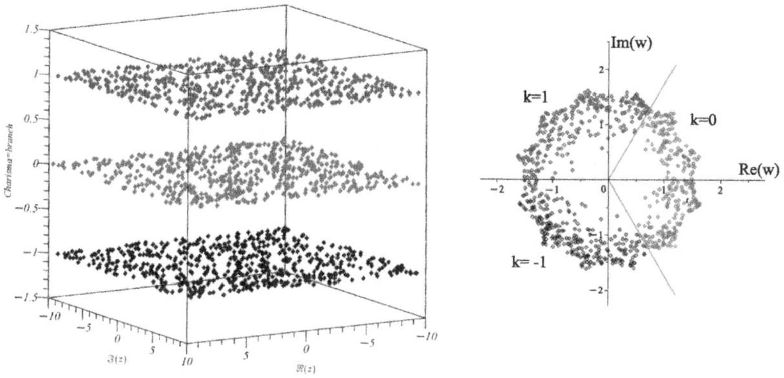

Fig. 3. On the left we see the domain of $w = z^{1/3}$ as a Riemann surface; on the right, the range of $z^{1/3}$. The sheets of a possible Riemann surface are separated by labelling them with charisma equal to the branch index. The sheets of the surface are coloured to match the branches of $\mathrm{cbrt}_k(z)$. The top sheet corresponds to $k = 1$ meaning all the values of z on this sheet map to $\mathrm{cbrt}_1(z)$ as shown by the corresponding colour in the range. Similarly for the other two branches. This choice of charisma is too crude, reflecting the discontinuous change in branch number when the point moves around in the range.

The phase is computed from the value of $w = z^{1/3}$, not from the value of z. This choice results in the surface shown in Fig. 4. Since we are now considering continuous variables, we change our method of plotting from point plotting to surface plotting. The right-hand axes repeat the range of $z^{1/3}$, now with colours that work better with the continuous surface, and the left axes display the corresponding smooth Riemann-like surface based on (5).

4.3 A Continuous and Periodic Charisma

The phase succeeds in creating a smooth surface, but we see in the range of $z^{1/3}$ that branch $k = -1$ joins $k = 1$ continuously, but in Fig. 4 there is a discontinuity between them. We have

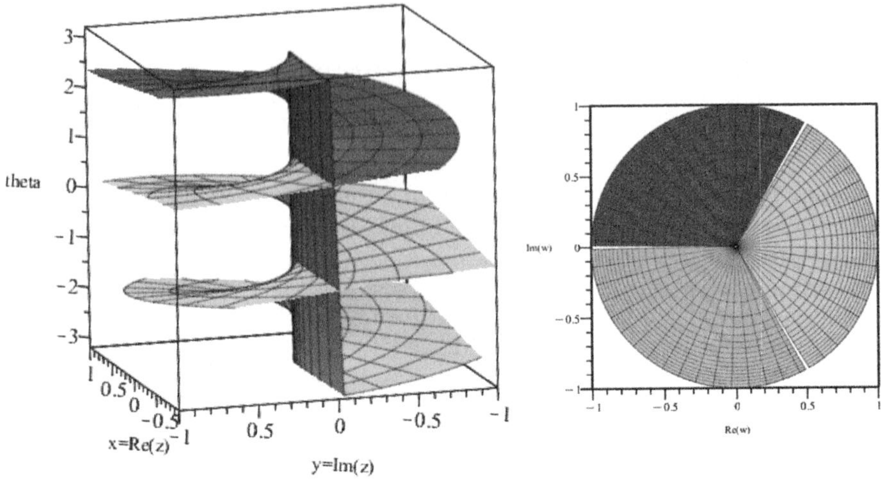

Fig. 4. The Riemann-like surface obtained by using the phase of the cube root as charisma. The surface rises from the minimum value of $-\pi$ to π with the colours showing the division into branches. The surface remains smooth where the branches change. Maple has joined the end of the surface at $\mathcal{C} = \pi$ discontinuously to $\mathcal{C} = -\pi$.

$$\lim_{y \downarrow 0} \mathrm{cbrt}_1(x + iy) = \lim_{y \uparrow 0} \mathrm{cbrt}_{-1}(x + iy) \ . \tag{6}$$

A function that has these properties is

$$\mathcal{C} = \sin\theta \propto \Im(w) \ . \tag{7}$$

In Fig. 5, the Riemann surface produced with this choice is shown. The surface is continuous and smooth everywhere. Unlike the previous surfaces, this one intersects itself in two places: branch $k = -1$ intersects $k = 0$ when $\mathcal{C} = -1/2$ along the negative imaginary axis, and $k = 0$ intersects $k = 1$ at $\mathcal{C} = 1/2$ along the positive imaginary axis. The intersections do not necessarily show function equality. For example, $\mathcal{C} = -1/2$ implies $\theta = -\pi/6$ or $\theta = 5\pi/6$. The different values of θ correspond to the different branches. The surfaces change colour (branch) along the negative real axis at $\mathcal{C} = -\frac{\sqrt{3}}{2}, 0, \frac{\sqrt{3}}{2}$.

4.4 An Alternative Continuous and Periodic Surface

The final Riemann surface for cube root uses charisma $\mathcal{C} = \cos\theta \propto \Re(w)$. The result is shown in Fig. 6. There are several æsthetic changes. The principal branch now is prominent at the top of the surface. Further, the surface intersections now line up with the real axis and complement the branch cuts.

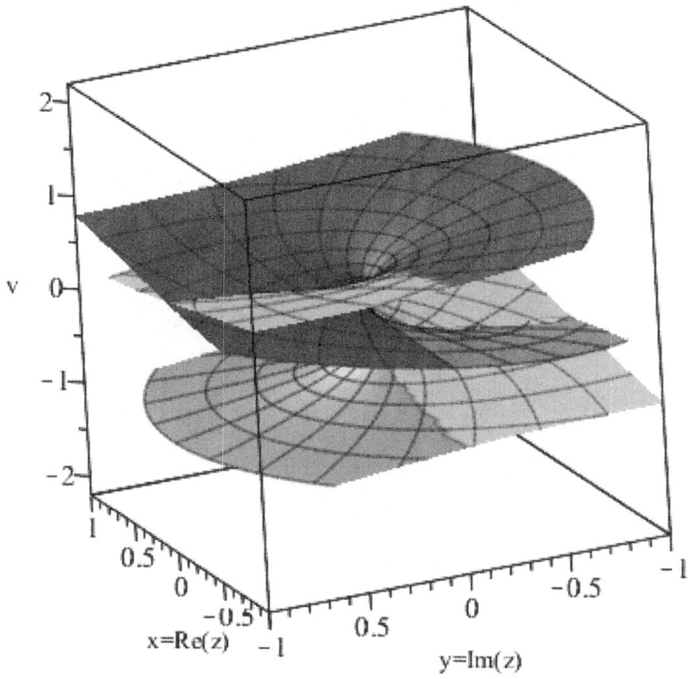

Fig. 5. A periodic Riemann surface for the cube-root function. The charisma is based on $\sin\theta$ where $\theta = \text{ph}(z^{1/3})$. This can equivalently be based on the imaginary part of $z^{1/3}$. Since the Riemann surface is plotted over the domain z, while being coloured based on the range $z^{1/3}$, the colours change along the negative real axis in the domain where $\mathcal{C} = -\sqrt{3}/2, 0, \sqrt{3}/2$.

5 The Logarithm

The first example had only 3 branches, with the consequence that the charisma was bounded, but the logarithm has an infinite number of branches, meaning the charisma will extend indefinitely. In [6], a contrast was drawn between different attempts to plot a Riemann surface for the logarithm. A first (failing) choice for the charisma was the real part of the value of logarithm; the surface was then coloured using the imaginary part. The attempt was unsatisfactory, as can be seen in Fig. 7.

By emphasizing the need to think in terms of the range of a function, we can see immediately why this is. In terms of charisma, the unsatisfactory choice was the real part of logarithm. Considering Fig. 1, we see that the branches separate in the imaginary direction, and not the real direction, and thus a charisma based on motion parallel to the real axis never leaves the branch of log in which the

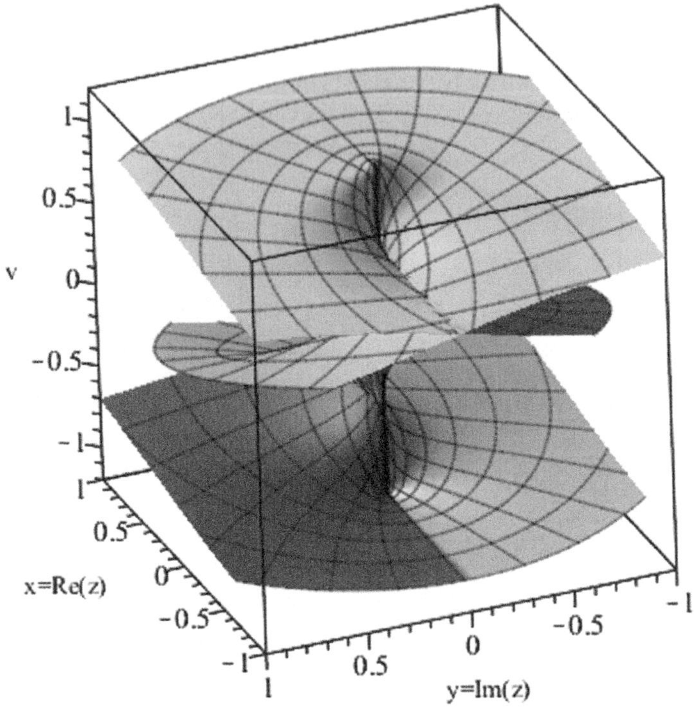

Fig. 6. The Riemann surface for cube root, using $\cos\theta$ for the charisma. The surface is of the same form as the one using the sine function, but the partition between the branches has changed.

point started. In order to obtain a surface for logarithm, we must move parallel to the imaginary axis, in order to cross from one branch to the next. This was shown to be the correct choice. We could try using the branch index of $\ln_k z$ as we did for cube root, but again that would result in flat segments separated by jumps. As shown in [6], a simple charisma for logarithm is its imaginary part. The result is shown in Fig. 8, where the colouring again changes with the branch.

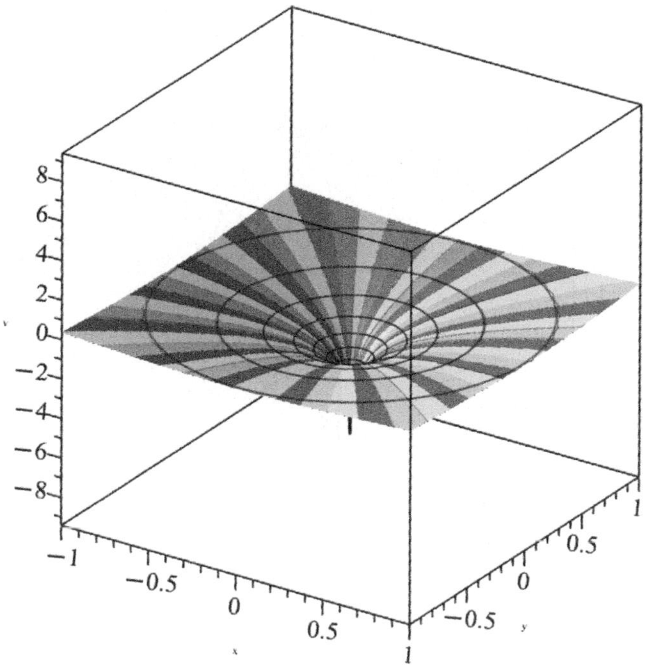

Fig. 7. An incorrect choice for the charisma function applied to logarithm. The choice of real part does not distinguish between branches, and therefore only one surface is created. The colour bands are the result of the colouring function creating circles of colour.

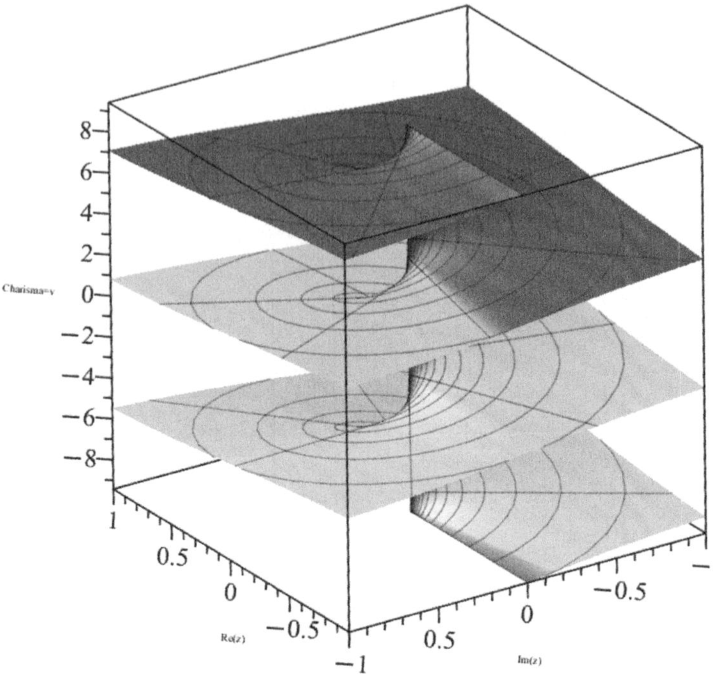

Fig. 8. A section of the infinite Riemann surface for logarithm, using the imaginary part of logarithm as the charisma. The surface is coloured according to the branch index.

5.1 Inverse Sine

The last example shows a function which is periodic in the real direction, and having two branch cuts. The inverse sine function does not have an agreed notation for its branches. In order to implement a branched function in Maple, we need to avoid any clashes with the built-in function `arcsin`. Therefore a function `invsin` is defined as follows

```
invsin := proc (z::algebraic) local branch;
  if _nparams <> 1 then
      error ``Expecting 1 argument, got'', _nparams ;
  elif type(procname, indexed) then
      branch := op(procname);
      branch*Pi+arcsin((-1)^branch*z);
  else
      arcsin(z);
  end if;
end proc:
```

Thus we have a Maple computation of different inverse sine values as follows.

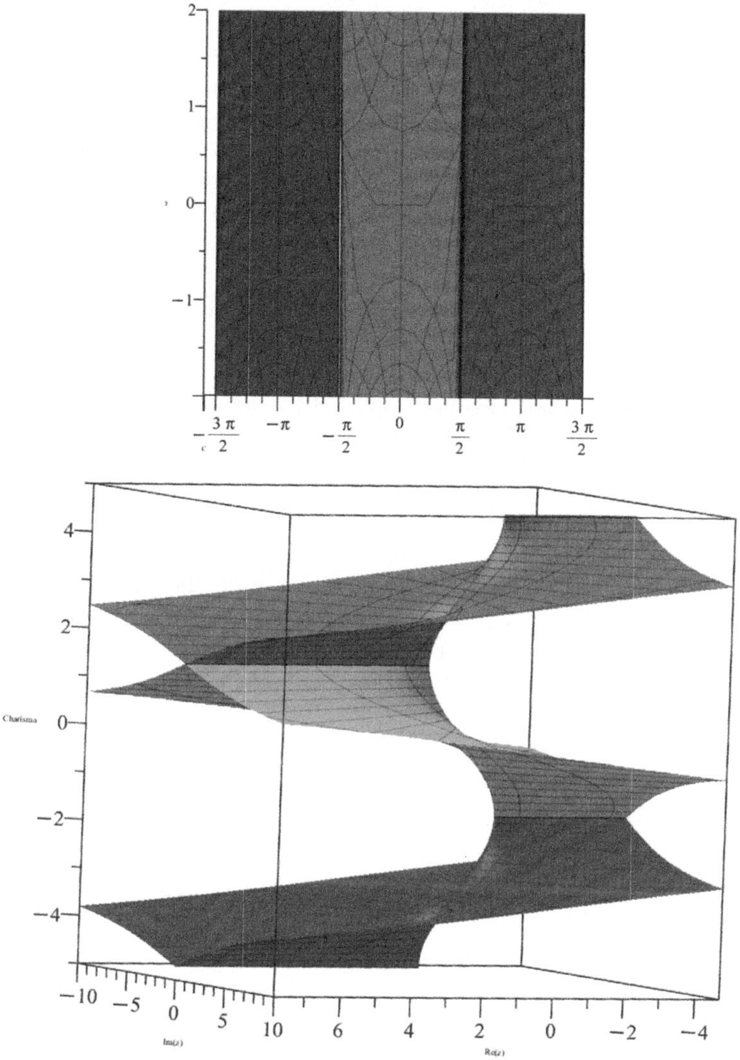

Fig. 9. The domain and range of the branched inverse sine, implemented as `invsin`. The Riemann surface in the domain is coloured to match the branches coloured in the range. The two branch cuts in the domain, $(-\infty, -1]$ and $[1, \infty)$, are clearly visible.

```
> [ invsin(sin(3*Pi/4)), invsin[1](sin(3*Pi/4)),
                               invsin[2](sin(3*Pi/4)) ] ;
    [Pi/4, 3*Pi/4, 9*Pi/4 ]
```

These results, which would likely puzzle mathematics students, become less puzzling with explicit branch notation.

The domain and range of inverse sign are shown in Fig. 9, where the range of the function is shown first, being the multivalued function driving the Riemann surface, while below it the domain of the function holds the Riemann surface itself. For efficiency, the Riemann surface is shown immediately, without the didactic display of the domain before and after imposing the charisma, which in this instance is the real part of inverse sine. The charisma for these plots, the real part of the value of arcsine (in its multivalue form $\operatorname{invsin}_k z$), stands in contrast to the example of logarithm, where the real part of the function failed to give a satisfactory surface.

The branch cuts are $(-\infty, -1]$ and $[1, \infty)$, which are discernable in the domain. To help with the interpretation of the figure, the conventional depiction of the branch cuts is shown in Fig. 10. Note that this example demonstrates that the methods described here are not confined to cases in which there is a single branch cut, but generalize to multiple branch cuts.

6 The Fourth Root

As a final example of a Riemann surface, we plot the fourth root function: $w = z^{1/4}$ in Fig. 11. The charisma is again the cosine of the argument of w. The principal branch $k = 0$ is the top blue surface. The bottom red surface is branch $k = 3$ and branches $k = 2, 4$ run between these surfaces.

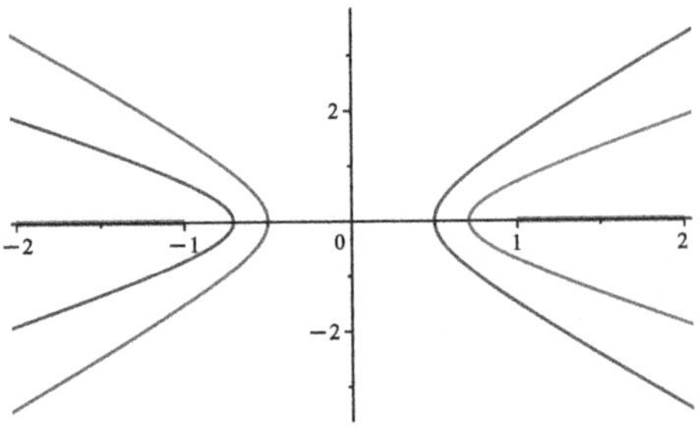

Fig. 10. The domain of inverse sine (arcsine) showing the branch cuts in their more usual depiction. The branch cuts are shown together with images under $\sin w$ of the contours $\pm\frac{1}{4}\pi + ti$ and $\pm\frac{1}{6}\pi + ti$ for $-5 \le t \le 5$.

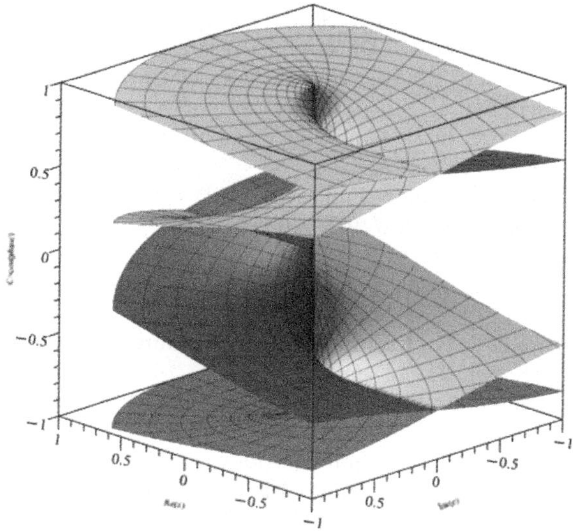

Fig. 11. The Riemann surface for $w = z^{1/4}$. The charisma is $\mathcal{C} = \cos\theta$, where θ is the phase of $w^{1/4}$.

7 Conclusions

Many treatments of multivalued functions concentrate on the domain of the function, and focus on branch cuts in the domain. See, for example, [1,4,12], where the functions are defined and illustrated only using branch cuts. This article hopes to demonstrate that thinking in the range as well as in the domain makes understanding easier. In this article, charisma was defined and used for conceptual purposes. As seen above, the charisma is not a uniquely defined quantity, but as a source of understanding, the lack of uniqueness is not an impediment. Whether charisma can be harnessed for computational purposes remains to be seen.

Acknowledgments. Disclosure of Interests. This work was supported by an NSERC Discovery grant. The author has no competing interests.

References

1. Abramowitz, M., Stegun, I.A..: Handbook of Mathematical Functions with Formulas, Graphs, and Mathematical Tables. US Government Printing Office, (1964), 10th Printing December (1972)
2. Beardon, A.F.: Complex exponentials and group theory. Math. Mag. **93**(3), 186–192 (2020). https://doi.org/10.1080/0025570X.2020.1736876
3. Beardon, A.F.: A Primer on Riemann Surfaces. London Mathematical Society Lecture Note Series, Series Number 78. Cambridge University Press (1984)

4. Olver, F.W., Lozier, D.W., Boisvert, R.: Charles W. NIST Handbook of Mathematical Functions, Cambridge University Press, Clark (2010)
5. Trott, M.: The return of the Riemann surface. Math. J. **10**(4) (2011). https://doi.org/10.3888/tmj.10.4-1
6. Corless, R.M., Jeffrey, D.J.: Graphing elementary Riemann surfaces. SIGSAM. Bull. **32**(1), 11–17 (1998)
7. Wegert, E.: Visual Complex Functions, ISBN 978-3-0348-0179-9, Birkhäuser (2012). https://doi.org/10.1007/978-3-0348-0180-5
8. Bradford, R.J., Corless, R.M., Davenport, J.H., Jeffrey, D.J., Watt, S.M.: Reasoning about the elementary functions of complex analysis. Ann. Maths Artif. Intell. **36**, 303–318 (2002)
9. Jeffrey, D.J., Hare, D.E.G., Corless, R.M.: Unwinding the branches of the Lambert W function. Math. Sci. **21**, 1–7 (1996)
10. Brown, J.W., Churchill, R.V.: Complex Variables and Applications, 8th ed. McGraw-Hill (2009)
11. Mathews, J.H., Howell, R.W.: Complex Analysis, 5th ed. Jones and Bartlett (2006)
12. Kahan, W.: Branch Cuts for Complex Elementary Functions. The State of Art in Numerical Analysis (ed. A. Iserles & M.J.D. Powell), Clarendon Press, Oxford, pp. 165–211 (1987)

Author Index

S. M. Watt and T. Ida (Eds.): SCSS 2024, LNAI 14991, p. 129, 2024.
https://doi.org/10.1007/978-3-031-69042-6

SPRINGER NATURE

GPSR Compliance

The European Union's (EU) General Product Safety Regulation (GPSR) is a set of rules that requires consumer products to be safe and our obligations to ensure this.

If you have any concerns about our products, you can contact us on ProductSafety@springernature.com

In case Publisher is established outside the EU, the EU authorized representative is:

Springer Nature Customer Service Center GmbH
Europaplatz 3
69115 Heidelberg, Germany

The manufacturer's authorised representative in the EU is Springer Nature Customer Service Centre GmbH, Europaplatz 3, 69115 Heidelberg, Germany. If you have any concerns regarding our products, please contact ProductSafety@springernature.com

Printed and bound by CPI Group (UK) Ltd, Croydon, CR0 4YY
01/10/2026
02225984-0004